The
MAKING
of a NATION

The MAKING *of a* NATION

South Africa's
Road *to* Freedom

PETER JOYCE

ZEBRA

Published by Zebra Press
an imprint of Struik Publishers
(a division of New Holland Publishing (South Africa) (Pty) Ltd)
PO Box 1144, Cape Town, 8000
New Holland Publishing is a member of Johnnic Communications Ltd

www.zebrapress.co.za

First published 2007

1 3 5 7 9 10 8 6 4 2

Publication © Zebra Press 2007
Text © Peter Joyce 2007

PUBLISHING MANAGER: Marlene Fryer
MANAGING EDITOR: Robert Plummer
EDITOR: Marléne Burger
PROOFREADER: Ronel Richter-Herbert
COVER DESIGNER: Angela Tuck
PAGE DESIGN AND LAYOUT: Natascha Olivier,
based on a concept by Janice Evans
PHOTO RESEARCHER: Colette Stott
PRODUCTION MANAGER: Valerie Kömmer

Set in 9.5 pt on 13.5 pt Minion

Reproduction by Hirt & Carter (Cape) (Pty) Ltd
Printed and bound by Craft Print International Ltd, Singapore

ISBN 978 1 77007 312 8

www.imagesofafrica.co.za

IMAGES OF AFRICA
PHOTO LIBRARY

Over 40 000 unique African images available to purchase
from our image bank at www.imagesofafrica.co.za

CONTENTS

TRAIN CAPTURED AT ELANDSLAAGTE BY VELDCORNET PIENA

CHAPTER 1

A WHITE MAN'S WAR

1899–1902

South Africa's two dominant white tribes greet the new century with a roar of guns. It is an epic struggle for power and privilege, a two-year duel between subcontinental giants in which the region's African people are all but forgotten.

$\mathcal{E}$arly in October 1899, a bewildered throng of mainly African migrant workers, 7 000 of them, jobless and hungry, set out from the bleak compounds of Johannesburg on the long road south to Natal, where many had their homes. Nothing remained for them on the Witwatersrand: Boer and Brit were flexing their muscles for an all-out war, and an eerie silence now lay over the dusty, deserted city streets. Mining headgear had ground to a halt, factory doors were closed; the English-speaking establishment had fled to the safety of the Cape, abandoning the 'natives' to the mercies and miseries of providence. Almost overnight, it seemed, thousands of black labourers, men who had helped build the golden citadel with their strength and their sweat, had become irrelevant, a nuisance, flotsam caught up in the currents of a conflict in which they were not involved and which they did not understand. There was no transport available for them. They decided to walk home.

Only one representative of authority, a servant of the Natal colonial government named John Marwick, took notice of this humanitarian crisis. Marwick told his superiors that unless something was done for the refugees, they would 'starve on the veld'. His plea was met with indifference.

So Marwick, armed with a safe conduct pass from the Boers and well aware that his personal intervention would embarrass his employers, asked to be suspended from his duties. The request was granted, and he joined the vulnerable but surprisingly cheerful procession (led by musicians) on its odyssey, often placing himself at the rear of the huge column, shepherding his flock, doing what he could to help the old, the sick and the weak. One diary entry tells of a typical day on the long march: 'During the morning trek a native who had suffered an amputation of his toe, was lagging behind his friends, so I led the pony while he rode. A native sickening with pneumonia rode the pony from the midday resting place to the homestead of Mr Horn where we slept that night … There was great suffering among the stragglers, some of them limping along miles behind the main body, it being impossible for them to reach the sleeping place until long after the others had cooked their food and retired for the night.' Eventually the column crossed the Natal frontier and reached the Pietermaritzburg area more or less intact.

It had been an epic journey of over four hundred kilometres of rough and often unfriendly terrain, a remarkable triumph of the human spirit in adversity. It caused hardly a stir in the newsrooms and salons of the colonial middle class.

Nobody cared. This was to be a white man's war – and, in the end, a white man's peace.

The seeds of conflict

The Anglo-Boer War had its origins in the discovery of fabulous deposits of gold in the Transvaal following the great migration of Boer families from the Cape in the 1830s and 1840s. There were many reasons for the exodus – economic pressures, the loss of cheap labour after the abolition of slavery, the 'liberal' British colonial policy in matters of race and, above all, British interference in the affairs of the independent-minded, often xenophobic Boer settlers in the frontier regions of the Eastern Cape.

But the Boers were not simply running from the unbearable. They cherished a vision of political independence, land to farm, good pastures, peace, solitude and the freedom to create a society stamped with their own cultural identity. All this, they knew from the early exploratory treks, could be found in the great spaces of the northern interior. Contrary to the myth that became an accepted fact by later generations of Afrikaners, they also knew that these regions were not empty of people, and that, at least in some areas, settlement would involve agreements with local tribal groupings and, on occasion, outright conquest. But the messages they received from their vanguard were encouraging. The ravages wrought by the *mfecane*, the

Boers, later called Afrikaners, on the move – their traditional answer to colonial oppression

great forced migrations triggered by the rise of the Zulu empire in the 1820s, had reduced populations and weakened tribal structures, leaving the north vulnerable to intrusion.

In due course, the Boers entered their Promised Land, suffered some tribulation and founded their republics – the Orange Free State between the Orange and Vaal rivers, the Transvaal between the Vaal and the Limpopo. Their objective all along had been to survive the pioneering phase and, having done so, preserve their Calvinist religion and community culture from all threats. In both these aims they succeeded well enough for some quarter of a century. Admittedly there had been and continued to be sporadic conflict with the resident African groups, notably with Mzilikazi's Ndebele and later with the Pedi and the Venda, but proto-Afrikanerdom's most feared spectre, the

meddlesome British imperialist, remained in the wings. The new republics, backward, pastoral and poor, had nothing to offer the covetous colonialist.

That all changed in 1866, when fifteen-year-old Erasmus Jacobs found a 'pretty pebble' on the banks of the Orange River. Three years later, a Griqua shepherd produced the eighty-three-carat stone that later became known as the 'Star of South Africa'. These were alluvial diamonds and the diggings were fairly profitable, but the real treasure house lay 160 kilometres to the south, in the giant kimberlite pipes around Klipdrift in Griqualand West. An avalanche of fortune-seekers, most of them British, descended on the new fields, and by 1872 an enormous tent town sprawled across the dry, flat, largely featureless veld. It accommodated some 50 000 miners – a population second only to that of Cape Town – and it was called Kimberley.

The lure proved too enticing. In 1871, on the pretext of settling a dispute between the Orange Free State and the Griqua community over the area in which the diamond fields lay, and after some crafty boundary rigging, Britain annexed Griqualand West.

Tensions mount

The Boers regarded the move as a cynical act of greed; the rights and wrongs of the matter were hotly (though peaceably) disputed, and the Orange Free State received compensation.

But the dynamics were rather more complex than a simple appetite for riches; they were bound up with Britain's wider imperial purpose and the drive to expand her territory and influence in the broader region. The seizure marked a basic shift in British colonial policy, one that envisaged the creation of a

Cecil John Rhodes: a flawed visionary

federation, or confederation, of southern African states with ultimate allegiance to a benevolent British Crown. Shortly afterwards, in 1877, and in terms of the new policy, Britain also annexed the Transvaal – a much more serious move that led, four years later, to war with the burghers and humiliating defeat on the bloody slopes of Majuba Hill.

Once again, it was the discovery of minerals that triggered further confrontation. In 1886, the newly-found gold of the Witwatersrand attracted a vast influx of businessmen, traders, diggers, drifters, adventurers and chancers, most of them English-speaking, into Paul Kruger's South African Republic (the formal name of the Transvaal). As the number of these *uitlanders* (outlanders or foreigners) grew, so the Boers began to fear for their cultural identity, even their independence. Republican president Paul Kruger saw only too clearly that the tidal wave of intruders threatened to swamp his young country and that non-Afrikaners might eventually take political control.

Paul Kruger, father of Afrikanerdom

A romanticised picture of the Jameson Raid: a farcical (though dangerous) adventure

Boer concerns were well founded. Cecil John Rhodes, the super-rich financier and quintessential nineteenth-century Empire Man, became prime minister of the Cape Colony in 1890, and when Johannesburg's *uitlanders* began clamouring for a bigger say in the republic's affairs, he listened to them, encouraged them and, finally, in late 1895, conspired with them to overthrow Kruger's government through a combination of military force and civil rebellion.

Herein, however, lay further humiliation for the British. The Jameson Raid, a comic-opera affair that involved the 'invasion' of the Transvaal by a 700-strong force of mounted Rhodesians and white policemen from Bechuanaland – a posse led by Rhodes's protégé Leander Starr Jameson – was a fiasco. The incursion had been timed to coincide with an *uitlander* uprising organised by a group of Johannesburg businessmen known as the Reform Committee, but everything that could go wrong did go wrong. The Boers had tapped into the telegraph wires, knew exactly what was planned and what was happening, and quickly rounded up the raiders. The uprising never materialised. Rhodes was disgraced, his political career destroyed.

Kruger acted magnanimously in victory, but the raid put paid to any chance of an amicable settlement. Boer suspicions had been dramatically confirmed. The British government, in the person of colonial secretary Joseph 'Slippery Joe' Chamberlain, had been complicit in the plot (though he kept a very low profile) and had lost face. More importantly, the issue became one of British national pride. Jameson was deported to stand trial in London, and by the time the court case ended he had become an instant folk hero to large numbers of ordinary Englishmen and women, who viewed 'Dr Jim's' military folly as an inspiring romantic saga. Rudyard Kipling helped create the myth with his stirring poem 'If'.

Relations between Boer and Brit now deteriorated rapidly.

The status of British subjects in the Transvaal remained the immediate bone of contention, but Chamberlain and his representative on the ground, Alfred Milner, were preoccupied with a much larger concern, namely the unification of the whole of southern Africa, an objective that, if achieved, would draw the gold-rich Transvaal into the imperial fold.

Alfred Milner: cold and calculating

Milner, at the time governor of the Cape Colony and British high commissioner in South Africa, was a highly efficient technocrat and a passionate imperialist, arrogant, patrician, a devout believer in the 'civilising influence' of the British Empire and its almost divine mission to provide justice, good order and economic progress for lesser peoples. He was also a very determined man: the Transvaal impasse would be resolved one way or the other, by negotiation if possible, but by force if necessary. And, he reckoned, it wouldn't take all that much force to bring a bunch of simple farmers to heel.

How tragically wrong this would prove to be!

Milner's stubborn insistence that the Boers capitulate to his demands was the principal reason for failure to reach a sensible compromise (one had already been worked out and widely accepted). He rejected out of hand the political concessions Kruger and his Volksraad (parliament) were prepared to make, choosing instead to raise the stakes as each hand was dealt. In the end, after long and wearying months of negotiation, Milner delivered his ultimatum: there was no way out, he told the beleaguered old president, except political surrender or war.

And on 12 October 1899, war it was.

British and besieged

The picture presented here is painted with a broad brush, and it would be wrong to suggest that a major conflict, the first of the twentieth century, erupted simply because the Boer nation was desperate to retain its independence and the British just wanted power and gold. It was a lot more complicated than that. Yes, the imperial government in London was insisting on 'paramountcy' in southern Africa (though that wasn't by any means the same thing as political control), but most British and Cape colonial leaders worked hard to avoid direct confrontation, even of the minor kind that the

General Louis Botha

Victorians had always so easily resolved with the help of a few gunboats and a couple of regiments of disciplined redcoats. And yes, the Boers did cherish the integrity of their republics, but many Dutch-speakers had become thoroughly urbanised and were as quick to flee the fighting as were their *uitlander* neighbours. Others prayed for a peaceful settlement. The *uitlander* leadership and its mine-owning friends did not, as has sometimes been perceived, press for war. They had no reason to do so: in 1899, gold shares were doing very well, thank you. English-speaking Cape liberals were highly critical of their titular overlords in London for the high-handedness with which British policy was being conducted. By the same token, Alfred Milner thought the Cape parliament a treasonable body, and said as much. And so on.

What it probably all came down to was plain old British muddle. Colonial affairs of the time floated on a sea of ignorance, incompetence, arrogance and indifference in which predatory fish – Milner, the calculating bureaucrat and amateur diplomat, together with a few well-placed 'jingo' warmongers – could swim freely. They received serious (though secret) support from Chamberlain, who was still smarting from the humiliation of the Jameson Raid and who, according to a former close colleague, had vowed 'to be even with Kruger'. All these people anticipated a quick, easy war with plenty of spoils for the victor.

The opening salvos shattered both the illusions and the confidence of the British. Within two months the brilliant young Boer general Louis Botha had penetrated deep into Natal, crippling the railway on which British commander-in-chief Redvers Buller depended for his northward advance across the Tugela River, even posing a threat to Pietermaritzburg and, in the mind of the more nervous colonial, to Durban itself. In fact, this was the Boer objective, and the port city could and should have been taken, which would have been a British disaster of *real* significance. Over the few December days that became known as 'British Black Week', imperial armies came to grief at Stormberg, Magersfontein and Colenso, and three key towns – Mafeking in the far north, Kimberley in the north-central region and Ladysmith in Natal – came under Boer siege.

These battles and sieges were relatively small affairs in the context of wider Victorian conflicts and later bloodletting. Casualties were light compared with, say, those of the American Civil War (1860s), and miniscule compared with those of the Flanders slaughterhouses (1914–18). But Britons did die on the broad plains of South Africa and were seen to do so. Campaigns were exhaustively covered by a new breed of on-the-spot war correspondents and their

Imperial troops on veld patrol

Boer artillerymen with their formidable 'Long Tom' siege gun

colleagues, armed with photographic equipment. Cinema had arrived, and it introduced, in graphic detail, the dramas, the defeats and often a distorted portrayal of glory to the ordinary folk far from the battlegrounds.

Much was made at the time, for example, of the courageous defence of the isolated siege towns, and indeed there was the occasional act of gallantry, though their inhabitants survived the long weeks more through stoicism and true British grit than heroics. Kimberley was notable for the presence of Rhodes, who made himself a thorough nuisance to the long-suffering garrison commander. The Kimberley siege also had its ironies: Rhodes instructed his American mining engineer, George Labram, to construct a field gun in collaboration with De Beers's chief draughtsman. It was called 'Long Cecil', and it was so effective that the Boers brought up their own 'Long Tom', one of whose first shells killed Labram! But Kimberley had a much darker side: its residents, both white and black, came close to starvation; 1 500 died, mainly of

enteric fever, many of them infants. Mafeking had its tragedies, too. Here, there was more than enough food for survival, but proper rations were denied to the 7 000-strong Tswana section of the community penned in the 'Native Stadt'. Those who complained were labelled 'grousers' by the town's commander, Robert Baden-Powell. Several blacks were executed for stealing food, others flogged. In due course, soup kitchens

Mafeking justice: flogging and hanging were among the punishments

made their appearance, but the soup had to be paid for. Money was scarce, and the hungrier and more intrepid blacks set out through the Boer lines, some to forage and others to make for the village of Kanye, 100 kilometres distant. One observer – Emerson Neilly of the *Pall Mall Gazette* – wrote that 'words could not portray the scene of misery ... I saw them fall down on the veldt and lie where they had fallen, too weak to go on their way. Hunger had them in its grip, and many were black spectres.'

Incongruously, though, Tswana raiding parties, known as the Black Watch, were sent out to steal Boer cattle and invariably came back laden with good meat for the white tables.

For the rest, the tribulations of Mafeking's defenders were largely a myth, and for the wider British public, a welcome one. The war was going badly; their armies had been soundly beaten by what had once been dismissed as a rustic rabble; the siege was tailor-made for the press, which told stories of bombardment, battle and bravery, and turned Baden-Powell into an instant hero. In fact, he did little more than organise a good system of trenches and dugouts and tell his people to 'sit tight and wait for [the Boers] to go'. Life then carried on much as usual, with concerts, theatricals, picnic parties and cricket enlivening the social calendar. Sunday cricket, though, had to be suspended for the duration – the Boer commander, JP Snyman, wouldn't tolerate such contempt for the Sabbath and threatened to shell the sports field. The siege was lifted after 217 days when the relieving force rode in, and the whole of Britain erupted in an orgy of patriotic joy.

Of far more strategic importance, and altogether grimmer, was Ladysmith, remembered by one beleaguered resident as 'an awful hole, celebrated for heat, dust, storms, wind and insects'. Adding to the problems were dysentery, enteric fever, typhoid, food shortages and bad water. The Boers battled hard to

Baden-Powell is lionised in the *Natal Mercury*

take the town; the garrison resisted stoutly and, to the south, Buller and his relieving army tried again and again to breach the Boer lines along the Tugela River. But neither the general nor his lieutenants seemed able to come to grips with the demands of modern warfare. The stolid, close-packed, parade-ground British regiments were repeatedly and bloodily repulsed by the enemy's advanced weaponry, notably the clip-loading Mauser rifle (contrary to popular perception, the Boers were not especially good marksmen: it was the sheer volume of firepower that did the damage), and by Louis Botha's ingenious system of trenches.

In due course the British did manage to cross the

British dead on the summit of Spioenkop – a pointless battle

Tugela and, on 28 February 1900, relieve Ladysmith. On the way, though, they fought one of the bloodiest and most pointless battles of the entire war on a hill called Spioenkop, which offered no particular military advantage. The British troops, in command of the heights, retreated after withstanding hours of murderous fire from Boer field guns, snipers and, wrote one Englishman afterwards, the 'great bearded warriors charging up the mountain, taking death as nothing …' But the Boers had also suffered, and they

Young Winston Churchill: his daring escape grabbed the headlines

too pulled back, only to reoccupy the abandoned field at dawn the next day. More than 2 000 soldiers had been killed or wounded; the defeat struck deep at the roots of British pride. In a weird piece of synchronicity, three men who would later leave their imprint on the course of human affairs – Winston Churchill, Louis Botha and Mohandas Gandhi – were present during the battle.

Meanwhile, Buller had been replaced as commander-in-chief by Lord Roberts of Kandahar, who chose as his chief of staff the imposing Horatio Herbert Kitchener, victor of Omdurman. Black Week and Spioenkop had pierced the heart of British national self-esteem. The imperial army had been massively reinforced and it now made its way implacably up the central front, through the western Orange Free State and beyond, sweeping all before it. Kimberley was relieved on 15 February; Bloemfontein fell after British forces defeated Piet Cronjé at Paarde-berg, in the process taking 4 000 of his men prisoner;

The Making of a Nation

Black recruits: uneasy allies

A great many black South Africans were profoundly and, in many cases, tragically affected by the conflict, the vast majority of them innocent civilians who knew nothing of its dynamics and cared little about the quarrel. As events unfolded and the news filtered through, those who harboured hopes of a better world tended to mourn British defeats and applaud British victories, but the great, vulnerable mass of ordinary, disinterested black folk of the northern regions were simply swept up by the winds of war, many of them being scattered across the country like chaff. The disruption was immense.

Some, however – and a lot more than has generally been supposed – were directly involved, hired by the British as drivers, herders, labourers, guides and, dangerously for them, scouts and spies. The British also encouraged tribal groupings, notably the Mfengu and Thembu in the south and the Kgatla and Ngwato in the north, to take up arms against the Boers. Despite a tacit agreement to the contrary between the two sides, blacks also fought as conventional soldiers. Kitchener admitted to recruiting and arming some 10 000 Africans and 3 000 coloureds, mainly, he said, to garrison his blockhouses (these guards were known as 'the watchers'), but in reality up to 20 000 more carried rifles and marched with his columns. Many were killed, singled out and shot by the Boers as neutrals who had turned traitor. The killings were not forgotten, adding one more brick to the wall of suspicion and hostility that was to divide African and Afrikaner for the next eighty years.

Not that the Boers themselves stuck to the agreement. Each commando had its black support personnel and, on occasion, its fighting men: commanders who took part in the sieges, for instance, assigned armed blacks to patrol and outpost duties. Most of them were conscripts, usually unpaid and technically liable to punishment (fines or lashes) if they refused to serve. The British approach was more civilised. Kitchener's agents canvassed impoverished areas for recruits, who were offered short-term contracts, monthly pay packets, rations and, sometimes, clothing and bedding.

These were the lucky ones. Black civil society as a whole, the huge majority of folk who remained outside the tenuous protection of the warring parties, suffered grievously as mines closed, farms ceased to function and normal economic activity ground to a halt. Thousands were laid off, with no money in their pockets, no food in their larders and, as often as not, nowhere to go in what Denys Reitz described as a region of 'blackened ruins and trampled fields, so that our course lay through a silent unpeopled waste, across which we navigated our wagon like a lonely ship at sea'.

A British soldier with black recruits

Mafeking was relieved on 15 May; British troops marched into Johannesburg on 31 May and entered Pretoria a week later. President Kruger evaded capture by making his way to the coast and sailing off into exile in Europe, where he was to die four years later.

The fighting, nearly everyone agreed, was just about over.

The informal war

The Boers, many of them, had other ideas. Led by a brotherhood of gifted generals, mobile, at one with their mounts and the terrain, able to live off the land and aided by their kinfolk, they took to the great sunlit spaces of the interior to carry on a guerrilla war. The commandos were coordinated by Louis Botha, but for the most part operated independently, blowing up bridges and railway lines, attacking isolated British detachments, seizing arms and supplies, hitting swiftly and hard and then melting away into the vastness of the veld. Botha, Koos de la Rey and Ben Viljoen fought with spectacular success in the northern regions; the

young lawyer and politician Jan Smuts took his men deep into the Cape Colony, at one point coming within sight of the sea. Especially successful was the Free Stater Christiaan de Wet, who became a kind of Scarlet Pimpernel of the African plains, a special target of the imperial fighting forces and, oddly enough, something of a charismatic to the British public in far-off England.

Horatio Herbert Kitchener

Kitchener, who had taken over from Roberts, reacted sharply and brutally to the guerrilla incursions, launching a counter-strategy that involved the erection of fortified blockhouses (8 000 of them), the laying of thousands of kilometres of barbed wire and the scorching of the earth. Some 30 000 Boer farmsteads were burnt to the ground, livestock driven off, and the white families and their black workers relocated to internment camps. Deliberate devastation and depopulation over huge swathes of countryside were designed to reduce the mobility of the commandos and deny them sustenance from their lands.

The strategy worked, eventually. The Boers in the field, hungry, some reduced

Three generations of Boers take up arms

The camps: 'methods of barbarism'

The no-holds-barred devastation demanded by Kitchener's scorched-earth campaign – the wholesale and deliberate destruction of Boer farmlands and rural homesteads – prompted the removal of thousands of Boer families and their black workers to internment or concentration camps. The British established some fifty such 'places of refuge' for whites and sixty-six for blacks, most of them in the Transvaal and Orange Free State. Altogether, more than 27 000 of their white inmates died, a tragically high percentage of them children. Disease killed one-tenth of the Brandfort camp's complement in just three weeks in October 1901. The Mafeking camp was among the worst: during one period the monthly toll here represented a 173 per cent annual death rate.

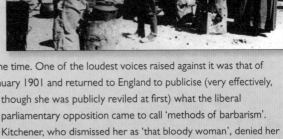

No records of black mortality were kept; the total number of deaths was officially pegged at around 14 000, but the true figure would have been much higher. The first, disorganised months were the most lethal. Often, inmates were simply dumped, without shelter and in some cases without sustenance, on a bare patch of open veld adjoining a white enclosure and left to survive as best they could.

History has condemned this aspect of British military strategy. So, too, did most thinking people at the time. One of the loudest voices raised against it was that of Emily Hobhouse, who visited many of the camps in January 1901 and returned to England to publicise (very effectively, though she was publicly reviled at first) what the liberal parliamentary opposition came to call 'methods of barbarism'. Kitchener, who dismissed her as 'that bloody woman', denied her access to the camps on her second visit, and then deported her under martial law.

Neither Miss Hobhouse nor Mrs Millicent Fawcett's touring commission – a group of busy ladies who believed the war justified drastic measures but, nevertheless, recommended some sound improvements to the system – set foot in any of the 'native' camps.

The concentration camps are associated only by name with the terrible death factories of Adolf Hitler's Third Reich. The earlier, Anglo-Boer–War kind were designed to intern, and in some respects to safeguard civilians (Louis Botha admitted, at one point late in the war, that 'one is only too thankful nowadays to know that our wives are under English protection'), not to exterminate them. Lack of proper planning, incompetent administration, poor food and unhygienic conditions led to pneumonia, and to epidemics of dysentery, cholera, measles and typhoid, which spread like bush fires through the crowded tent towns.

Abraham Carel Wessels, Bloemfontein concentration camp

Kitchener's solution to predations of the ghost-like guerrillas – burn their farmsteads, destroy their crops and livestock, herd their families into concentration camps

to wearing grain bags for clothes, fought grimly on, but their numbers dwindled as the months passed. Some, the so-called *hensoppers* ('hands-uppers'), surrendered; others simply melted away; still others actually joined the British, many because they felt morally obliged to bring the futile killing to an end. The latter, among whom were the brothers of popular generals Christiaan de Wet and Piet Cronjé, were organised as the National Scouts, whose 2 000 members were distributed among the British fighting units and who, during and for a long time after the war, were treated as pariahs by their countrymen.

Peace feelers

Finally, both sides had had enough. For the British, there seemed no sure road to a conclusive victory; the war had become increasingly unpopular with the voting public at home, and it was proving immensely expensive. The Boers had even more compelling reasons to come to terms. There were serious divisions at leadership level and within their ranks: by the end of 1901, almost a third of their fighting men were in the service of the British. Moreover, the exhausted republican commandos were being hemmed in by the great 'drives' mounted by Kitchener's overwhelmingly superior forces. They were being harried, too, by hostile black groups in remote rural areas.

Kitchener, despite the ferocity of his military methods, had always been willing to talk peace. It was Milner who stubbornly insisted on unconditional surrender. In any case, Kitchener, latterly satrap of all Egypt, was tired of unglamorous mopping-up campaigns and yearned to go on to bigger things. He invited the rumps of the two republican governments, which had somehow managed to maintain forms of administration while on the run, to a peace conference at Vereeniging, south of Johannesburg, on 15 April 1902.

In fact, Kitchener had already met Louis Botha, now the spokesman for Afrikanerdom, at Middelburg a full year before, but the Boers had not been willing to concede their independence. They had also held out for a general amnesty for colonial (Cape) rebels, something the British had refused to consider at the time. But a basis had been laid for future talks.

As delegates from both sides gathered to talk peace, the Boers fought, and lost, the last set-piece battle of the war – a defeat that perhaps helped persuade the republican waverers finally to settle. The largest of the remaining Boer commando concentrations was operating on the bleak plains of the Western Transvaal, and their leader, the brilliant and elusive Koos de la Rey, had chalked up a number of notable victories. But De la Rey had left for the peace conference, and his subordinates were not nearly as competent. They were, however, brave men. At Rooiwal they led their cavalry in a massed charge, across open country, against Ian Hamilton's well-positioned, well-armed columns, and they were cut down in their hundreds.

While the Vereeniging forum was in session, senior Boer spokesmen – Botha, Jan Smuts, JBM 'Barry' Hertzog, Koos de la Rey and Christiaan de Wet – met with the British in Pretoria for the decisive round. De Wet, always the uncompromising nationalist, wanted to carry on the fight. This, to Smuts, would amount to

The colour of courage

Among the more unlikely heroes of the war was Abraham Esau, a blacksmith by trade and a coloured

man who was both deeply religious (he was a Wesleyan) and fiercely loyal to the British cause. Esau moved to Calvinia in the Great Karoo and attempted to enlist, but was turned down by the imperial army, which considered the conflict to be a whites-only affair. Nevertheless, in the later (guerrilla) phase of hostilities, he managed to raise his own militia (armed with swords), and organised an intelligence network that covered much of the vast, bleak northern Cape region.

When a Boer commando eventually attacked the town, Esau and his followers offered sturdy resistance, but were defeated, captured and taken prisoner. Esau was brutally tortured for two weeks without either betraying his agents or renouncing his allegiance to the British. He was then shot. At his funeral, his coffin was shrouded in the Union Jack.

'a sacrifice of the Afrikaner nation itself upon the altar of independence'. Most of Smuts's colleagues concurred, and an agreement was hammered out.

The Boer delegates at Vereeniging were left with a simple choice of 'yes' or 'no', and after a tense, dramatic conference the proposals were accepted (the vote was 54 to 6 in favour).

On 31 May, in the elegant reception rooms of Melrose House, Pretoria, the British and Boer leaders signed a peace treaty, and the guns finally fell silent.

PEACE WITHOUT HONOUR

1902–1909

*The war, ironically, brings Boer
and English-speaker closer together.
They are united by their common fear of
a non-white majority that is just beginning
to flex its muscles, and their determination
to retain control firmly in white hands.*

The peace terms are read out to Imperial troops in Pretoria's Church Square

The Treaty of Vereeniging gave the Boers pretty well everything they had asked for. They agreed to surrender their independence and return to the imperial fold as colonies, but were promised responsible government in what was clearly understood would be the not too distant future. The British would take no punitive measures against the rank-and-file colonial rebels – the issue over which the 1901 Middelburg talks had broken down – although those in Natal would have to answer to their own government. The burghers would be allowed to keep their rifles, and their property rights would be respected. Dutch, and by extension the Afrikaans language that was evolving from it, would be safeguarded for use in the law courts and schools. Britain would extend generous loans to war-stricken Boer families, help cover war debts and rebuild the shattered economies of the two former republics.

It was all very conciliatory, but beneath the surface there remained a wellspring of bitterness that would define, often poison, Boer–British relations for generations to come, feeding the flow of Afrikaner nationalism until, in the end, it swept its adherents to the pinnacles of political power. Kitchener's concentration camps would, in Lloyd George's words, erect 'a barrier of dead children's bodies' between the two white tribes of Africa. So would the devastation of the Boer lands. And whatever concessions the peace treaty made to Boer sensibilities, there had already been reprisals, most notably (and visibly) against the Cape Afrikaner rebels after Roberts's successful advance up the central front. Hundreds were sentenced to death, some executed – publicly, in a festive atmosphere loud with the cheers of largely non-white crowds.

More significantly for the future, perhaps, the treaty betrayed the trust the black people had placed in the British government. They had been promised the vote (by, among others, colonial secretary Joseph Chamberlain), albeit a limited, non-racial franchise such as the Cape Colony had enjoyed for the past half-century. In the event, the peacemakers agreed to postpone the question 'until after the introduction of self-government', which, since independent northern whites were hardly likely to concede an iota of power, meant the denial of African voting rights in perpetuity.

Boer prisoners under cover in Green Point, Cape Town

Roots of apartheid

The pattern of race prejudice was imprinted early in the story of modern South Africa. The Cape Dutch settlers, and the British that followed them, legally owned almost all the land they formally occupied. They were militarily dominant and they remained in authority at every level of the administration and the economy within the colonial boundaries. People of colour – the descendants of slaves brought in from other parts of Africa and the East, the indigenous Khoisan, the Bantu-speakers to the east – could rarely rise above the rank of servant or labourer. Had the economy grown more quickly and in more sophisticated fashion, had there been an early demand for those skills that define a middle class, the human and political landscapes would have been very different.

As it was, the region began as a rural backwater and remained so for more than two centuries as segregation became deeply entrenched. The rights of slaves were, by definition, severely restricted until abolition in the 1830s; by the end of the eighteenth century, black and 'coloured' people had become subject to strict legal controls on their working lives and mobility (the ancestral 'pass' system). In the circumstances, social mixing, once a refreshing feature of the Cape community, quickly became taboo. Even the Dutch Reformed Church, for more than a century the only official religious institution, drew ever sharper racial distinctions, until, in due course, it began to hold separate services for its colour-coded congregations.

All this left a devastating psychological legacy: slavery, cheap labour and a submissive non-white population led the early colonists to the conviction that they were an innately superior race, preordained to rule, chosen by God to create a race-based social order. This righteousness, bequeathed to succeeding generations, eventually lent moral force to the creation of the most immoral of societies.

The infection of race prejudice was more virulent in the Boer-dominated northern regions than in the two nineteenth-century self-governing colonies of the Cape and Natal, some of whose politicians subscribed to the fundamentals of high Victorian liberal thought, Whitehall's ideas on 'trusteeship' and the need to 'civilise' backward peoples. This did not deter the British from first helping to 'pacify' the troubled Xhosa-occupied areas of the Cape in a series of brutal frontier wars that pushed the colonial boundaries ever farther eastward, though it was argued that conquest was simply part of the 'civilising' process (in other respects it was an outright land grab).

Colonial governance remained technically colour-blind throughout much of the nineteenth century. Britain's rulers had expressed their earnest desire that all of Queen Victoria's subjects at the Cape, 'without distinction of class or colour, should be united by one bond of loyalty and common interest, and we believe that the exercise of political rights enjoyed by all alike will prove one of the best methods of obtaining this object'. These sentiments were given substance when the colony gained representative government in 1854, at which point the vote was granted to all adult males who owned or occupied property worth at least £25 – that is, every man with a stake in the community. Initially the number of non-whites able to meet the qualification was small, but black and coloured voters were flexing their electoral muscles, and it was only a matter of time before they would be in the majority. White interests, of course, were fully aware of the threat, and their representatives made quite sure, notably by passing the restrictive 1887 Registration Act, that it would never reach serious proportions.

Other benignly intended British-inspired measures failed largely because they were motivated by high-minded but essentially impractical paternalism, and because powerful local leaders had their own agendas. The Glen Grey Act of 1894, for example, conferred the rights of individual land ownership and a modest form of self-government on the people of the Transkei, a region seen by the British as a territory in which traditional cultures could develop unmolested. But the law did nothing for the black franchise, even though it brought half a million additional people into the Cape Colony, since the plots allocated were too small for their owners to qualify for the vote (the calculation was deliberate). More important were the long-term consequences. Liberals viewed the legislation as the first step towards delivery of full civil rights, but what it really did was reinforce the widespread belief that black and white could not live comfortably together, a conviction that would one day fashion the malevolent philosophy and machinery of 'separate development'.

Boer and black

Division along racial lines ran deepest in the two northern Boer republics. As early as the mid-1850s, the Transvaal constitution reflected a desire by the burghers 'to permit no equality of status between the coloured people and the white inhabitants, either in Church or State'. This proto-apartheid is perhaps understandable in human, if not in moral, terms. After all, only a few years earlier the Boers had trekked into the wilderness because they found meddlesome British officialdom and its liberal race policies intolerable. There was also a profound collective fear of being overwhelmed by the great masses of African people who inhabited the interior, and a fierce determination by the Boers to defend their newfound independence, community identity, evolving language and Calvinist religion against all threats. Essentially they regarded the land as theirs by right of conquest; their relationship with black Africans was autocratic and dismissive, unqualified by any thoughts of 'trusteeship' or of sharing resources through some form of land reservation. That was to come much later.

Splendid isolation, however, eluded the Boers. The discovery of diamonds near Kimberley and gold in the Transvaal ushered in the industrial age and changed the patterns of settlement. The mines and factories needed cheap labour, so blacks had to be brought into the mainstream economy without being integrated into society as a whole. In white minds, ethnic 'purity' was essential to cultural survival, and anyway, they asked themselves, why part unnecessarily with other than the smallest slice of their emerging wealth? The two races, though more interdependent than ever, had to be kept apart, so compounds were built around the mining centres for the huddled masses of the new black proletariat, rigidly controlled places whose inhabitants enjoyed few of the ordinary amenities of life and none of the civil or political rights. In legal terms they were temporary workers, migrants whose homes and families were in distant rural areas.

The social edges, though, remained blurred. Adding to white fears was the very real threat of what might be called integration by stealth. Well before the end of the century, a 'poor white' class had emerged, rural, landless, mostly Afrikaans-speaking, often illiterate people who were being driven from the rural areas by drought, stock disease and the ravages of a brutal war. There were also the urban poor, former labourers who had found jobs on the mines when the wealth was near the surface and digging it out was easy, but who hadn't the skills for the more technically demanding, deeper work. The new underclass tended to gather on the squalid fringes of the mining centres, where, at first, they mixed freely with a black workforce prepared to accept breadline wages.

The birth of protest

What opposition there was to nineteenth-century white supremacy came initially from the Eastern Cape, and it was remarkably moderate. Highly educated, devout Christians like John Tengo Jabavu and, for a time, the more radical Alan Soga had soaked up colonial culture. Respectable, patriotic, royalist by

John Tengo Jabavu (centre) believed, too optimistically, in the white man's innate sense of fair play

inclination, quintessentially English in their lifestyle and values (cricket was their favourite game, and they kept Queen Victoria's portrait in their conventionally furnished living rooms), they believed in the power of reasoned argument and in the white man's sense of fair play. They fought their battles against the unequal administration of justice, the hated pass laws, the liquor laws and other racist legislation in the excellent newspapers they created and ran. Jabavu, doyen of the new 'civilised' elite, tried to stay neutral during the Anglo-Boer confrontation, throwing in his lot with a group of English-speaking 'independents' who had joined the pro-Boer Afrikaner Bond.

These gentle 'modernists' had good friends in high political places and they remained influential in the intricate game of Cape politics. But they made little practical headway. More muscular were the new religious pressure groups, independent churches led by ministers who had become disenchanted with the paternalistic arrogance of the missionary establishment. Nehemiah Tile founded his Thembu National Church in 1884, while Mangena

Mokone established the Ethiopian Church, taking the name from a biblical reference that equated Ethiopia with the whole of Africa. Of the two, the charismatic Ethiopians, with their separatist preaching and their 'Africa for the Africans' war cry, were the more powerful, especially after they merged with the American-driven African Episcopal Methodists in 1896.

The followers of these and other independent churches provided the backbone of the nationwide South African Native Congress (SANC), an organisation founded in 1898 by 'Africanists' disillusioned with Jabavu's pro-white, rather gentlemanly leadership. The SANC, distant forerunner of the South African Native National Congress (1912), renamed the African National Congress in 1925, rejected Jabavu's confidence in the power of the Cape liberal establishment to effect change, and instead placed its faith in direct British intervention. After all, it argued, blacks had proved their loyalty in the furnace of war, and they were entitled to some of the fruits of peace.

In this, the SANC's members and their allies were to be grievously disappointed. Alfred Milner, the architect of war and newly ennobled (he was created viscount in 1902), was appointed governor of the two

Alfred Lord Milner with some of his bright young men, collectively known as the 'Kindergarten'

Boer captives on remote St Helena. They created self-contained communities complete with shops, theatres and newspapers

through scientific farming, forestry and irrigation projects, the provision of rural roads and so forth. Buchan himself was in charge of resettlement – getting the mass of displaced farming families and their labourers back onto the land and working productively. It wasn't an easy task, the difficulties compounded by the start of a savage five-year drought.

Large numbers of Boer breadwinners were prisoners of war, a fair percentage of them held in camps established in such exotic places as St Helena, Bermuda, Portugal, India and Ceylon (Sri Lanka); all had to be repatriated. Far from home, thrown on their own resources, the exiles had withstood the later war years with admirable fortitude and not a little ingenuity, creating self-contained little communities that boasted a surprising variety of amenities and comforts – churches, shops, newspapers, homecraft industries, social clubs, improvised theatres and sports fields. It was all very pleasant, but underneath the surface of normality ran a current of sadness, well expressed by Joubert Reitz in his poem 'Searchlight', whose beam 'when it throws its rays upon my tent/Then I think of home and comrades/And the happy days I spent/ … And only then I realise/How much my freedom meant'.

Reconstruction and resettlement were expensive undertakings; fund-raising became a priority. Soon after the guns fell silent, three of the most senior Boer generals – Louis Botha, Koos de la Rey and Christiaan de Wet – took themselves off to Europe to plead the cause of their impoverished people. Wherever they went they were welcomed as heroes, lionised by the public, their presence coveted at society functions laid on by the great London hostesses of the time. On their last evening they dined at Buckingham Palace. They

former republics – now known as the Transvaal Colony and the Orange River Colony – and charged with the daunting task of post-war reconstruction. The ravaged land needed to be repaired, the denuded areas resettled, the gold mines brought to full production, the railway system extended, a customs union negotiated, Boer and Brit reconciled – huge challenges that Milner met brilliantly, gathering together a group of clever young Oxford graduates, his so-called 'Kindergarten', to spearhead the recovery programme.

Few coteries of civil servants contained such a richness of individual talent. Among its members were Geoffrey Dawson, later to edit *The Times* of London (and, before that, Johannesburg's *Star*); Richard Feetham, future South African appeal court judge; the Marquis of Lothian (Philip Kerr), later British ambassador to Washington; Patrick Duncan, who was to become governor general of South Africa, and Lionel Curtiss, author of the crucial Selborne Memorandum that drafted the Union constitution. Best remembered of these young bachelors, perhaps, is John Buchan, who went on to write a string of adventure novels, among them *The Thirty-Nine Steps*, and eventually, as Baron Tweedsmuir, to serve as governor general of Canada.

Much of the Kindergarten's energy and expertise were directed towards upgrading the country areas

Boer generals Christiaan de Wet,
Koos de la Rey and Louis Botha

were even offered knighthoods, but, fierce republicans to a man, refused the honours. They also brought back some money. Not much, but every little helped.

Milner's post-war reconstruction record was by no means unblemished. African workers, scattered by the winds of war, were slow to return to the mines, so he imported labour from China. It was a clever attempt to help solve the immediate problem, but politically it backfired badly.

The first of the Chinese, known as the 'Celestials', began arriving on the Witwatersrand in 1904, and their presence in numbers (some 63 000 at their peak), though harmless enough, triggered all sorts of local resentments, and there were plenty of wild rumours about crime, banditry, murder and mayhem. More important to Milner's reputation and self-esteem was the impact of the Chinese issue in London's corridors of power. The British government was accused of encouraging slavery and brutality. Indeed, the 1906 British general election was fought (and lost) on the

question. In due course the labourers were repatriated, the last of them departing South Africa's shores in 1910.

This was something of a side issue, though. On the whole, Milner's administration of the economy was successful. He couldn't have engineered recovery, however, without the active support of both the Boers and the English-speaking population, the two politically articulate groups which, whatever their differences, were united on a single, all-consuming preoccupation: the need to retain white dominance. This Milner guaranteed, his stated aim the creation of 'a self-governing white community supported by a well-treated and [a] justly governed labour [force] from Cape Town to the Zambezi'.

The divided society

The tripartite alliance between Milner and the two white groups laid the foundations of the future Union, though it was in some respects a fragile partnership, vulnerable to Milner's wider imperial ambitions for an 'anglicised' South Africa. Indeed, his scheme to settle 10 000 English-speaking farmers on

The 'Celestials' – brought in by the British to get the
mines going, and the source of much false rumour

the land and his interference in the Dutch schooling system – 'Dutch should be used to teach English,' he pronounced, 'and English for everything else' – provoked dangerously sharp reaction from Boer cultural and political leaders. They also gave impetus to the ultimately successful Afrikaans language movement.

In this pressurised context, black political rights remained well down on Milner's priority list, perhaps against his natural inclinations. But these he kept to himself. A product of the classic British imperial school, clever, cool, paternalistic and, above all, pragmatic, his belief in racial equality and gradual advancement of the black people towards political emancipation seems to have been genuine enough, and had he been able to deal with the race issue in isolation, he would probably have included an extended vote, based on some sort of 'civilisation' test, among his reforms. But the alliance of vested white interests proved too strong; Milner's hands were tied. His sole concession to what was later to become the central issue was the appointment, in 1903, of a Native

Affairs Commission, headed by Sir Godfrey Lagden and composed wholly of English-speaking white men.

Lagden, a conscientious colonial administrator of the old school and author of *The Native Races of the British Empire* (1924), was instructed to recommend a 'native policy' acceptable to all four colonies. His massive report, produced in 1905, proved a disaster for future race relations in South Africa. It was based on the assumption that whites were of 'superior intellect' to people of colour, and it recommended, among many things, the formal separation of the races, creation of race-based urban 'locations', and the establishment of reserves that corresponded approximately to the existing 'tribal homelands' of the Sotho, Zulu and Xhosa peoples. It was to serve as a blueprint for some of the most divisive laws ever to appear on any country's statute books.

At about the same time, a Zulu group in Natal staged an armed protest against colonial authority generally and, in particular, a poll tax that was onerous enough to force villagers to seek unwelcome work

Rebel chief Bambatha: ready for war

on the mines. The revolt, the so-called Bambatha Rebellion, never became a general uprising. It was just the final, faint flicker of the Zulu flame that had once burnt so brightly, and it was swiftly and brutally extinguished. But the slaughter in Natal's hills and forests had its lessons: it showed the whites, at least those in Natal, just how fragile was their authority over the black underclass and how much the colonies needed each other (and Britain) if whites were to remain in charge.

And it told the black people that armed insurrection was a futile option; that their hopes of a better future could be realised only through peaceful pressure.

The road to Union

Practically nothing was done to satisfy even the most modest of black aspirations in the crucial, tragically wasted post-war years, a period that saw steady progression towards unification of the four colonies.

In 1905, Alfred Milner was succeeded as high commissioner in South Africa by the more approachable Lord Selborne, who immediately set about introducing a form of responsible government to the Transvaal and Orange River colonies. He also gave his name to a crucial memorandum, authored

Smuts: ascetic and brilliant

by the gifted young Lionel Curtiss, which examined the concept of a united South Africa and, ominously, favoured the kind of single, centrally administered 'native policy' that the northern Afrikaners had

been so insistently urging. Inevitably, such a policy would simply cement race segregation and the exclusion of blacks from the political process in the former Boer republics, and, just as surely, erode and eventually destroy the relatively liberal Cape franchise.

Hertzog: passionate nationalist

Selborne looked on benignly as the movement for self-government gathered strength and, in 1907, entrenched Boer administrations in both of the northern colonies. The victorious Het Volk party, founded by Louis Botha and Jan Smuts, had fought and won the Transvaal election on two major issues: the unpopular presence of Chinese mineworkers and Britain's assault on Afrikaner culture, typified by Milner's approach. Het Volk's counterpart in the Orange River Colony was the Orangia-Unie, led by JBM Hertzog, a passionate Afrikaner nationalist and by no means an admirer of things British. Like Het Volk, though, Orangia-Unie had opened its doors to English-speakers. Reconciliation between South Africa's two politically dominant groups, barring those republicans with the bitterest memories of scorched earth and military defeat, was almost complete.

These three white men, each a distinguished military commander, each an Afrikaner but with different world views of the *volk* and its place in the scheme of relationships, would stride the South African political stage through successive and sometimes turbulent administrations for the next forty years.

Botha, the hero of the Tugela River battle line and an audacious guerrilla leader, was something of an anglophile and a politician whose natural leanings tended towards compromise.

Smuts was a lawyer (armed with an outstanding Cambridge academic record, he had served as Transvaal state attorney while still in his twenties) and also a soldier, philosopher and naturalist. Like Botha, he was an Empire Man who evoked dislike and distrust from the diehards among his compatriots because he believed in conciliation between the two white cultural groups and in friendly, mutually profitable links with the colonial power. On race, he was ambivalent. Though deeply compassionate by nature, he was a child of his times, subject to the prejudices and pressures of a generation for which racial segregation was a fact of life. On the other hand, he knew just how complex, and dangerous, the race problem was. As early as 1906 he foresaw the doom-laden decades of the later twentieth century when he remarked that

'when I consider the political future of natives in South Africa, I look into shadows and darkness'.

In sharp contrast was Barry Hertzog, an ardent republican who had endorsed the Vereeniging peace treaty not out of conviction, but out of respect for his exhausted Free State commandos. His guiding principles at this time, and right up to the eve of the Second World War, were summarised in a duality of catchphrases: the self-explanatory 'South Africa first', and a 'two-streams' policy that sought to protect each of the two white tribes from domination by its rival and, by definition, from the then distant threat of the non-white peoples.

Doing a deal

Confusion and damaging rivalry on the economic front gave impetus to the drive for territorial unity. In May 1908, Smuts proposed that a national

The road to Union: middle-aged white men chart the country's future

The Making of a Nation

convention of delegates from each of the four colonies consider and devise a constitutional formula for unification. Optimism among whites, at least those who subscribed to the policy of reconciliation, ran high. The Vereeniging peace terms had been more than generous to the Boers; Britain had handled post-war recovery with aplomb, then granted the two former republics a healthy degree of independence, and by 1907 Transvaal premier Louis Botha could say with a certain smugness that he had 'the fullest faith that I shall be able to make of those two great races of South Africa one solid, united and strong race'.

Over the seven months from October 1908 to May 1909, the National Convention met in Durban, Cape Town and Bloemfontein. The four colonial governments and their parliamentary oppositions were represented in more or less equal measure. There were no black delegates.

On the race issue, the northern leaders, as expected, dug in their heels. Apart from the post-war interregnum, they had monopolised regional political power for sixty years, and they were not about to bow to the liberal sentiments of older colonies that allowed non-whites the vote, even if it was a largely cosmetic one. The convention recommended that the voting systems in the four future provinces remain the same, that the Union adopt the Westminster model, comprising a strong central government, a sovereign all-white parliament of two chambers, and the recognition of English and Dutch as the country's official languages. A governor general would represent the Crown.

Only the Cape leadership – notably William Schreiner (the rather stodgy but fair-minded brother of the feminist writer, Olive) and the enlightened Afrikaner François Malan – pushed for the inclusion of blacks in the future constitutional arrangement. They wanted a 'civilisation' test in which property, income and education, not race, were the measuring rods – in effect, a system that would enfranchise some blacks and disenfranchise some whites.

Support for these moderate proposals from the British officials and the Natalians ranged from cool to lukewarm. The Natalians, even though they considered themselves part of British culture, could not bring themselves to share British liberal values. In their colony, more than anywhere else, blacks were in the overwhelming majority. But there were a few concessions, notably an assurance that the existing and, in practice, very limited black vote in the Cape would be retained until such time as a Union parliament decided otherwise. The coloureds of the Cape were luckier: their vote would be guaranteed by the new constitution, and they would be allowed to seek election to the provincial council.

Luckiest of all were the white, largely Afrikaner, conservatives. The Union's country constituencies were to have 15 per cent fewer voters than the average urban divisions (rural Afrikaner voters would be able to elect disproportionately more parliamentary representatives than the more numerous English-speaking townsmen). This weighting would have profound significance for the future, because most rural whites were Boers, and they would eventually, perhaps inevitably, prevail at the polls.

The activist from India

One of the stronger voices raised against the draft proposals of the National Convention came from the sidelines. Mohandas K Gandhi, future architect of modern India, was a young lawyer who had come to Natal in 1893 on a private brief. His arrival coincided with the introduction of laws that restricted the freedom of the Indian community and, of more immediate concern to him, threatened the prosperity of its merchants. He decided to stay on and help lead the political struggle.

Gandhi, later to be known as the Mahatma ('Great Soul'), was a key figure in the founding of the Natal Indian Congress in 1894, devoting himself in the following years to a relentless campaign of letters and petitions on behalf of the Indian traders (he had yet to embrace the common man). During the Anglo-Boer War he led a team of stretcher-bearers, known as 'bodysnatchers'. After conclusion of the war's first phase he discarded his uniform and visited his homeland before returning to South Africa to found *Indian Opinion*, a newspaper printed at and distributed from his Phoenix self-help settlement north of Durban. *Indian Opinion* played an important role in spreading Gandhi's evolving philosophy of *satyagraha*, loosely translated as 'keeping firmly to the truth', which in essence held that nothing could be achieved through violence, that in the end love and truth would prevail. *Satyagraha* was to exert a powerful influence on the South African freedom movement, at least for a time.

The Indian protest campaign enjoyed some, but not complete success. In due course Gandhi turned his attention from Natal to the Transvaal and formed the British India Association, to fight both the proposal to remove coloured folk to 'locations' and the 1907 pass law, which, among other things, forced Asians to carry registration papers bearing the owner's

Mohandas Gandhi:
from quiet lawyer to Asian colossus

thumbprint. More than 3 000 protestors publicly burnt their documents and hundreds were imprisoned. Gandhi himself twice went to jail. Eventually he and Smuts agreed on voluntary registration, a laudable enough compromise, though it attracted criticism from radical Indian elements that still regarded Gandhi as something of an elitist, a man who drew his support largely from the wealthier members of the community. It was only after Union in 1910 that he sought a following among the labouring classes and that his passive resistance movement gained real impetus.

Coloured and black protest

In the Cape, other opposition forces were flexing what muscles they had. Their moving spirit was a handsome young Scottish-trained doctor named Abdullah Abdurahman, the grandson of slaves and, although based in Cape Town, an advocate for a middle-class northern coloured community that had been subjected to much more restrictive race laws than their southern compatriots and who had hoped that, with the British peace, the British promise of an equitable dispensation would be fulfilled. At first Abdurahman expressed exclusively coloured aspirations, campaigning for a fully integrated Cape society (the social barriers were high) and expressing admiration for the Cape's 'colour-blind' voting system, but fearful that the poison of northern race segregation would leach into and destroy it.

In 1905, Abdurahman became president of the fast-growing, though somewhat ineffectual, African People's Organisation (APO), a body narrowly focused on coloured interests until he led a delegation to London in 1906 to protest the granting of self-government to the 'barbarous' northern colonies. The APO, he said, spoke for all non-whites – blacks and Asians as well as coloureds – in its quest for 'equal rights for all civilised men'.

All these efforts to influence the debate during

Abdurahman: 'Equal rights for all civilised men'

the run-up to Union were both modest and fruitless. Black and coloured in the Cape tended to rely, rather complacently, on their white parliamentary representatives to safeguard their privileges. Others elsewhere were more forceful, though no more organised or successful. They reacted to the 1909 draft Union proposals with disappointment tinged with anger, even though they had known full well what to expect. Non-whites in the northern areas had long been denied rights and, far from showing signs that the laws would be relaxed, the political bosses had been loud in their insistence on maintaining the status quo.

But the proposals had their positive effect, prompting the first moves to unify the coloured and black opposition movements. A number of regional congresses were held around the country, while the national South African Native Convention, chaired by churchman and newspaper owner Walter Rubusana, convened in Bloemfontein to express the black people's hostility to the draft constitution. Their views were echoed by Abdurahman's APO in Cape Town, which finally buried its mildly racist stance. Both bodies then agreed to send a mixed delegation to London to 'secure an extension of civil and political liberty to all qualified men irrespective of race, colour or creed'.

Voices in London

Three missions sailed to Britain in mid-1909. First to arrive was the mixed-race delegation led by William Schreiner, followed by a supportive delegation that included Walter Rubusana and John Tengo Jabavu, and finally a heavyweight party of unionists. Among the latter were Cape prime minister John X Merriman, Louis Botha, Jan Smuts and that consummate political survivor, Leander Starr Jameson.

The unionists, and especially Merriman, had done their worst to discredit Schreiner and his liberal colleagues. In fact, Botha and Smuts had prepared the ground very well indeed. On earlier visits they had made considerable headway with their hosts: Smuts, with his razor-sharp mind and patrician bearing, was clearly a man worth listening to. Botha had an endearingly friendly manner, and his pretty daughter (who proved attractive to, among others, an up-and-coming young Winston Churchill) created all the right impressions among London's political elite. Both generals had fought the British skilfully and honourably a few years earlier, but both were now steadfast Empire Men, part of the Club, each of them 'one of us'. Approval of the Union arrangement was a foregone conclusion.

The Schreiner mission was received politely but achieved nothing. Its message had been sabotaged, and it was further weakened by Schreiner's erstwhile Cape liberal colleagues, who now thought good Boer–British relations and the prospect of a profitable Union were more important than non-white rights.

The Colonial Office's measured but basically negative response to Schreiner's plea for an amended constitution, said delegate Abdurahman, was 'the most hypocritical piece of humbug I have ever listened to'.

MAJOR EVENTS

October 1899: Boers and Brits go to war. **February–June 1900:** Imperial troops occupy Bloemfontein, Johannesburg and Pretoria. Boer guerrilla commandos take to the veld. **May 1902:** Peace treaty of Vereeniging. **1905:** Lagden Commission recommends race segregation. Het Volk wins election in Transvaal Colony, which gains self-government a year later, followed by the Orange River Colony. **1907:** White miners strike in protest against imported Chinese labour; 50 000 Chinese repatriated. SA Native Congress and African People's Organisation plan campaign against Union proposals. **1908:** Gandhi leads massive Indian anti-pass campaign and is imprisoned. National Convention meets to chart course to Union. **1909:** South Africa Act (creating Union) passed by British parliament. Non-white delegation travels to London to protest (fruitlessly).

PEOPLE

Cecil John Rhodes, Victorian imperialist, tycoon and a visionary who, whatever his faults (and they were many), was a powerful force in southern African affairs, dies at his Cape seaside cottage in 1902. His body is taken north across the Limpopo River to be buried in the Matobo Hills near Bulawayo. Two

years later, Paul Kruger, the father of Afrikanerdom, passes away in Clarens, Switzerland, where he had lived in exile since fleeing his beloved, embattled Transvaal in 1900.

The much-publicised hero of the Mafeking siege, Robert

Campaigner Charlotte Maxeke

Baden-Powell, is promoted and goes on to found the worldwide Boy Scout movement. Charlotte Maxeke returns from the US in 1903 to campaign against the pass laws and eventually to found the ANC Women's League. Cecilia Makiwane becomes South Africa's first black registered nurse.

PLACES

The first official 'African township', Pimville, is proclaimed in 1901. Pimville is the grandfather of a conglomerate of urban settlements later consolidated as Soweto.

Not too far away, the Premier mine, near Pretoria, yields the biggest diamond ever unearthed, in 1905. Weighing in at 3 025 carats and named the Cullinan, it is believed to be part of a much bigger stone. It is presented to King Edward VII and then cut into ninety-six small brilliants, seven gems and two of the most famous jewels in the British crown collection.

TECHNOLOGY

Among local pioneers of the period is Alfred Jennings, a Port Elizabeth instrument-maker who, according to the records but largely unremembered, invents wireless telegraphy independently of the lionised Marconi. In 1899, he builds a transmitter that achieves an offshore signal distance of 12.5 kilometres. Also all but forgotten is Natalian John Goodman Household, who dies in 1900. Thirty years earlier, Household had constructed a primitive glider and, with the aid of Zulu helpers, ran it down a hill to become airborne for 230 metres.

ARTS AND ENTERTAINMENT

Schoolteacher Enoch Sontonga dies in the early years of the decade. His moving hymn 'Nkosi Sikelel' iAfrika' (God Bless Africa), first sung in 1899, later becomes the unofficial anthem of the liberation movement and, in the 1990s, part of the new South Africa's national anthem. Another song of the time, 'Sarie Marais', is extemporised during a wartime Boer singalong and inspired by Saré Marais, a romantic young farmer's wife who settled *in die wyk van*

The Making of a Nation

Author Rudyard Kipling

die *Mooirivier* (in the region of the Mooi River) and who died in childbirth.

Notable writers of the period include Rudyard Kipling, who is a close friend of Cecil Rhodes and spends much of his time at the Cape, and John Buchan, a member of Milner's Kindergarten post-war task force. Buchan's sojourn in South Africa inspires his first novel, *Prester John*. As enduring a literary work will be *Jock of the Bushveld*, which recalls Percy FitzPatrick's adventures as a transport rider plying his wagon between the gold-rich town of Barberton and the coastal centre of Delagoa Bay (now Maputo) in company with his intrepid terrier, Jock. FitzPatrick originally tells his stories to his children, but Kipling persuades him to publish them in book form in 1907.

The silver screen is all the rage during the century's first decade. Initially the movies – mostly shorts of great diversity and dubious quality – are shown in a motley collection of auditoriums, ranging from shabby warehouses to barns, but in 1909 impresario Frederick Mouillot launches his chain of 'electric theatres'. A year later, Wilhelm Wolfram opens his plush 565-seat Bioscope in Cape Town.

SPORT

Both major white sports come of age in 1906. South African cricketers record a 4-1 series victory against Sir Pelham 'Plum' Warner's MCC tourists; Paul Roos's rugby side, the first to be known as Springboks, return triumphant from its inaugural tour of the United Kingdom. The football squad also tours with success, beating Argentina 2-1 in 1906.

South Africa's first Olympic gold comes courtesy of Reggie Walker, who breaks the 100-metre tape at the 1908 London Games. Walker is not part of the official team and competes only after his Natalian friends raise funds for his passage.

Non-white boxing hits the back-page headlines when Cape Town's Andrew Jeptha fights his way to the top in the international arena. He becomes British welterweight champion in 1907, but from then on it is all downhill. He is exploited by unscrupulous promoters and, his body tired and eyes damaged, he returns home to the Cape. He dies in his fifties, penniless and blind.

Last-man hero Percy Sherwell: led the first African team to win a test match, in 1906. He helped Dudley Nourse put on 43 runs for the last wicket

Reggie Walker going for gold

The South African Native National Congress delegation to London, 1914.
From left: Thomas Mapikela, Walter Rubusana, John Dube, Saul Msane and Sol Plaatje

CHAPTER 3

UNION, CONFLICT AND POLITE PROTEST
1910–1919

A series of racist laws entrench white domination in the first years of a united South Africa. The war-torn decade also brings the first determined move towards the creation of a united opposition.

The decade between the convening of the first Union parliament and the death of Louis Botha, the country's first premier, was a turbulent period of in-fighting among white politicians; armed conflict at home and cataclysmic war abroad; of industrial unrest and profound social change; and of the steady erosion of black rights.

Botha's South African National Party comfortably won the first general election in September 1910, taking 66 of the 121 parliamentary seats, although Botha himself, rather embarrassingly, lost to rival candidate Percy FitzPatrick, author of the bestselling *Jock of the Bushveld*. In due course the premier entered the chamber via a backdoor by-election.

In the following months, Botha, with the help of his like-minded colleague Jan Smuts, gathered around him those who favoured close ties between Afrikaners and English-speakers, a bi-ethnic group that also sought to resist British imperial interference (after all, the two senior Union politicians had just fought a war over this very issue) and, above all, to make no further concessions to black political aspirations.

All the signs appeared to point to a stable white future, one that was underpinned by a racially conservative government and an apathetic non-white majority.

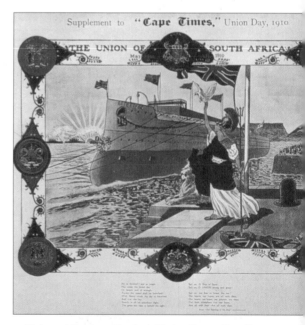

Union celebrations. *Top:* In Adderley Street, Cape Town. *Above:* Front cover of the *Cape Times*

The Making of a Nation

But fault lines lay beneath the political landscape. There were many who thought that the racist Union arrangement was in fact too kind to people of colour. It allowed Cape blacks the vote, for example (though not to stand for parliament), and this was seen as a danger; remote perhaps, but one that would grow to the point where white supremacy could be seriously challenged.

Racial angst also lay in the minds of the white labour unions and the expanding community of poor whites, their fears fanned by economic recession and an accelerating poor-white migration from the drought-stricken countryside. Finally, there were the militants of the Afrikaner republican movement, small in size and influence in the first years of Union but, feeding on insecurity and deep racial anxiety, destined to strengthen and, far in the future, to overwhelm.

Botha and Smuts consolidated their support under the umbrella of the newly formed South African Party in 1911, by which time divisions had already become apparent. They would grow quickly. Hardliner Barry Hertzog was not given a cabinet seat and, in 1914, left the SAP to form the first National Party, which claimed to represent 'the convictions and aspirations of the South African [white] people, under the guidance of God' – the core definition of Christian nationalism. More specifically, the NP enjoined the two white groups to forge a single nation, to respect each other's language, lifestyle and moral values, and, crucially, to prohibit any mixing of the races.

Daniël François (DF) Malan, leader of the NP's Cape branch and editor of its newspaper *Die Burger*, went even further, pressing for a republic outside the British Empire and the pre-eminence of Dutch, from which Afrikaans was rapidly evolving, as the principal medium of communication.

Small beginnings

It took nearly two years for the deep disillusion of Union, an arrangement imposed both against non-white wishes and contrary to non-white interests, to be translated into some sort of coherent action. In January 1912, delegates from black communities around the country – 'chiefs of royal blood and gentlemen of our race' – met in Bloemfontein to launch the South African Native National Congress (SANNC), later to be renamed the African National Congress. This was a watershed event: hopes that Cape liberalism would flow north to soften the harshness of institutionalised segregation had been crushed – the river seemed to be running in quite the opposite direction. Now, for the first time, black leaders admitted they could no longer depend on the goodwill and good offices of liberal white politicians to advance their cause. They were on their own.

Among notables at Bloemfontein was the young, impulsive, foreign-educated (Columbia, USA, and Oxford, England) lawyer Pixley ka Isaka Seme, who

Pixley Seme: spurred on by the 'demon of racialism'

had already been shocked by the 'demon of racialism' contained in such early legislative broadsides as the Dutch Reformed Church Act (this consigned blacks to the status of second-class worshippers); the Native Labour Regulation Act, which prescribed punishments for black workers who broke their contracts; and, most far-reaching of all, the Mines and Works Act, which formalised job reservation by excluding blacks, on the grounds of competency, from numerous categories of work on the mines and railways. Seme was the most prominent of an enterprising group of black South Africans working within the legal system. Among his brighter junior colleagues were Alfred Mangena, George Montsioa and Richard Msimang.

The measures these men opposed passed through the statutory process without much fuss. The black opposition movement was grievously fragmented, rival groups choosing to fight each other rather than confront injustice. Seme recognised the problem, stating bluntly that internal squabbles had already 'shed among us sufficient blood … These divisions, these jealousies, are the cause of all our woes and all of our backwardness and ignorance today.' Seme belonged to the movement's conservative wing, and would eventually (in 1930) serve as the ANC's president general. He also founded *Abantu-Batho*, the country's first national newspaper for black readers.

An older, steadier, less publicity-conscious but equally dedicated delegate to the Bloemfontein forum was the remarkable Sol Plaatje, a Tswana man of little formal education. He had advanced no further than primary school, but possessed great talent and a vast intellect. Plaatje was fluent in eight languages, had served as a court interpreter during the turn-of-the-century siege of Mafeking, went on to found two newspapers and edit a third, translate two of Shakespeare's plays into Tswana, and to write a number of books, among them *Native Life in South Africa*, *Mhudi* and *The Mote and the Beam*. This latter work, a novel, was subtitled,

The remarkable Sol Plaatje, founding member of the ANC

'An epic of sex-relationship twixt white and black in British South Africa'. Plaatje was elected founding secretary general of the SANNC, later embarking on two overseas expeditions to plead its case.

The man chosen as SANNC president was something of a compromise. John Dube was of the old school, a teacher, mission worker, founder of the influential newspaper *Ilanga Lase Natal* and a political moderate. He was also somewhat naive: he stressed the need for strength and vigilance in the quest for black rights, but was still able, in 1912, after all that had happened, to put his trust in 'the sense of common justice and love of freedom so innate in the British character'. He was convinced that 'perseverance, reasonableness, the gentlemanly tendencies of Africans' would ultimately prevail. How wrong history would prove him to be!

The Making of a Nation

The great land robbery

Botha's government began pondering the stricter division of South Africa's land along racial lines immediately after Union in 1910. It was five years since the Lagden Commission had recommended that reserves be set aside for black groups; the time had come to implement this thorniest of measures.

Oddly enough, the black opposition drew some encouragement from the government's initial manoeuvres – the introduction of and debate over a 'Squatters Bill', which sought to restrict land ownership by blacks and to remove them from 'white' farmland. The term 'squatters' covered, among others, the myriad peasant families who paid rent for the few acres they were free to till. The bill was finally abandoned after strong representations from Sol Plaatje and John Dube, who made the most of their triumph at the 1912 forum that gave birth to the ancestral ANC. In truth, opposition from absentee landlords and other special interests had probably done more to scupper the proposals.

The Natives Land Act of 1913, however, was a different matter altogether. Fast-tracked through parliament without serious opposition, it set aside 7.5 per cent of the country for exclusive black occupation. At the time, blacks made up around 67 per cent of the population; many of the 'scheduled areas' were in the already crammed tribal lands that eventually evolved into the homelands of Transkei, Ciskei and KwaZulu, and would one day form the bedrock of the apartheid state's network of Bantustans.

Black people were now prohibited from owning land elsewhere, a right they had previously enjoyed in the Cape and Natal. They were allowed on land designated as 'white' only as labourers. More than a million rural residents would either have to pack up and move, or stay on in conditions not far removed from serfdom. One SANNC leader, TM Dambuzu, put the malignity of the arrangement in poignant terms:

'The Natives Land Act,' he said, 'breaks our people and puts them back in the rearing of their stock and ruins what they term their bank. It causes our people to be derelict and helpless. There is winter in the Act. In winter the trees are stripped and leafless …'

No South African with a modicum of sense and sensibility believed the allocation was equitable, or even workable. It was obvious to anyone of reason that the reserved areas were far too small to sustain a rapidly expanding black society, and in due course the Beaumont Commission of Inquiry recommended an increase to 17 per cent. Twenty years later, after the commission had reported desperate overcrowding and degradation, the slightly more generous Native Trust and Land Act was passed.

The land law dispelled what remained of a number of black illusions, most notably the belief that South Africa's borders embraced a coherent society holding to a common vision, and an assumption that its lawmakers were basically decent people who would strive for fairness. Thousands of humble folk were forced to trek; rural schools and churches closed their doors. The SANNC accused government of deliberately destroying the means of self-reliant subsistence in order to expand the pool of cheap labour. In May 1914, its domestic appeals and petitions ignored, the SANNC sent emissaries to London, but there, too, its protests aroused little interest. Britain, having helped create a stable, white-controlled state south of the Limpopo, was more than happy to leave things to the men on the spot. With war clouds gathering over Europe, British politicians had other, much more serious matters on their minds.

Challenges from below

During the immediate post-Union years, Mohandas Gandhi had been campaigning for Indian rights. Hitherto he had moved in somewhat elitist circles, his main preoccupation the interests of merchants and other relatively affluent Indians. Now he was marshalling support among the labouring classes, organising strikes on the coalfields of Natal, stoppages that quickly spread to the sugar plantations and other sectors. His passive resistance movement received its final and most compelling impetus from the Immigration Bill of 1913.

Much of Gandhi's newfound mass appeal was engineered by his more pragmatic lieutenant, Thambi Naidoo. Gandhi himself had quarrelled with the Natal Indian Congress, and his overall leadership was under serious question. But he did provide the charisma, a quality that intensified when, daring the government to arrest him – indeed, asking it to: martyrdom is a powerful weapon when you're a revolutionary, even a pacifist one – he led waves of followers across the Transvaal border. In Natal there were riots and incidents of arson; a number of strikers were shot dead, many others injured, and by the end of November 1913, commercial life in the province was at a standstill and Gandhi behind bars.

The authorities had initially tended to dismiss the protest movement as a minor blip on their radar screens, but the unrest concentrated their minds

wonderfully. It prompted Interior Minister Smuts to appoint the Solomon Commission of Inquiry, and in June 1914 he and Gandhi reached an agreement that produced the Indian Relief Act, a relatively minor measure that scrapped a tax on labourers who had completed their contracts. Gandhi, believing that his work in South Africa was done and sensing opportunity in the impact that the impending war in Europe would have on the structure of the British Empire, returned to India. 'The saint,' said Smuts, 'has departed our shores.'

Trouble in the workplace

Smuts had a great deal to contend with on the protest front during these pre-war years, most of it reflecting discontent among working-class whites. Trouble on the Witwatersrand goldfields began in earnest with the first outburst in 1907, when skilled and semi-skilled miners downed tools in protest against cost cutting. The threat to their jobs from cheap and docile Chinese, black and 'poor white' (mainly Afrikaner) labour was real enough, and although this particular strike was easily broken, similar upheavals would be a depressingly familiar feature of industrial life throughout the first quarter of the twentieth century. Underlying all was a single, inescapable constant: white fear of non-white encroachment.

The biggest of all pre-war troubles erupted in July 1913, when 18 000 mineworkers from sixty-three of the Rand's sixty-nine mines walked out in sympathy with five sacked colleagues. Rioters set fire to Johannesburg's Park Street railway station and to the *Star* newspaper's premises. In the vanguard of the mob was the feisty feminist Mary Fitzgerald, known as 'Pickhandle Mary' since leading a violent group of protestors, armed with pickhandles, two years earlier. Although government forces killed more than a hundred strikers and bystanders, it was the bosses who finally caved in. The five men who had caused all the trouble were reinstated.

Indian protestors cross the Transvaal border

White miners battle police during the 1913 strike

However, the strike gave Botha's administration an excellent reason to pass the Riotous Assemblies Act, an efficient instrument of control and coercion that would be amended and effectively used in the following year, when Smuts mobilised 70 000 troops throughout the country (10 000 on the Witwatersrand) to arrest union leaders and smash a general strike.

The Boer rebellion

With Europe on the brink of all-out conflict and the sons of Empire rallying to the flag (albeit for reasons few of them understood), the SANNC defined its patriotic duty and resolved to cease all criticism of the government. It also offered to raise a force of 5 000 black soldiers. The offer was refused. This, again, would be a white man's war.

In marked contrast were the attitudes and actions of the hard-line republicans, men whose minds were filled with bitter memories of their own fight for freedom, against the imperial power they were now being asked to support, little more than a decade earlier.

Botha formally declared war on Germany on 8 September 1914 after much angry debate about the respective merits of neutrality on the one hand and loyalty to the empire on the other. Among leading Afrikaner anti-war figures were Christiaan Beyers, incumbent commandant general of the Union Defence Force; the erstwhile guerrilla leaders Koos de la Rey and Christiaan de Wet, and serving officers Manie Maritz, JCG Kemp and Jopie Fourie, all of them intent on declaring independent Afrikaner republics and raising the Vierkleur once again over Pretoria and Bloemfontein.

Of the dissidents, De la Rey was probably the most politically influential and least extreme, and probably the only man who could have stopped a direct confrontation. But De la Rey was mistakenly, tragically, shot to death at a police roadblock at Langlaagte (set up to catch the notorious Foster gang of armed robbers), and hopes of a peaceful outcome disappeared as rebel commandos led by Kemp, Fourie, Chris Muller, Jacques Pienaar and others took to the field. Together, they mustered some 11 000 men. Maritz and 500 of his troops defected to the Germans in South West Africa.

Public support for the rebels failed to materialise and, ill-armed, poorly organised and too few in number, they were easy prey for the disciplined government forces. Beyers fled, but was drowned attempting to cross the Vaal River (this was the official explanation; he may well have been executed on the spot). Christiaan de Wet, once hero to thousands in Europe as well as South Africa, went to jail; Jopie Fourie was arrested, tried, convicted and faced a firing squad. He died singing the hymn 'Als wij de doodvallei betreen' ('Though we walk in the valley of death').

Marching to victory

It wasn't until February 1915 that Botha and Smuts were free to lead their Union troops against the Germans in South West Africa. Botha and his 12 000-man force landed at Swakopmund, Smuts and his 6 000 at Luderitz Bay. Other Union troops marched into the neighbouring territory from the Orange River and quickly overcame resistance. By May it was all over.

Pushing through the rugged East African terrain. Heat, disease and vast distances were the main enemies

Smuts calls for volunteers

The chief enemies had been heat, the hostility of the desert, the mines and the poisoned wells that the retreating Germans had left behind them.

Not nearly so swift and sure was Smuts's long-running cat-and-mouse East African campaign against the wily – indeed brilliant – German general Paul von Lettow-Vorbeck's largely *askari* army, a scratch force that became adept at living off the land and improvising to keep itself armed, fed and supplied. In fact, Smuts, so successful himself in the art of informal warfare, was only a mediocre commander of a conventional operation that was never really brought to a victorious conclusion: Von Lettow-Vorbeck led the South Africans a merry dance back and forth across the vast, heat-hazed, trackless, fever-ridden terrain until 25 November 1918, when his soldiers formally laid down their arms – two weeks after the armistice in Europe.

Perhaps the finest collective South African feat was the savage battle for Delville Wood, part of the great Somme offensive of 1916. Here, far from the sunlit spaces of Africa, 121 officers and 3 042 men of the SA Brigade of the 9th Division had advanced to the edge of a key tactical position and, on 15 July, they stormed the wood, occupied it, and held it for almost a week against murderous German artillery fire and infantry counter-attack. Just five officers and 750 other ranks walked away unscathed. Said the German Kaiser: 'If all divisions had fought like the 9th, I would not have any troops left …'

Coloured, Indian and black soldiers also served – nearly 90 000 of them, for the most part as non-combatants. Especially enthusiastic were the young coloured men from the Cape, who flocked to recruiting centres in their thousands. Many were turned away, and only two infantry battalions of the Cape Corps were formed (or rather, re-formed: regimental history went back to the 'pandours' who fought the British invaders of 1795). They saw service in Nyasaland (now Malawi), East Africa and the Middle East. The corps' finest moment, perhaps, was the capture of Square Hill from the Turkish army in Palestine. Men of the Indian and Malay Corps also did honourable duty, as did the 80 000 black volunteers of the Native Labour Corps, which suffered disaster when 700 of its members went down with the troopship *Mendi*, torpedoed off the Isle of Wight early in 1917. The men stood quietly in ranks

Black troops in the French war zone

as the ship sank. Eerily, news of the tragedy reached the victims' families in the remoteness of Africa before the official announcement was made.

Post-war politicking

The two South African leaders duly joined other Allied statesmen at the 1919 Paris Peace Conference. Botha was deeply shocked by the savage terms forced on an astonished, but by now powerless, German delegation: it was so very different from the way the Boers had been treated nearly two decades before. But he signed the Treaty of Versailles; to do otherwise would have

The devastation of Delville Wood

been futile. 'Today,' he wrote on his agenda paper, 'my thoughts go back to the 31st May 1902.' Smuts told the British that 'This treaty breathes a poisonous spirit of revenge, which may yet scorch the fair face of Europe.'

And South Africa did come away with some of the spoils of war, though they were not quite so valuable, or permanent, as Botha would have wished. What he really wanted were the vast spaces of South West Africa (now Namibia), Southern Rhodesia (Zimbabwe), Portuguese East Africa (Mozambique), and the High Commission territories of Bechuanaland (Botswana), Swaziland and Basutoland (Lesotho). What he got was the future Namibia, and even here it wasn't a simple transfer of ownership, but rather a League of Nations mandate to administer the former German territory. The prize proved to be of dubious long-term worth and the source of endless controversy and conflict until its final transition to independence in 1989.

Ironically, it was a white South African who had perhaps done most to create the League, predecessor of the United Nations. Jan Smuts produced its blueprint, insisting that the body be given real teeth and that its obligation to use force when necessary had to be 'absolute'. In the event, it proved to be a toothless agent of international peace. Indeed, its actions, or rather, its inaction, contributed directly to the emergence of those predatory states that destroyed so much of the world in the mid-twentieth century.

The SANNC also sent a deputation to Europe in 1919. It was led by Sol Plaatje, and it didn't come away with any political plums, but it did do something for Plaatje's image abroad. He was warmly received, colonial secretary Lloyd George pronouncing himself impressed. 'It is evident,' he wrote to Smuts, 'that you have in Africa men who can speak for native opinion and make themselves felt … If they do suffer under disabilities and if they have no effective mode of expression, it is obvious that sooner or later serious results must ensue.'

MAJOR EVENTS

1910: Four colonies come together as the Union of South Africa. Louis Botha becomes first prime minister.
1911: Botha and Smuts launch the South African Party. The racist Mines and Works Act denies blacks skilled jobs.
1913: Natives Land Act passed. White miners riot on Rand. Gandhi launches passive resistance campaign. **1914:** Barry Hertzog quits Botha's government, forms National Party. Union declares war on Germany. Boer rebels stage short-lived uprising. **1915–18:** South African troops sent to German South West Africa, East Africa, Palestine, Western Front.
1919: Botha and Smuts attend Paris Peace Conference. Botha dies soon afterwards.

HEALTH

Pioneer nursing icon Henrietta Stockdale dies (1911). She had spent her adult life working among the miners of Kimberley; launched training programmes; started a nursing school; founded a maternity home; and was instrumental in gaining international recognition for nursing as a profession. In 1891, the Cape parliament was the first in the world to formally confer this status on the discipline. Nurses are badly

Pioneer nurse Stockdale

needed seven years later when the global influenza pandemic, known as the 'Spanish Lady' because it started in Spain, kills 140 000 South Africans (this was the official figure; the real one was much higher). Commerce and industry grind to a halt; thousands of dead are buried in mass graves.

ACTIVISTS

Among the more prominent feminists of the time is Mary Fitzgerald, known as 'Pickhandle Mary' after she leads a demonstration by militant Johannesburg women armed with pickhandles. She is in the vanguard of violent strikes in 1913 and 1914, inciting workers to burn down Park railway station and the *Star* newspaper premises. Later she serves as Johannesburg's first woman councillor. Mahatma Gandhi returns to his native India (1914). During the preceding decade he has been a painful thorn in Jan Smuts's flesh, but the two men, one an Asian rebel, the other a supremacist Afrikaner, develop strong bonds of mutual respect, even affection. Smuts refers to his old adversary as 'the saint'; while in prison, Gandhi fashions Smuts a pair of sandals as a gift, which he treasures all his life. Back in India, Gandhi leads the independence movement. India gains freedom in 1947; Gandhi is assassinated a year later. Less admirable are the activists who incite anti-German mobs to rampage through South African city streets after the sinking of the passenger liner *Lusitania* (1915). Much German (and non-German) property is destroyed and blood spilt; citizens with German-sounding names are hounded.

CRIME

The notorious Foster gang break out of their Cape Town prison and embark on a countrywide orgy of robbery and murder before being cornered in a cave overlooking the Johannesburg suburb of Kensington. One of the gang is wanted American gunman John Maxim. A crowd gathers to watch the shoot-out. Foster's wife Peggy, her baby and her father are sent in to talk sense to the fugitives. The father and child re-emerge; shots are heard; the four inside are found dead.

ARTS & ENTERTAINMENT

Avant-garde South African artist Irma Stern stages the first of her 100-plus one-person exhibitions in Berlin (1919). The paintings receive critical acclaim in Europe, but it will be more than a decade before she sells a single work in her home country, where the canvases are declared 'immoral', even 'revolutionary', and Stern is investigated by the police. The local movie industry is launched when the Springbok Film

The Making of a Nation

Irma Stern's 'revolutionary' art

A scene from the early epic *Die Voortrekkers*

Company releases its first full-length feature, *The Star of South Africa* (1911). It is written off as an 'amateurish' melodrama. Five years later, though, the epic *Die Voortrekkers* is a huge success. Radio broadcasting also makes progress early in the decade, with dozens of hams on the air and installations (mainly for shipping) erected near Cape Town and Durban. War intervenes and the airwaves reopen only in 1919.

SPORT

South African distance runners triumph at the 1912 Stockholm Olympics. In the rugby arena, the incredible Morkel family of Somerset West, ten of whom earn Springbok colours, with twelve more playing at provincial level, plan to send a full family squad overseas to take on Europe's best. Unhappily the tour is cancelled when war threatens (1914).

The extraordinary Morkels could have fielded a world-beating family team

The Making of a Nation

CHAPTER 4

THE CITY AND THE MODERN AGE

*The country's main urban centres
are the first in Africa to modernise.
By the time of Union in 1910,
most of the infrastructure of
a twentieth-century industrial
society – telecommunications, power,
transport – is firmly in place.*

Kimberley's manual telephone exchange in 1905. By 1910 South Africa had 112 exchanges and 13 650 telephones

Quiet and cosmopolitan Cape Town, first of the settler cities

*I*n the early years of the twentieth century, the country's principal urban centres enjoyed much the same ranking as they do today, although Kimberley has slipped down the scale somewhat. The town is now a quieter, much more respectable place than the rugged, frontier-type diamond camp that ushered in South Africa's industrial revolution. The largest mine, the Big Hole, finally closed down in 1914, by which time it had reached a depth of more than a thousand metres and yielded more than three tons of precious stones.

The oldest and arguably most attractive of the cities was Cape Town, set beneath the beautiful, sometimes menacing, always imposing heights of Table Mountain in the far south-west. Founded by the first Dutch settlers in 1652, it had grown gracefully, and by Union in 1910 was one of the southern hemisphere's busiest port cities, genial host to steamers and the last of the ocean's tall ships. It was also the newly unified

country's legislative capital, a role to which it was well suited, having served for decades as the seat of government of the Crown Colony of the Cape of Good Hope. The first elected parliamentarians took their seats as far back as 1854.

Cape Town's was a diverse and cosmopolitan society, its affairs controlled by a white elite, its soul

The Mother City's Parliament Street

The Making of a Nation

The cobbled and bustling Bo-Kaap

enlivened by a resident coloured community that traced its origins to three main sources:

- the indigenous Khoi, whose distinctive identities had long disappeared beneath the twin onslaughts of smallpox epidemics and colonial encroachment;
- the Malay slaves, imported from various parts of the East by early settlers;
- a fair degree of miscegenation, settler and aborigine mixing freely in the early years.

Many coloured people lived in the pretty little Islamic suburb of cobbled streets and flat-roofed cottages that graced the slopes of Signal Hill, just west of the city centre; others in District Six on the eastern fringes.

By 1910, District Six was already a slum, overcrowded, crime-ridden, unsanitary, joyful in its celebration of life, home not only to mixed-race Capetonians but also to a growing number of black migrants from the far eastern regions and haunt of merchant seamen from a score and more far-flung lands. Part of it had been demolished (and rebuilt in ramshackle fashion) after the outbreak of bubonic plague in 1901, a frightening episode that led to the removal of black residents to the first of the 'locations'. This was Ndabeni, which consisted of 500-person dormitories, seven-man huts and tents (no liquor; all-male; no female overnight visitors allowed).

This was Cape Town's seamier side. Slums had proliferated with prosperity, growth and population pressure, and very little had been done to clear them – understandably, perhaps, since many of the Victorian city fathers were profit-driven property owners, but hardly excusable. Cholera and smallpox were endemic killers. Not until the 1890s was the first health officer appointed, and it was only in 1895 that a modest system of waterborne sewerage was introduced to the wealthier areas.

In those days, sea and city were still intimately linked. Massive harbour redevelopment and the reclamation of the land known today as the Foreshore lay in the future. Palm-fringed Rogge Bay, later covered by tarmac and concrete, was both a prime playground for the people and functional host to fishing boats. Author Lawrence Green remembered 'a beach of oars, tackle boxes and snoek *kerries*, anchor ropes and stone anchors. It was a memorable sight when the whole fleet put to sea under spitsails and jibs, and the scene on their return was even more vivid. For then the old Malay priests and grey-bearded hajis, all the bright-skirted womenfolk and fezzed small boys, seemed to be waiting on the sand. Then

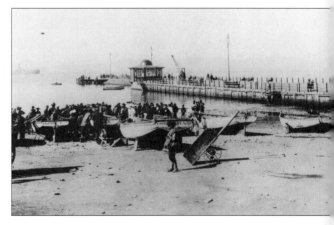

Rogge Bay: a busy beach of oars and tackle boxes

the fish carts were piled high and the fish horns sounded triumphantly …'

City life, though, was changing. At decade's end horses and hansoms still plied the streets, but electric trams were very much part of the scene, and now there were a few motor cars, too.

Cars, trams and telephones

South Africa's first 'horseless carriage', a single-cylinder 1.5 horsepower Benz Voiturette manufactured in Germany, had appeared in Pretoria before the turn of the century. Guest of honour on this auspicious occasion in 1896 was Transvaal's President Paul Kruger, who must have wondered at the pace of progress. (As a boy of ten, he and his family had set out by ox-wagon on the Great Trek.) Thereafter the motor trade developed, slowly at first, rapidly from the second decade.

The first two service stations, or 'motor work-shops', were established in 1901 in Cape Town and Johannesburg respectively. A year later, the Johannesburg Motor Company, agents for the Cudell marque, and the Continental Garage, representing De Dion and also in Johannesburg, began trading, and the country's first motor show was staged at the Wanderers

Electric trams in Adderley Street, Cape Town

Club in Johannesburg in 1908. By the immediate post-Union period, more than 4 000 cars were being imported into the country each year, most of them Model T Fords, or 'Tin Lizzies', which had replaced the almost equally famous Model As. Car registrations climbed to well over 100 000 in the late 1920s, by which time South Africa's first assembly plant had opened in Port Elizabeth.

It was the trams, though, that caught the eye (and assaulted the ear) of the city dweller. One contemporary described them as 'monstrous masses of rowdy tin', but they served their purpose well enough for nearly half a century. All the main centres operated tramway systems; in 1920 Johannesburg had 110 kilometres of track in use, and that year its trams carried 53 million passengers – a figure that, despite the growing automobile presence, grew to 58 million over the next twenty years.

Well before the end of the nineteenth century, too, businesses and the richer private citizens were enjoying the benefits of electricity. Cape Town's Table Bay harbour had installed arc lamps as early as 1881; the first power station began generating (in Kimberley) a year later; the Victoria Falls & Transvaal Power

The first horseless carriage, a Benz Voiturette

Company, which fed the giant Witwatersrand goldfields from 1906, ranked among the world's largest electricity undertakings. Domestic supply systems were slower to develop, though, and for some time remained the preserve of the middle and upper classes. The majority of South Africans, the black people who huddled in urban ghettoes and their families in the country areas, remained literally in the dark for decades to come.

Similarly, early telephones were very much a symbol of wealth and status. Port Elizabeth gave the new technology impetus when it built the country's first exchange in 1882 (before then, a number of companies and private lines were connected directly to each other); other cities soon followed, and by the close of the old century, all the major urban hubs had their own networks. Telephone services expanded rapidly after Union in 1910.

Seaside centres

Port Elizabeth started life in earnest in the second decade of the nineteenth century as a kind of filter for British immigrants. The newcomers, some 4 000 of them, were part of a dual-purpose strategy, a scheme both to help anglicise a colonial territory that had, not too long before, belonged to Holland, and to bring stability to a region over which settler and Xhosa were still fighting bitterly. In due course the settlement

became a busy little port, outlet for shipments of beef, butter and the products of the wool-rich merino sheep. By 1861, when the town received full municipal status, substantial buildings (including a grand new city hall) and elegant colonial homes, designed in styles reflecting the settlers' rural British roots, graced the town's thoroughfares. Port Elizabeth pioneered South Africa's motor industry, with Ford's first plant, established in the mid-1920s, turning out twelve Tin Lizzies a day. A splendid new artificial dock basin was completed in 1938.

Quite different in origin, extent and character was Durban, founded on land granted (or apparently granted) to a party of British traders and hunters by a surprisingly amiable Shaka Zulu in 1824. But despite its wonderful natural harbour, strategic position and inviting hinterland, the settlement was slow to grow. The last of the wild elephants that roamed what would become the modern city's precincts were dispatched as late as the 1850s. Still, Durban was the first to enter the railway age (1860), and when the sandbar that obstructed the harbour entrance was finally removed after decades of costly effort and the first ocean-going steamer sailed in at the end of the 1890s, port and town began to develop in earnest.

Durban's white population had been expanding steadily since mid-century, after the Natal territory had

Graceful Port Elizabeth: pioneer of the motor industry

been annexed to the Cape Colony and a clever Irishman named Byrne had launched his ambitious immigration scheme. Most of the newcomers were sober, hardworking Britons, but Durban always functioned as a natural bolt hole for upper-crust English remittance men, gentleman farmers, second sons and adventurers of various sorts, and the place took on a peculiar, ultra-royalist, enthusiastically British character that lasted well into the twentieth century.

Not long after the first of Byrne's shiploads arrived came the vanguard – 107 men, 89 women and 54 children – of the Indian community, indentured (contracted) labourers and their families brought from the subcontinent to work the great new sugar-cane plantations of the sunlit, lushly humid coastal belt. In due course, ordinary immigrants, known as 'passenger' Indians, followed. They were British subjects, able to travel freely within the empire, and many of them chose to make Natal their permanent home.

At the time of Union, the former colony's Indian population numbered around 150 000, most of them Hindus and Muslims from the Madras area, together with a significant element of Gujarati traders from Bombay. It was to protect the interests of the latter that the lawyer Mohandas Gandhi, later known as the Mahatma, came to South Africa in 1893.

Durban's personality drew much from this exotic influx: the immigrants added a vibrant, colourful element to the city's human landscape, a distinctiveness at its most visible just to the south of the central district. Here, around Grey Street, the air was strangely un-African, filled with the scents of sandalwood and spices and alien with the semi-tonal sounds of the *tanpura* and the beating of Eastern drums. It was an integrated community, kept separate from the colonial mainstream not only by social and regulatory segregation, but also by choice: Durban's (and Natal's) Indians cherished their cultural legacy, their religions and languages, customs, music, cuisine and special

Durban's early rickshaws: plain and practical at first

(and among women, marvellously attractive) modes of dress.

A singular feature of Durban's streets was the rickshaw, a lightly-built, man-pulled cart introduced from Japan by local sugar baron Marshall Campbell in the 1890s. Well over a thousand of them were serving city commuters at Union. Competition intensified as the years went by, and the 'drivers' became ever more decorative in their bid for custom, man and carriage elaborately adorned with feathers, beadwork and streamers. But other, more modern means of transport – trams, the petrol-driven omnibus, its electric cousin the trolley-bus and the motor car – were taking over the thoroughfares, and the rickshaws were eventually reduced to the status of tourist attraction.

Tourism indeed was already a major money-spinner by 1910. Holidaymakers, mostly from the inland industrial wastes of the Witwatersrand, had favoured Durban as a relaxing seaside destination for at least two decades, but it was only after the Anglo-Boer War, when the rail connection had been made, that the place really began to develop its reputation as a prime resort. In 1907, the provincial parliament set aside an eight-kilometre-long stretch of Indian Ocean frontage to be transformed, as the city's mayor put it, into 'the playground of the people from the interior'. This became a 'Golden Mile' of white beaches, pavilions, pools and piers that would host generations of leisure-bent white South Africans.

The indigenous black people, the Nguni of the eastern seaboard, were excluded from these amenities. They were present in number during the city's infancy and adolescence, but, as an underclass, restricted to unskilled and menial work, and accommodated in the shabby and ill-served perimeter settlements that began to appear as Durban entered the modern age. It was a shocking status in the context of their proud heritage: less than a hundred years earlier, Shaka had refashioned the tiny Zulu clan along highly disciplined military lines and, in a series of brilliantly conceived and conducted campaigns, brought the entire eastern region under Zulu control. Wars waged by Shaka's successors over the following decades – against the Voortrekkers at the end of the 1830s and the British redcoats in 1879 – had been fought honourably and with plenty of mutual respect, but, inevitably, they had led to the decline and eventual destruction of the Zulu empire. In 1906, the so-called Bambatha Rebellion was swiftly and brutally crushed, and it would be nearly a century before the Zulu reclaimed their place in the sun.

Boer capitals

Bloemfontein, set on the high, bleak, windswept savannah between the Orange and Vaal rivers and the new Union's judicial capital, was born in the 1840s as the hub of the old Orange River Sovereignty, soon to become the Boer republic of the Orange Free State. And a modest hub it was, too: just a tiny cluster of houses and some land that the local British Resident had bought for petty cash (£35.10s to be exact). The first state parliament convened in a simple thatch-roofed building that had done duty as the village school.

But Bloemfontein had two major advantages: it sat astride the major routes (road, later rail) between the Cape ports and the northern interior, and it was close to the great Kimberley diamond fields that, from the 1870s, were generating the wealth that began the region's economic transformation. The town grew steadily, if unspectacularly, and with a certain grace. In the late 1890s a visiting British traveller could describe the place as 'very quiet … one of the neatest and, in a modest way, best appointed capitals in the world'. At Union it functioned as a major railway centre.

Another Boer settlement, perhaps more deeply rooted in Voortrekker history and more wedded to its mythology, was to become the new executive capital of the Union. Pretoria's name honoured Andries Pretorius, victor of the brutal 1838 Battle of Blood River between the eastern Trekkers and a brave Zulu army unable to cope with modern firepower. It was a stately town whose focus was Church Square, a splendid piazza that had served as the region's main venue for *nagmaal* (Dutch Reformed communion) and as a marketplace before its eventual conversion into a tramway terminus. Among the fine buildings erected around or near the square were the Renaissance-style (with classical touches) Old Raadsaal, or parliament, and the elegant Palace of Justice.

Much of the city's attractiveness, though, lay in its wealth of greenery and its bright flowers. During its infancy, it was known as the 'City of Roses' for the ramblers that decorated 'every garden, hedge, stoep and even water-furrow …' Later came the lovely jacarandas for which the city is famous, and which clothe the streets in a billowing mantle of purple blossoms every spring.

Overlooking it all was a hill called Meintjeskop on which, three years after unification, the grand, crescent-shaped Union Buildings would stand. They were designed by the noted architect Herbert Baker and constructed to exalt the fragile new unity of South

Pretoria, graced by jacarandas and the heart of Afrikanerdom

Africa's white tribes. Eighty years later they would house a different kind of administration and celebrate a different triumph of unity.

Gold-rush town

Pretoria's brash new neighbour, just sixty kilometres to the south, was in its adolescence at Union. It still had plenty of the rugged mining camp about it – predictably so, since its fabulous golden lode had been discovered by an itinerant Australian prospector not much more than two decades earlier, in 1886. But its growth had been explosive. Just six years after its birth, Johannesburg accommodated 40 000 white residents, a figure that by 1905 had risen to 150 000, plus a huge and expanding population of temporary black workers crammed into adjacent settlements.

During the town's first years it was generally thought that the gold deposits, though rich, were limited to the surface areas and would soon be mined out, so few plans were made to secure the future. Streets ran strictly north–south and east–west with no respect for the land's contours, and the first tents and shacks gave way to barely more durable wattle-and-

daub structures. But in due course the proven ore reserves grew larger, the mines deeper, the new cyanide recovery process revolutionised mining methods and the locals began to build for permanence.

First of the amenities were Turffontein racecourse and the stock exchange (their prompt appearance throws some interesting light on the priorities of the time), followed in 1888 by a school, a hospital, the Globe Theatre and the famed Wanderers Club recreational complex. By the early 1890s, the Randlords – clever entrepreneurs such as Barney Barnato, his friend and rival Cecil Rhodes, the Beit brothers, the Wernher family, the unpopular JB Robinson and others – were adding hugely to their fortunes, creating business empires that would become household names. In upmarket Parktown and elsewhere they built grand homes 'with skylights and turrets, scrolled verandahs and gilded tips to their fences'. Most of the mansions had electricity well before the turn of the century. The central area, too, now had a certain dignity, the broad thoroughfares flanked by wide pavements and substantial, stone-faced edifices designed in classical style.

Johannesburg: founded on gold, aggressively rugged, and deeply racist

The families of Parktown could afford a coach-and-four; other Johannesburgers couldn't, and the talk around such moderately affluent suburbs as Doornfontein and Hospital Hill focused on the need for a horse-drawn tramway service. Several such were introduced without much success, to be followed by a steam roadster line between Yeoville and Berea. The first electric trams appeared on the streets four years before Union.

The darker side

For the black people, though, civic comforts remained pitifully inadequate. Restricted to the locations (or compounds) that had proliferated around Johannesburg and its mines, they were kept, by law and prejudice, strictly apart from the social mainstream. Accommodation for 'mine boys' was primitive, overcrowded, squalid, the streets unpaved, unlit, crime-ridden, the whole a vast factory for such diseases as cholera, typhoid and dysentery. The work, too, took a savage toll on those who went underground. Accidents, lung disease and malnutrition were the enemies; during the first years of the century the death rate among miners hovered around the 6 per cent per year mark.

During the decade that had passed since imperial troops marched into the city, the welfare and fate of the Transvaal's black people had been the responsibility of a British government that prided itself, at least in its public utterances, on an even-handed approach to the race issue. But most of this was hollow rhetoric.

Viscount Milner, post-war administrator of the two former Boer republics, was at base a hard-headed civil servant who was more concerned with keeping the whites on side and protecting short-term British interests than he was with dispensing British justice. He had revealed the cold face of *realpolitik* when he clinched a deal with the English-speaking leadership of the Transvaal in 1897. The *uitlanders* were violently opposed to concessions to black interests, political or economic; Milner, with his eyes firmly fixed on the Transvaal's gold, set aside all notions of race equality.

'You have only to sacrifice the nigger absolutely,' he told his far-off prime minister, 'and the game is easy.' Britain's disdain for black people became even clearer from the very moment its troops entered Pretoria at the end of May 1900. Many of the city's blacks had gathered to cheer their perceived liberators as they paraded through the streets, but, as Thomas Pakenham noted in his excellent book, *The Boer War*, the new regime's priority 'was to get them off the pavements and back into the locations. This was one set of Transvaal laws that the conquerors had no intention of changing.'

These were ominous signs for the future of white–black relations, and the next ten years brought little or no progress on the racial front. The Transvaal was now the richest place on earth, its gold output exceeding that of Australia, Russia and California combined, and the new British administration spared nothing in its efforts to keep the whites happy. The harsh pass laws were retained, as was the medieval practice of flogging. The death sentence remained the automatic penalty for certain offences (rape, for example, but only when the perpetrator was black, the victim white). Labour laws created working conditions that came very close to legitimised slavery.

Taxation added to the misery. It was both high (relatively) and inequitable. Of the £450 000 collected by Milner from the 'native' workforce during his post-war regime, a mere £5 000 was directed towards improving the locations. Wages stayed at a level just high enough to sustain a working black man, but too low for him to take any savings back to his family at the end of the seasonal contract period. Nor could he easily escape his soul-destroying predicament even if he wanted to: desertion was classed as a criminal offence, and in any case, rural poverty invariably forced him to sign on for a further spell. Perhaps the most brutalising element of location life, though, was the lack of family. A man had no home to nurture his self-esteem and nothing to bring cheer to him, except maybe a drink or two (or ten).

At first, alcohol was a legal township commodity. In fact, mine owners actually encouraged consumption, on the principle that a drinking worker was an impoverished worker, and poor workers were hostage to their jobs and their employers. But here the owners overstepped the mark. Drinking not only became a catastrophic social problem, but an economic one as well. It affected productivity, and this, to the company, was much more serious.

If any advantage derived from the dismal plight of the urban black at this time, it lay in the very thing that was destroying family life – detribalisation. Group distinctions within the broad black community, traditional loyalties, even the languages that provided the glue that kept rural societies together, broke down in the great, turbulent melting pot of the northern townships. From this disintegration would evolve, slowly at first, a national consciousness, a pride, not only in self and clan, but in race as well.

Linking up

The major centres and many smaller ones were connected to each other by a rail network that was born relatively late and occasionally with pain, but was performing well by the end of the century's first decade.

Durban inaugurated the country's railway age in 1860, when a 3.2-kilometre track was opened with great fanfare between the town and The Point. Cape Town's railway-building programme, forerunner of the national system – a 72-kilometre stretch from the city to Wellington – had in fact started somewhat earlier, but incompetence delayed progress and it was only in 1862 that the line managed to reach Eerste River, a little way north-east of the city. By 1875, when Kimberley's glittering wealth had begun to enrich the Cape, the colony was served by 246 kilometres of track. During the next quarter-century, some 7 000 more kilometres

The young, exciting era of rail

were laid across the country.

In the century's later years there was bitter competition – notably between Paul Kruger's independent but vulnerably landlocked Transvaal and the British colonies of Natal and the Cape – to establish rail routes linking the new goldfields to the sea. Kruger lost the race. His line through Komatipoort to Lourenço Marques (now Maputo) suffered setback after setback and took a devastating toll of human life (it was reckoned that one man died for each sleeper laid through the fever-ridden lowlands of the coastal plain), and the track finally reached Pretoria only in 1894. By that time, Cape trains had been steaming into Johannesburg for a good two years.

The national road system, however, had yet to be modernised and the horse remained king of the overland routes. Although the internal combustion engine had made its appearance, the few motorists there were kept to the relative safety of city limits. Beyond them, the distances were vast, the terrain rugged, river bridges flimsy or non-existent, and petrol stations as yet unheard of.

Nevertheless, by 1905 cars had managed to negotiate the Cape's formidable Sir Lowry's Pass, a Mercedes had made the 225-kilometre run from Johannesburg to Potchefstroom in just 3.5 hours, and Count Revertera, an Austrian aristocrat farming in the Transvaal, had driven his single-cylinder six-horsepower De Dion more than two thousand kilometres from Johannesburg to Cape Town in eleven days. During the decade that followed, a succession of intrepid adventurers opened up the overland routes, initially within southern Africa and then across the continent (the final challenge was met by Frenchman Captain Delingette, who drove his wife in a twelve-tyre Renault from Algiers to Cape Town in 1925).

Air travel, of course, was still in the future, although Albert Kimmerling, another Frenchman, had piloted his 'Flying Matchbox', a Voisin aeroplane, at an altitude of six metres above the gentle countryside near East London in 1909. The country's first air passenger was Thomas Thornton, who paid Kimmerling £100 to fly him from the top of Lydenham Hill near Johannesburg in 1910. Little more than a year later, Evelyn Driver carried 729 postcards from Kenilworth to Muizenberg, on the Cape Peninsula, in his Blériot monoplane to complete the first airmail delivery. The Aviation Age had arrived.

Kimmerling's 'Flying Matchbox' takes to the air

The tank which played a prominent role in suppressing the 'Red Revolt' in Johannesburg in 1922. It is seen passing Corner House, the Head Office of the Chamber of Mines and the Johannesburg Consolidated Investment Corporation

CHAPTER 5

THE AGE OF THE GENERALS

1919–1939

*The middle years of Union
are a troubled time of drought
and depression, urban revolt,
Afrikaner poverty, growing deprivation
among black communities and
a sinister groundswell of
racist white nationalism.*

The period between the end of the First World War and the beginning of the second was a complex one, marked by divided loyalties and shifting alliances, the political stage dominated by two Afrikaners who differed, essentially, only in the degree to which they shared the concept of white supremacy. Indeed, at one point they actually came together to form a 'fusion' government.

It was also an era in which Afrikanerdom gathered strength, while what remained of black political rights was steadily eroded.

Louis Botha, the Union's first premier, died on 17 August 1919, shortly after his return from the Paris Peace Conference. The cause of death was pneumonia, but for some time he had been suffering from heart problems and dropsy, or oedema, a condition characterised by the accumulation of body fluids and obesity. His natural successor, Jan Smuts, inherited a country with an economy that had been both stimulated and stretched by global conflict. The huge wartime demand for commodities and matériel had galvanised industrial growth, but the inevitable post-war recession had now set in; mine owners were planning reductions in output and, much more worrying for white workers, they proposed replacing some 2 000 semi-skilled men with cheap black labour. Wages, moreover, had not kept up with the rising cost of living. It was a tinderbox situation, inflamed by the dangerous messages coming out of a Russia still convulsed by its workers' revolution.

White and red rebels

Industrial unrest, the so-called 'Red Revolt', was Smuts's first big challenge, and he handled it so badly that it would contribute in a major way to his eventual loss of office. On 28 December 1921, white workers walked off the job, and when they were joined by engineering, power-station and foundry employees two weeks later, industrial life on the Witwatersrand came to an abrupt halt – a crisis that even Smuts's personal intervention failed to resolve. All his attempts at mediation proved abortive, and in February 1922, the barricades went up.

Ideology of a kind underpinned the uprising, the strikers forming themselves into paramilitary commandos controlled by the all-white Federation of Labour, a sinister group without formal standing that had been infiltrated by a Marxist element. The federation enjoyed the support of the Communist Party of South Africa (CPSA), whose leader, Bill Andrews, called for a general strike. Looking back at these events, it is hard to understand how Andrews and his colleagues could reconcile their egalitarian beliefs with what was, essentially, a racist stance.

At first the rebels attracted a fair degree of public sympathy, but this quickly evaporated in mid-March when the confrontation erupted into outright violence. There were calls for the establishment of a republic; workers stormed police stations, mines, railway installations, the Johannesburg post office and the power station. Reaction was swift and savage. Smuts called out the military and ordered the fledgling South African Air Force to strafe rebel strongpoints.

A demonstration outside the Johannesburg Court House on the eve of the 'Red Revolt'

Mounted Police clearing Rissik Street, March 1922

Altogether, 153 people were killed, including 72 of the state forces, with 534 injured. A few of the rebel leaders were executed, others deported, and about 15 000 white workers lost their jobs.

Smuts had always walked a fine line between liberal principle (he valued both the non-racial Cape franchise and his international reputation for fair-mindedness) and the demands of the racially obsessed white electorate; between respect for individual freedoms on the one hand and the need for public order on the other. In the event, his ruthless suppression of the uprising alienated large sections of the white working class. Nor was he popular among Afrikaners as a whole. Most regarded him as a sell-out to British interests and to English-speaking, mainly Jewish, big business.

All of which his political colleague and rival Barry Hertzog cleverly exploited, principally through an alliance with Frederick Cresswell's small Labour Party. Initially this 'pact' also involved the Communist Party, which at the time comprised a strange mix of members ranging from hard-line Leninist reds to barely pink liberals. The communist connection, though, was clearly an embarrassment and quickly abandoned. The 1927 general election swept the Pact Government to power. Its leader, Hertzog, would remain in office for the next fifteen years, until the very eve of the Second World War.

The dismal journey

Whatever his scruples – and they were well advertised; he certainly liked to project a moral image to his British friends – Smuts was convinced that the stability and prosperity of the Union depended on tight control of the movement, settlement and economic welfare of the black majority. It was government's moral duty to exert this control, he believed, in the interests of a backward but evolving society. 'The qualities of this childlike human,' he said of the black man, 'must be preserved and gradually developed.' Some of the biggest building blocks of institutionalised segregation – what would later be called apartheid – were laid during Smuts's first term of office. Hertzog then continued along a path that had been clearly charted.

The 1920 Native Affairs Act created separate community-based councils, their members appointed by central government, to represent the interests of black South Africans. The measure, modelled on the much earlier Cape colonial Glen Grey Act, was a significant step on the long and dismal journey to full racial separation. It allowed a form of self-government within the rural reserves through a network of forums comprising traditional leaders, government-nominated representatives and some elected members, and thus had its modest merits. Its urban counterpart had none. The 1923 Natives (Urban Areas) Act, probably the inter-war period's most far-reaching piece of race control legislation, defined and established locations. It gave local authorities the power to exclude blacks from designated white towns and suburbs, and even from the locations themselves when, for example, a resident was deemed to be 'idle, dissolute or disorderly' or 'surplus to requirements'. The statute prepared the ground for the future, hugely divisive Group Areas Act, for the forced removals of whole communities and for the increasingly draconian application of the pass laws.

There were other race-based measures, important ones. The Industrial Conciliation Act (1924) denied black workers the right to bargain collectively for better wages and conditions, restricting certain types of work to apprentice-trained employees at a time when there were no black apprentices.

The Industrial Conciliation Act fashioned the framework for a second measure, enacted in 1937, that entrenched comprehensive job reservation. 'Native' policy was fleshed out and standardised nationally by the Native Administration Act (1927), a monstrous weapon of segregation that elevated the governor general to the paramount chieftaincy of all black South Africans, and established a central Native Affairs Department with absolute powers to create 'tribal areas', move entire communities from place to place, rule by proclamation, appoint local leaders, and punish anyone who promoted 'feelings of hostility between natives and Europeans'. The department, autocratic and seemingly accountable to no one, soon began to function as a kind of state-within-a-state that would eventually, from the 1950s, serve as the agency through which Hendrik Verwoerd would erect the hideous structures of what was to be called Grand Apartheid.

Finally, the Immorality Act of 1927 banned sexual relations across the colour line. Mixed marriages remained legal for the time being, but in 1949 they, too, would be prohibited.

The ebb tide of protest

All these supremacist statutes were an affront to the dignity and well-being of the black majority and should, in hindsight, have provoked a fierce backlash. But the story of opposition to the government's race policies between the two World Wars is not a happy one. The African National Congress, renamed as such in 1925, decided to maintain its cooperative stance, preaching moderation to a black audience stunned into apathy by the ease with which strikes were broken and protests stamped out.

Indeed, the most dramatic confrontation of the period had little to do with straightforward politics. It was played out in May 1921 in the Queenstown area of the Eastern Cape, when a religious sect known as the Israelites illegally occupied a stretch of land and, placing God's instructions above those of the authorities, refused to move. After a lengthy stand-off, a heavily armed police contingent, including artillery, moved in and was attacked, with stones, by the devotees. More than 160 Israelites died.

Less well remembered is the savage suppression of a minor tax protest in rural South West Africa. In one incident, the military reported, more than fifty 'rebels' were killed, just one wounded – a virtual admission of massacre.

On the political front the decade began with a small but significant victory for the opposition when Charlotte Maxeke, the first black South African woman to gain a university degree and founder of the Bantu (later ANC) Women's League, campaigned vigorously against laws that forced women to carry passes. The rules were relaxed after she contrived a face-to-face meeting with Jan Smuts, but her success is memorable largely because it was so unusual.

What strength the extra-parliamentary movement did have lay not with the ANC and its predecessor, but rather in the labour-based Industrial and Commercial Union, founded among the dockworkers of Cape Town in 1919 by the young Malawi-born firebrand Clements Kadalie. This organisation thrived from the start, expanding from city to city and into the country areas until, by 1927, it boasted a membership of some 100 000. For a brief period the ICU provided the focus of opposition, but poor management, financial scandal, pressure from its communist wing to adopt radical

The charismatic trade unionist Clements Kadalie

policies and, more than anything else, in-fighting among the leadership – notably between Kadalie and the versatile Natalian George Champion (born Mhlango) – led to its rapid decline.

In due course both these men joined the ANC, which continued to remain faithful to its moderate principles. It had done its best to diffuse the Israelite crisis, accepted what the segregationists had already done to restrict black rights and was now, in the early 1920s, proving indecisive about proposals to eliminate the Cape black vote. The forces of opposition, it seemed, had been well and truly tamed.

Nevertheless the legislative onslaught did provoke a reaction, nudging the different and often quarrelsome elements of the movement towards unity. Its leaders – Sol Plaatje, Davidson Don Jabavu (son of the illustrious John Tengo), the up-and-coming ZK Matthews and other heirs to the fine traditions of the Lovedale Mission and the new Fort Hare University – were losing patience with a supremacist regime. They were especially appalled by a prime minister (Hertzog) who could say that parliament belonged to a 'civilisation in which the Native does not share'.

But in the later 1920s the ANC summoned its courage and moved sharply (if temporarily) to the left. Moderation, clearly, was going nowhere. Soviet communism was pointing the way to a New Jerusalem, and in America, Marcus Garvey, a controversial Jamaican character, was preaching a heady brand of militant Black Nationalism. The Negro race, Garvey asserted, was a gifted one with a splendid heritage, and its members must put aside all feelings of inferiority, take pride in the past and develop a distinctive culture. Much of his message foreshadowed what Steve Biko would tell black South Africans half a century later.

Josiah Gumede, a left-leaning founder member of the SANNC, had already visited Russia, and on his return, full of enthusiasm for the Soviet way of doing

The admirable John Tengo Jabavu and his son Davidson

ebb, its formal membership numbering just a few hundred, its wider constituency – the great mass of black people around the country – crushed by the global economic crisis and the poverty it brought. The last straw was the government's proposals, first expressed in the so-called 'Hertzog bills' a decade earlier, to deprive Cape blacks of their vote.

In fact, the Cape vote was by now a merely symbolic one, enjoyed by a tiny minority and useless as a political instrument. Still, Hertzog's proposals were seen by middle-class blacks, in the ANC's words, as 'a direct threat to the African community', and their imminence galvanised non-white opposition over a broad front. Representatives from myriad organisations – political, civil, religious and labour – met in Bloemfontein at the end of December 1935 to launch the All-African Convention. Prominent among the groupings present were the ANC, the CPSA, the African Peoples' Organisation and the South African Indian Congress. Davidson Jabavu, arguably the country's

things, he called for the creation of a workers' republic in South Africa. In 1927 he was elected president general of the ANC and, two years later, president of the African League of Rights, a communist-inspired popular front for liberation. The league attracted a fair amount of immediate popular support – enough to launch a lively campaign against social inequality – but collapsed abruptly when its Soviet masters, certain that economic depression would scuttle capitalism soon enough, forbade all alliances with non-communist bodies.

All this was just too much for the chiefs and the black clergy, conservative to a man, and for the moderates within the ANC. Led by Pixley Seme, they ousted Gumede and his followers, who then went on a mass pass-burning spree.

Demise of the black vote

By the early 1930s, Seme was an old man, set in his ways, autocratic and inclined to favouritism in his appointments. The tide, for the ANC, was at its lowest

Josiah Gumede – wanted a 'workers' republic'

leading political intellect, was elected president, with Alfred Bitini Xuma, a medical doctor and the first black South African to earn a PhD from the London School of Tropical Medicine, as his lieutenant.

For all the eagerness and optimism, though, the mood was still one of compromise, despite calls from the communists and various radicals for militant action. Xuma merely asked white South Africans to invite into its 'institutional precincts' all those who could enrich the nation 'by their different cultural and temperamental origin', and stressed his loyalty to country and Crown. Delegates also agreed that perhaps there should be a qualified vote based on some form of 'civilisation test', and then launched a programme of prayer, petition and polite protest. The government took virtually no notice, and on 6 April 1936 parliament abolished the Cape African franchise, passing the Representation of Natives Act by an overwhelming majority.

Whites and poverty

These were the years of the Great Depression, the global financial meltdown triggered by the Wall Street crash of October 1929. It did as much damage to the South African economy and caused as much misery to its people as it did elsewhere, and probably more, the crisis compounded and extended by a series of savage droughts. Mines and factories closed down; farmlands lay idle; wages (for those lucky enough to hold on to their jobs) plummeted; the soup kitchen queues grew long; hunger stalked the countryside.

None of this was entirely new to South Africa, although the sheer scale of the disaster was unprecedented. The country had its special vulnerabilities; deep faults had lain beneath the economic terrain ever since the industrialisation process had begun in earnest in the 1890s.

Rapid urbanisation and periodic recession had proved devastating to traditional black society. However,

A 'poor white' family. During the depression, fully one sixth of South Africa's white population lived below the poverty line

it was the plight of marginalised white folk – mainly refugees from the increasingly inhospitable country areas now living, in the words of a contemporary observer, in 'wretched shanties on the outskirts of towns' – that caught and held the government's attention. In 1931, at the depth of the depression, a Carnegie-funded survey found that, of 600 white homes visited, fewer than a quarter were fit for human habitation, and that 300 000 whites – a sixth of South Africa's total white population – fell into the 'very poor' category. Most were Afrikaners. Suffering among black South Africans, terrible though it must have been, went largely unrecorded.

The rise of Afrikanerdom

South Africa's relationship to the other dominions and to the once all-powerful mother country was defined, to the satisfaction of most, at the 1926 Imperial Conference held in London. According to its chairman, Arthur (Lord) Balfour, the bigger components of the brotherhood were 'autonomous communities within the British Empire, equal in status, in no way subordinate one to another in any aspect of their domestic or internal affairs, though united by a common allegiance to the Crown, and freely associated as members of the British Commonwealth of Nations'.

The life-saving soup kitchen. The 'poor white' problem was well documented; the suffering of blacks ignored

This was the most that local loyalists could have expected, the least that Afrikaner republicans could hope for. And for the latter, there was icing on the cake, namely the trappings of full independence that Hertzog pushed through – a flag (the old Netherlands *prinzenvlag*, with a miniscule British emblem tucked

The language of power

It was in the context of the poor-white crisis that white nationalism, and Afrikaner nationalism in particular, gained new momentum, its bedrock a linguistic phenomenon.

Afrikaans is the world's youngest language, its evolution a testament to the national consciousness and passionate pride in cultural identity of a major segment of South African society. Its origins lie in the words and phrases of the first Dutch settlers, most of whom came from Zuid-Holland (South Holland), though over the years and decades its structure and vocabulary changed. The colonists were isolated from their homeland and, as the outpost expanded its borders, even from the principal Cape settlement itself (where pains were taken to maintain the purity of spoken and written Dutch, or Nederlandic). Immigrants – German, French, English, South Asian – added to its vernacular richness, as did the indigenous peoples.

After the British took control of the Cape in the early 1800s, there were serious attempts to ban Dutch as a teaching medium, part of an 'anglicisation' process that for a time looked as though it might succeed. But in the end the new culture proved too tough. Moreover, the British were busy evolving their ideological commitment to the basic human liberties, and in the late 1820s they granted the private press its freedom. Dutch journalism, and in due course Dutch literature, began to flourish.

Meanwhile, the vernacular version of the language steadily developed, the campaign to promote what had become known as Afrikaans beginning in earnest in the 1860s, when periodicals such as *Die Zuid-Afrikaan* and *Het Volksblad* started using it in print. Up to then it had been regarded as the preserve of the uneducated, spoken privately, and the formal means of communication remained Nederlandic. But such early pioneers as Louis Meurant were making rapid inroads.

The linguistic struggle intensified when Boer and Brit found themselves at odds after the annexation of the Kimberley diamond fields in 1871 and, more traumatically, of the Transvaal six years later. By now it had become a fiercely patriotic issue among the leading protagonists, who included Arnoldus Pannevis, a teacher at the newly established Paarl Gymnasium, Casparus Hougenhout, perhaps the first significant Afrikaans literary figure, Jan Hendrik Hofmeyr (the celebrated 'Onze Jan'), and the Reverend Stephanus Jacobus du Toit, who, in 1874, wrote a series of powerful articles in *Die Zuid-Afrikaan* defending the infant language on religious as well as linguistic grounds. Shortly afterwards he produced a into it); a Foreign Affairs Ministry; the appointment of ambassadors, and so forth. There was also a new national anthem – 'Die Stem van Suid-Afrika', a stirring piece written by CJ Langenhoven and later set to music by ML de Villiers – but until the 1950s, this would only be sung in conjunction with 'God Save the King'.

Meanwhile, there were a great many poverty-stricken Afrikaners, most of them huddled on the fringes of the northern industrial centres, and their welfare was a priority for Hertzog and his colleagues. A growing arsenal of race laws protected their political privileges and labour legislation was loaded in their favour. What they needed, what Afrikanerdom wanted, were material security and opportunities to advance.

These were duly provided. The public service expanded to include a social welfare department. Relief, vocational training and land grant schemes were launched. Powerful Afrikaner business and publishing enterprises had begun to emerge, at first mainly in the Cape, among them Nasionale Pers and its newspaper *Die Burger* (1915), with a youngish DF Malan in the editor's seat; and the giant Santam insurance company and its investment arm, Sanlam. A little later the northern manufacturing scene entered a dynamic new phase with the establishment of the Iron and Steel Corporation (Iscor). Financial muscle was added with the creation of Volkskas bank in 1934.

A host of service organisations, associations and clubs, all with exclusive Afrikaner motivation and membership, complemented the commercial and

---

set of basic grammatical rules and went on to write, among much else, the first Afrikaans history book and to edit *Die Afrikaanse Patriot*, in which he declared that true national identity and language could not be separated.

CJ Langenhoven

Eugène Marais

Du Toit also used *Die Patriot* as a platform from which to launch the Afrikaner Bond, a Cape cultural group that had offshoots in the northern territories and played a key role in the language movement. Du Toit's friendship with the eccentric arch-imperialist Cecil Rhodes, though, eventually proved his nemesis – his membership of the Bond, his very own creation, was terminated in 1899.

Meanwhile, Dutch had become the second language of the Cape parliament and an official medium in the courts, the public service and the schools, helping to trigger the surge of enthusiasm that propelled the second Afrikaans language movement forward in the years after the Anglo-Boer War. Much of the support was in reaction to Alfred Milner's tactless attempts to turn the country into a cultural extension of his own Anglo-Saxon world. Some traditionalists, among them Hofmeyr and Marie Koopmans-De Wet, the formidable Cape Town matron, had been urging the reacceptance of Dutch; radicals such as writers Gustav Preller, CJ Langenhoven, and the mystic poet and naturalist Eugène Marais, championed Afrikaans.

In 1909, representatives of the various pressure groups merged within the umbrella Zuid-Afrikaanse Akademie voor Taal, Letteren en Kunst, but even though the 1909 Act of Union entrenched English and Dutch as the country's two official languages, it was Afrikaans that was striking the real chords. A year into the new era, Langenhoven, writing in *Ons Land*, called on his countrymen to choose between the two Nederlandic tongues, lobbied in the political corridors on behalf of Afrikaans and, in 1914, successfully pressed for its introduction in schools. A little over ten years later, on 8 May 1925, the Union parliament formally enacted the establishment of Afrikaans as South Africa's second official language.

Jan Smuts (third from right) and Barry Hertzog (third from left) with their 'fusion' cabinet

industrial developments, the most significant of them the Broederbond. This secret and sinister society, which was both nationalistic and socialistic (early leaders foreshadowed the thinking of Adolf Hitler), began to infiltrate and eventually dominate every arm of government and the professions. Oddly enough, the Broederbond was also committed to the preservation of coloured rights. The Broeders perceived blacks and English-speaking whites as their natural enemies; most coloured folk spoke Afrikaans in the home. Operating in tandem with the Broederbond – indeed its creation and biggest baby – was the Federation of Afrikaans Cultural Organisations (Federasie van Afrikaanse Kultuurvereniginge, or FAK), which was not in the least secret, openly promoting the ideas and ideals, myths and mystique, of the *volk*.

By the end of the 1930s, the poor white problem was largely a thing of the past, and the national economy, underpinned by rising gold prices, had been restored to health (the gross national product had grown by 70 per cent since 1933). In the process a great many unskilled jobs had also been created for urban non-whites.

By contrast, the rural black communities felt grievously short-changed. Crammed into reserves, their numbers increasing, their lands devastated by overcrowding, over-grazing and erosion, the black people of the countryside were, according to one contemporary report, victims to wholesale 'poverty, congestion and chaos'. Their principal lifeline was

the money sent home from migrant breadwinners working on the mines of the Transvaal.

Unity and division

There had long been divisions between the pragmatic nationalists represented by Barry Hertzog, who valued unity within the Commonwealth and the integrity of his 'two-streams' policy (mutual respect among Afrikaners and English-speakers) on the one hand, and the radical republicans on the other. The moving spirit among the latter was the portly little ideologue and *Die Burger* editor DF Malan, who was speaking to working-class white hearts with his militant Afrikaner chauvinism, his hatred of Jews, his admiration for what was happening in Nazi Germany and, above all, his dedication to comprehensive race segregation.

These divisions more or less forced Hertzog and his Nationalists into a coalition with Jan Smuts's SAP, and in 1934 the two political parties merged, or fused, to form the United Party and its 'fusion government', a sometimes uncomfortable but generally workable arrangement that endured for the next five years.

For Malan, the deal was a betrayal of nationalist principles. He departed to form the Purified National Party (Gesuiwerde Nasionale Party) and to launch his people's quest for the promised land – a Christian national republic that cherished its Afrikaner heritage, marginalised English-speakers (they were to have 'associate status') and excluded non-whites.

Centenary of the Great Trek:
ox-wagons make their way to Pretoria

This was the future nation, given expectant expression during the centenary year (1938) of the Great Trek.

The centenary celebrations were the product of Broederbond inventiveness, their two central features the faithful recreation of the odyssey and the planned erection of an imposing granite memorial that would rise from a hill just outside Pretoria. Pilgrims in period costume – bonneted women and bearded, slouch-hatted men – guided their ox-wagons northwards from Cape Town, following the routes and outspanning at the hallowed sites used by the nineteenth-century trekkers. They were greeted everywhere with enthusiasm, often with hysteria. When they finally got to the site of the Voortrekker Monument, they and the thousands who had gathered there were told by Malan that the time had come 'to make South Africa a white man's land'.

The call to arms

During these years, Europe, and the world, were marching relentlessly towards all-out conflict. Hitler had been gobbling up chunks of the continent – Austria, the Sudetenland, Czechoslovakia – without hindrance from the timid, unfailingly appeasing French and British. To Smuts, veteran of the First World War against Germany and of the Versailles peace deliberations, the rape of Czechoslovakia was especially unacceptable, a threat to the general stability of Europe and, less obviously perhaps, to Britain and her Commonwealth. Hertzog, on the other hand, had some sympathy with a German regime and people who, in his perception, had been humiliated, oppressed and were struggling, just as Afrikaners were, to regain national pride. He favoured neutrality in the coming clash of titans.

It was a disagreement between colleagues that could be settled only in parliament. When Britain declared war on 3 September 1939, Hertzog asked members to endorse his hands-off policy; Smuts counter-proposed that South Africa acknowledge its historic loyalties, sever relations with Nazi Germany and join the mother country in the struggle.

The new premier (Smuts) and the old (Hertzog)

Smuts's motion was carried by an 80-67 majority. Hertzog, 'looking aged and drawn' according to a local newspaper, conceded and, lonely and embittered, resigned his office. He was replaced as prime minister by Smuts.

On 6 September 1939, South Africa, for the second time in the century, went to war with Germany.

The Making of a Nation
The Age of the Generals: 1919–1939 **73**

SPECTRUM 1920–1939

MAJOR EVENTS

1920: Jan Smuts succeeds Louis Botha as South African premier. Transvaal Native Congress protests pass laws. Racist Native Affairs Act passed. **1922:** White workers stage 'Red Revolt' in Johannesburg. **1923:** Racial segregation extended with the passage of the Natives (Urban Areas) Act and, in the following year, of job reservation statutes. **1924:** Barry Hertzog and his Nationalists form government. **1927:** Native Affairs Department, a 'state within a state', is created; Immorality Act passed. **1930:** White women over thirty get the vote. The ANC's radical wing, led by Josiah Gumede, is ousted by Pixley Seme and his moderates. Beginning of the Great Depression, compounded by prolonged drought. **1931:** Statute of Westminster confers full law-making powers on South African parliament. **1934:** Smuts and Hertzog form 'fusion' government. **1935:** All-African Convention founded. **1936:** The few remaining black voters are removed from the common roll. **1938:** Paramilitary Afrikaner underground Ossewabrandwag is founded. **1939:** South Africa goes to war with Germany; Hertzog retires to the opposition benches.

GETTING AROUND

Huge strides are made in the realm of aviation. Two South Africans, Pierre van Ryneveld and Christopher Quintin Brand, set new benchmarks when they conquer the London–Cape Town route in 1920 using three Vickers Vimy aircraft (the first two crash, one on the Cairo–Khartoum stretch, the other near Bulawayo). Towards the end of the decade, Lady Mary, wife of Johannesburg financier Sir Abe Bailey, breaks more new ground (she already holds the world light-plane altitude record of 18 000 feet) when she flies solo from London to the Cape and back again

Lady Mary: aviatrix *extraordinaire*

in her miniscule De Havilland Moth. On the return flight she takes the mostly unmapped route along the west coast. The privately run Union Airways, the country's first airline, is launched during the following year, but suffers a succession of disasters and is taken over by the government, and renamed South African Airways, in 1934. It is the beginning of the end for the great age of steam when five electric trains begin their fast, smoke-free service between Ladysmith and Estcourt in Natal (1925). There's rapid progress, too, in the world of road travel: the country's first petrol pumps are installed in Cape Town (1924); the city also gets South Africa's first electric trolley-buses (1930); and British driver Sir Malcolm Campbell makes a determined effort on the world land-speed record on the desolate Verneukpan salt flats of the Northern Cape in his car *Bluebird* (1929). The altitude is against him, but he does manage to better the five-kilometre and five-mile marks.

DISCOVERY

The scientific fraternity is split down the middle when Wits University's Raymond Dart identifies a fossilised skull, unearthed at Taung in the Northern Cape, as that of a million-year-old apeman (1924). He names the immensely primitive species *Australopithecus africanus* and asserts that southern Africa, not the northern hemisphere (as nearly all the experts thought at the time), was the 'cradle of humankind'. Another fossil, this time a living one, is netted off the East London coast in 1938. The coelacanth was long thought to be an ancient fish that became extinct at least sixty million years ago. Of more immediate import are the discoveries of diamonds in the desert terrain near Port Nolloth on the upper Namaqualand coast (1925).

The Making of a Nation

Raymond Dart with his southern man-ape
– a shock for the scientific world

Prospectors pour into the area; one man (Hans Merensky) finds 487 glittering stones beneath a single flat rock. A year later, diamonds are also found far inland, near the isolated little farming town of Lichtenburg, triggering the last of the country's great rushes. Over 100 000 diggers scratch away at the alluvial ground; 30 000 take part in a single, frenzied claim-pegging race across the dusty veld.

JLB Smith with the coelacanth

PEOPLE

South Africans are charmed by the handsome young Prince of Wales, who pays a three-month visit to the subcontinent (1925). Everyone wants to host or meet him, and his itinerary is ferociously punishing. His advice to other touring royals: 'Only two rules really count. Never miss a chance to sit down and rest your feet. Never miss an opportunity to relieve yourself.' Emily Hobhouse, the Englishwoman so beloved of the Afrikaners of the Orange Free State for her selfless

support during the Anglo-Boer War, dies in England (1926). Her ashes are later taken to Bloemfontein and interred at the splendid National Women's Monument. The first woman member of parliament, the feisty little lawyer Bertha Solomon, takes her seat in 1933.

Pioneer politician Solomon

ARTS & ENTERTAINMENT

Sound comes to South African silver screens in 1927 when Johannesburgers see their first talking film, *The Jazz Singer*, starring Al Jolson. Radio broadcasting also moves ahead. The first regular station, Johannesburg's JB, goes on the air on the evening of 1 July 1924, quickly followed by independent broadcasters in Cape Town and Durban. Capetonians listen to their first rugby commentary (from Newlands) in 1925. The wonders of television are demonstrated to the public at Johannesburg's Empire Theatre in 1937, although it will be almost four more decades before the first South African service is launched.

SPORT

The Comrades Marathon, honouring the fallen of the Great War, is inaugurated in 1921. The following year, Arthur Newton, who is forty years old, covers the nearly 100-kilometre route so quickly that he catches the finish-line officials unprepared, and this despite stopping for an invigorating glass of brandy at the Star & Garter pub en route. Newton goes on to break every distance world record during the next fifteen years. Springbok rugby more than fulfils its early promise, sharing the inaugural series against the New Zealand All Blacks (1921). Led by the noted Bennie Osler, the Springbok team plays dour ten-man rugby to triumph against all four UK Home Unions (1931), while the 1937 squad, which features scrumhalf Danie Craven and his famous diving pass, overcomes both Australia and New Zealand.

The Making of a Nation

CHAPTER 6

DARK CLOUDS AT HOME AND ABROAD

1939–1948

*South Africans join the free
peoples of the world in their great
fight for liberty, and they serve with
distinction. But on the home front,
moves towards the creation
of a 'white' South Africa
are gathering momentum.*

Black troops were needed to defend the country during World War II, but were not allowed firearms

For South Africa, it would be a 'volunteers-only' war. Barry Hertzog, now leader of the opposition in parliament, protested vehemently that, as its name suggested, the Union Defence Force was designed for protection of the home country and should not be sent on overseas adventures. His views found strong support in both public and certain political circles.

Smuts thereupon launched a recruiting campaign, and the nation responded magnificently. Fully a third of white males of military age, a great many Afrikaners among them, stepped forward during the next five years, together with 80 000 blacks and 45 000 coloureds and Asians, all of them prepared to serve 'anywhere in Africa' and later, some of them, in Europe.

Subversion by torchlight: the
Ossewabrandwag (OB) on parade

Calls for volunteers

Pro-war sentiment, though, was by no means overwhelming. Many whites would have preferred neutrality. A small percentage – anti-British Afrikaner republicans of fiercely militant mind – was determined to sabotage the war effort by any means, violent or otherwise. These were members of the Ossewabrandwag ('ox-wagon sentinel') or OB, a pro-German under-ground movement conceived in the Orange Free State in 1938, the Great Trek centenary year, and initially led by Colonel JC Laas, later by Dr Hans van Rensburg.

The latter was a gifted lawyer, fanatical admirer of Adolf Hitler and opponent of all things British. During the war years, the OB's military wing, the 'Stormjaers' (stormtroopers), waged a brutal, though broadly speaking ineffective, campaign in which stealth, assassination and street-killings featured with depressing regularity.

The OB's most notorious recruit was probably Sydney Robey Leibbrandt, a heavyweight boxer who represented South Africa at the 1936 Berlin Olympics and fell under Hitler's spell. Leibbrandt underwent military training in Germany and, in 1941, made a secret landfall on the Namaqualand coast. His mission was to take command of the movement and topple the pro-Allied government, but he was eventually captured near the Limpopo River

Hitler's disciple:
the OB's Robey Leibbrandt

and sentenced to death (this was later commuted). Many of the OB's cadres, including future prime minister BJ Vorster, were interned for the duration, though Van Rensburg himself remained free and the movement was never formally banned – Smuts deemed it to be a comparatively harmless outlet for anti-war feeling.

South African troops march through captured Addis Ababa

At the front

Union troops served in all the major Western war theatres, but most notably in eastern and northern Africa, Italy and in the air.

General Brink plans African conquest

Major General George Brink's 1st Division, well supported by squadrons of the SA Air Force, spearheaded the offensive against Mussolini's Italian armies in Abyssinia; Dan Pienaar's troops, backed by British colonial elements, swept into Italian Somaliland, and in April 1941, South African units occupied Addis Ababa, restoring Emperor Haile Selassie to his ancient throne. The Italian commander-in-chief, the Duke of Aosta, surrendered in the following month, though it wasn't until mid-July that the 22 000-strong garrison of the almost impregnable fortress at Gondar capitulated. It had been a swift, comprehensive and physically taxing campaign. The 1st SA Brigade, for example, covered more than four thousand kilometres in just one hundred days or so over some of Africa's most forbidding terrain.

A South African stretcher-bearer in the desert

The battle of El Alamein: South Africans fought on the southern flank

South African gunners in Fortress Tobruk.
Most of the garrison were captured

A little later, the 1st and 2nd South African divisions joined the British Eighth Army in its great tank battles across North Africa, fighting in see-saw

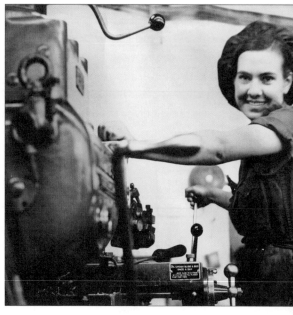

War meant work for women;
the munitions industry boomed

Armoured Division troops hand out sweets
in occupied Florence, Italy

fashion over the empty, featureless, unforgiving wastes of the western desert. They suffered humiliating defeat (notably at Tobruk, where the 2nd Division was lost) before the final breakthrough at El Alamein in October/November 1942. The 6th SA Armoured Division, in company with units of a dozen and more other Allied nations, then slogged its way up the mountainous spine of Italy – terrain that Winston Churchill perceived, astonishingly, as 'the soft underbelly of Europe' – in what was arguably the most thankless campaign of the war.

Civilian South Africans suffered a lot less than other peoples of the combatant countries (with the notable exception of the USA). They remained far from the front lines, faced no invasions or raids, and experienced few shortages. In fact, local industry was galvanised by the Free World's demand for foodstuffs, metals and minerals, armaments and munitions. Jobs were relatively plentiful, especially for white women.

The Making of a Nation

Smuts: the enigma

South African premier Jan Smuts was very much a world figure during the war years, a status reinforced by his close friendship with the British leader, Winston Churchill. The two were bound together by their shared memories of a war that had been fought forty years before. They had served on opposite sides, of course, Smuts as a top Boer commander, Churchill as a newspaper correspondent and latterly an officer with the South African Light Horse. Churchill, who loved all things military, admired the fighting qualities of the Boers. He recalled with nostalgic fondness the heady days of his youth and his adventures in the great sunlit spaces of the African veld when, for an instant, he had enjoyed modest fame and even, after his dramatic escape from a Pretoria prison, a moment of personal glory. Now, in a different kind of war, he valued Smuts as a trusted advisor on matters of Allied strategy and command, especially those touching on the Middle East theatre of operations. Smuts made frequent trips to Cairo and London. In May 1941, he received the rank of Field Marshal in the British Army, a singular honour.

Smuts and Churchill: sharing a heroic past

South Africans, said Smuts in the early years of the war, were fighting for 'the freedom of the human spirit, the free choice of the human individual to shape his own life according to the light that God has given him'. Fine words, but what he was really referring to, it seems, were the freedoms of white people. This ambiguity was one of the constants in the leadership of this great and complex political figure. He never could reconcile his genuinely felt commitment to the basic liberties with the hard practicalities of governance in a multiracial, multicultural society. The most serious of domestic issues seemed intractable, best put aside if not forgotten, so while the majority of his countrymen continued to suffer the abuses inherent in a segregationist system, he spent a great many of his days preoccupied with international issues, finding time, for instance, to lecture British parliamentarians in 1943 on world affairs and the future of the Commonwealth. Later on, he helped refine the mechanisms of the future United Nations (although he always had doubts about the big-power right of veto) and personally drafted the UN Charter's Declaration of Human Rights. An ambiguous man indeed.

In August 1941, Churchill and US President Franklin Roosevelt hammered out a document that became known as the Atlantic Charter, a 'blueprint for the future' that placed strong emphasis on civil liberties. The great powers of the world, it affirmed, would do their utmost 'to afford assurance that all men in all lands may live out their lives in freedom from fear and want'. The South African government maintained a low profile on the issue. Smuts was of the opinion that the declaration was directed against Nazi-style oppression, not race supremacy in his own country. An official spokesman did eventually concede that the freedoms 'were intended for the African people as well', but omitted any mention of the specifics or of a timetable for conferring them.

Then, early in 1942, Smuts seemed to make an astonishing about-face when he spoke against the separation of the races and told a crowded Institute of Race Relations meeting in Cape Town that he regarded white and black 'as fellow South Africans, standing together in the hour of need'. He also said, a little later, that 'every black and coloured man who can be armed, will be armed'. Shortly afterwards the influx control measures were relaxed, a move justified by an equally surprising report on segregation tabled by the Secretary of Native Affairs. The report drew attention to the massive disruption caused by and the 'tremendous price' the country was paying for the pass laws, and went on to call for their abolition.

This sudden benevolence, however, proved short-lived. It had little to do with a newfound conscience or the message sent by the Atlantic Charter. Two months earlier, on 7 December 1941, the Japanese had entered the war by attacking the American naval base at Pearl Harbor, and their apparently irresistible armies were in occupation of the Pacific Islands and large parts of South-East Asia. The threat to the Indian Ocean, and to South Africa itself, seemed very real at the time, and Smuts's concessions were made during a period of perceived national crisis. He needed everybody's loyalty.

Just how far the pendulum swung back was dramatically illustrated four years later, in August 1946, when Smuts ruthlessly crushed a miners' strike. On one mine, hundreds were injured, six were shot dead, six others died in the panic. On another, police and strikers fought savage battles in the stopes (passages) deep underground before the protestors were forced to the surface.

The Young Lions

Early in the war years a young Nelson Mandela arrived in Johannesburg to study by correspondence for, and gain, a bachelor's degree, going on to earn a law degree from the University of the Witwatersrand. Before his move north he had attended Fort Hare University, where he met and made friends with Oliver Tambo. Both had been active in student politics and both were expelled.

Tambo joined Mandela in the Golden City and, together, they established the country's first wholly black legal practice. They were also members of the by now largely dysfunctional African National Congress and, together with Walter Sisulu (a trade unionist who had worked as a miner, baker's assistant, domestic help and factory hand), they helped create and launch the Congress Youth League (CYL).

These three, and others like them, represented a new breed of extra-parliamentary politician – dynamic, large in vision, no longer tolerant of the manifest injustices that afflicted their people, and worlds away from the passive, class-conscious, perennially optimistic Old Guard of the movement.

Oliver Tambo: among the founders of the youth brigade

Alfred Xuma: ousted in
favour of the 'radicals'

Anton Lembede: gave ideological impetus
to the resistance movement

Presiding over the ANC's affairs during the whole of the war period was Dr Alfred Xuma, a skilled organiser and by nature a somewhat conservative man, though he was fully aware of the movement's need for young blood and of the mounting pressures for transformation. Rather reluctantly, perhaps, he backed the formation of the CYL and, in doing so, more or less signed his own political death warrant. However, Xuma's decline would be gradual and his eventual fall a matter largely of his own choosing. It wasn't until the end of the decade that the radical Young Lions of the CYL, who had no lingering illusions that political change could be brought about through polite discussion with the establishment, finally ousted him.

The new generation consisted of uncompromising Africanists who drew much of their inspiration from the ideology of Anton Lembede. This youthful visionary, the son of a humble farm worker, grew up in the countryside near Durban before going on to become a schoolteacher and, in due course, a key figure in the CYL's leadership and its top thinker. His philosophy, which anticipated the Black Consciousness Movement of the 1960s, was summed up in his 1946 statement that 'Africa belongs to [us] … The basis of national unity is

the nationalistic feeling of the Africans, the feeling of being African irrespective of tribal connections, social status, educational attainment, or economic class.' The nature of African society, Lembede said, was basically socialistic, the liberation struggle a race rather than a class conflict, and therefore by implication excluded both communists and liberal white sympathisers from the battleground. Tragically, Lembede died in 1947 at the age of thirty-three, but his legacy endured.

In July 1949, after rejecting a compromise offer put to him by Mandela and Tambo, Xuma was replaced by James Moroka as leader of the ANC. Walter Sisulu was elected secretary general. The movement then adopted a Programme of Action, which, though perhaps mild compared with what was to follow in later years, was a radical document for the times. The objectives, it stated, were to work for 'political independence', to reject both racial segregation and white leadership, and to these ends to embark on a course of strikes and civil disobedience.

The rise of the right wing

Since the Voortrekker centenary celebrations of 1938, DF Malan's Purified National Party, reinforced at the

In Gandhi's footsteps

Early in March 1946 the South African Indian leadership launched its Passive Resistance Campaign with a day of prayer. Shortly afterwards a delegation travelled to India to meet with and get the backing of both Mahatma Gandhi and the Viceroy, Lord Wavell. The campaign received their blessing; there was massive support at home.

The hated object of the protest: Jan Smuts's Asiatic Land Tenure and Representation Bill, which prohibited Indians buying land from non-Indians, a cynical move to keep as much wealth as possible in white hands. It also proposed a 'communal' system of voting.

The campaign manifesto called for united action, asserting that 'Any man or woman who ... obstructs the struggle, in any way whatsoever, will be guilty of an act of despicable treachery.' Thousands gathered in non-violent protest, many were assaulted by white thugs; many more were arrested. The Indian High Commissioner was withdrawn.

Nevertheless the bill, soon to be known as the Ghetto Act, became law. Half a century later Nelson Mandela remembered the campaign as 'an epic in our struggle for liberation'.

outbreak of war by its coalescence with the anti-war Hertzog faction and renamed the Reunited (Herenigde) National Party (HNP), had steadily been gaining ground with its promises of a white South Africa. It was a sinister progression of the forces of prejudice that the United Party and its illustrious leader, bent on striding the world stage, barely seemed to notice. Smuts entirely underestimated the attraction to both white language groups of a movement whose ideological cornerstone was race segregation.

Economically, there had been real progress since the Great Depression of the early 1930s; the poor white problem had largely been solved; the unemployed now had jobs. Nevertheless, the old fears remained as potent as ever. Wartime industrialisation had stimulated demand for cheap labour, for a large and regular flow of temporary migrant workers between the mines and rural reserves that could be regulated only by applying strict influx controls. These controls antagonised a black opposition that was growing ever stronger and bolder, and its new militancy frightened the white working class. Moreover, the controls were only effective to a degree; they simply could not stem the mass migration to the cities of impoverished rural blacks desperate for work and who, once they arrived, tended to stay – which frightened less-skilled whites even more.

Nor were feelings of insecurity confined to the lower strata of white labour. The introduction of ever more efficient production methods – mechanisation – threatened the artisan class, which, with peace, was having to compete in the job market with a horde of demobilised ex-servicemen.

Smuts's sudden though temporary mid-war about-turn on influx control and the status of the black majority had done nothing to ease white insecurities. Moreover, the government-appointed post-war Fagan Commission's report on 'native laws' (tabled in the run-up to the 1948 general election) dismissed a wholly segregated racial landscape as 'totally impracticable' because the black reserves simply could not cope. Fagan also declared that urban drift was inevitable and irresistible, and that a large black presence was now a permanent feature of industrial South Africa. Indeed, his report stated, this was probably a good thing, since mines and factories needed a large, easily accessed pool of labour. Fagan simply stoked the fires of white fear.

The Purified National Party had also appointed a commission, headed by the politician and ideologue Paul Sauer, and its report on native policy was much more reassuring to white families. It focused sharply on the colour issue, its conclusions arguing the necessity for a whites-only vote, for the strict protection of the jobs, privileges and status enjoyed by whites, and institutionally entrenched segregation at all levels. A mechanism for all this – a vast supremacist master plan – would be needed.

In fact, the two reports were not all that dissimilar; or rather, they differed in degree rather than kind, and of course in tone as well. Fagan had not condemned segregation outright; he had simply recommended a blurring of the edges for hard, practical reasons. Sauer's report, on the other hand, was unambiguous and quite uncompromising.

Predictably, race dominated the 1948 election. But DF Malan and the Purified National Party had other weapons in their arsenal, most notably a United Party policy that encouraged skilled immigrants from Europe. The newcomers, they said, would squeeze local whites out of their workplace niches. And to the Afrikaans-speaking segment it was a threat that had another, deeper dimension – most of the incoming migrants were British, and if the trickle became a flood, Afrikanerdom itself would become a minority within the ruling minority.

Finally, there was the weighted vote, entrenched within the Union constitution and subsequently refined, which favoured the rural electorate over the urban. Most white residents of the countryside were Afrikaners. But still, the watershed election turned out, as Wellington said of Waterloo, 'a damned close-run thing'. Malan, aged seventy-four and wholly lacking in charisma, made a deal with Nicolaas Havenga's small Afrikaner Party and sneaked in with a majority of just five parliamentary seats to form the country's first entirely Afrikaner government on 28 May 1948. The political landscape had changed dramatically; white nationalism of an extreme kind was now the norm.

The time had come for the social engineers to begin their work in earnest.

DF Malan – launched the era of codified apartheid

MAJOR EVENTS

September 1939: South Africa follows Britain and France to war against Nazi Germany. **1940:** Alfred Xuma elected ANC leader. **1941:** South African troops capture Addis Ababa, reinstating Abyssinian (Ethiopian) emperor Haile Selassie. SA 1st Division takes part in Cyrenaica (Libya) offensive. **1942:** Tobruk falls to German Afrika Korps; thousands of South African troops taken prisoner. Pro-German underground Ossewabrandwag members interned, including future South African prime minister BJ Vorster. **1943:** ANC Youth League founded. **1944:** The 6th SA Armoured Division takes prominent part in Italian campaign, captures Florence. **1945:** Smuts helps launch United Nations. **1946:** Fagan Commission reports on 'native policy'. Indian Passive Resistance Campaign launched. Asiatic Land Tenure (and amended Indian Representation) Act passed. **1947:** British royal family tours southern Africa. **1948:** DF Malan forms the first Purified National Party all-Afrikaner government, launching the four-decades-long era of codified apartheid. He simplifies the name to the National Party in 1951.

Jan Smuts, leading architect of the UN, signs the Charter

WAR HEROES

Among wartime Victoria Cross recipients are southern Africans QGM Smythe (North Africa), CGW Anderson (Malaya), GR Norton (Italy), E Swales (Germany) and John Nettleton, who leads the famed RAF bombing raid over Augsburg in 1942. Black South African soldier Job Mosego, taken prisoner at

Tobruk, escapes to creep aboard and place home-made explosives on an enemy ship. The vessel is destroyed; Mosego wins the Military Medal, among the highest decorations awarded to non-officers.

On a lighter (but still dramatic) note, SAAF fighter-pilot Bob Kershaw lands his single-seat Hurricane in the middle of a fierce battle for control of an East African airfield to rescue his stranded flight commander. The two men just manage to squeeze into the cockpit and take off under fire; Kershaw is awarded South Africa's first Distinguished Service Order.

PEOPLE

German bombs claim the life of black missionary and writer John Henderson Soga in the British port city of Southampton in 1941. During the 1930s, John Henderson, son of the equally respected and better known Tiyo Soga, produced a number of works on the culture of his people. He also completed his father's Xhosa translation of John Bunyan's *The Pilgrim's Progress*. He and his wife Isobel eventually retired to England. Isobel and their young son were also killed in the air raid.

DISCOVERY

The fossil-rich Sterkfontein cave complex near Krugersdorp yields (1947) the almost complete skull of a million-year-old

Robert Broom (right) uncovers the treasures of Sterkfontein

female hominid who becomes known as 'Mrs Ples' (from its original scientific name *Plesianthropus transvaalensis*). The find provides the crucial link between the primitive, ape-like Taung species and early hominids. Discoverer Robert Broom describes it as 'the most thrilling [find] in all my experience'. Sterkfontein continues to produce new fossil treasures for the next half-century and beyond.

ARTS & ENTERTAINMENT

A fifteen-year-old girl gives her first solo performance in 1947 in front of the visiting British royal family. Her name is Miriam Makeba, and she will go on to sing with leading jazz bands; play the lead in the ground-breaking musical *King Kong*; charm the world with her 'click song' and a myriad other numbers; marry acclaimed American civil rights activist Stokely Carmichael; embark on world tours (notably with singer Harry Belafonte); and represent the state of Guinea at the United Nations. She will also marry another South African master musician, Hugh Masekela.

Eastern Cape artist George Pemba – known as 'the painting grocer' – is turning out a succession of sensitive portraits, striking landscapes and cityscapes. One of the leading visual artists of the era, Pemba will have to wait decades for the formal recognition he deserves. Literary giants include Herman Charles Bosman and Alan Paton. Bosman, who at the age of twenty-one was condemned to death (the sentence was subsequently commuted) for shooting his step-brother, publishes *Mafeking Road* (1947), a collection of stories featuring the endearingly simple characters of the countryside around Marico, who, although they spoke in English, conveyed the very essence of rural Afrikaner life. Paton's *Cry, the Beloved Country* appears on the shelves in the following year. It tells the moving story of a black priest in search of his son in the concrete wastelands of Johannesburg and becomes an instant and enduring bestseller.

FASHION

The new and rather shocking bikini swimsuit (named after the Pacific atoll destroyed by one of America's experimental nuclear bombs) makes its tentative appearance on the beaches of a still largely puritan white South Africa in the late 1940s. The scanty costume proves highly controversial; some of the more relaxed sun worshippers adopt a compromise outfit, linking the two-piece with a bit of see-through netting. Cape Town finally lifts its formal bikini ban in 1965, sunny Durban only in 1969.

SPORT

Shortly before the Second World War (March 1939), the cricketing world stages its one and only 'Timeless Test' when the England side plays South Africa in Durban. The game lasts more than twelve days, during which 5 070 balls are bowled, 1 981 runs scored and 19 records shattered. In the end the match is declared a draw because time has run out and the tourists are late for their voyage home. South Africa's amateur boxers do their country proud at the 1948 London Olympics, coming away with two gold medals (G Dreyer, lightweight, and G Hunter, light-heavyweight). Greatest of the immediate post-war South African sportsmen, though, is probably golfer Bobby Locke, who won the SA Open in 1935 at the age of just seventeen. He captures the first of his four British Open titles at the end of the 1940s, and becomes one of the very few pros of the time to be elected an honorary member of the Royal and Ancient at St Andrews, Scotland. He is known to the golfing world as 'The Maestro'.

Bobby Locke: 'The Maestro'

The 1948 cabinet. DF Malan is seated third from left. His successor, JG Strijdom, is seated second from right

CHAPTER 7

THE SOCIAL ENGINEERS
1949–1960

*DF Malan's new National Party
regime, elected on a platform of
guaranteed white supremacy,
ushers in the era of codified apartheid.
After decades of peaceful protest,
the opposition movement
finally loses patience.*

The National Party (the prefix 'Herenigde' was dropped in 1951) took over the reins of government with an unswerving commitment to white supremacy and, in particular, Afrikaner supremacy, and to the construction of an all-pervading, all-powerful system of institutionalised apartheid. Throughout the 1950s, it pursued these objectives with vigour, indeed with almost Jesuitical passion, under the successive leadership of DF Malan (until 1954), JG Strijdom and, finally, from 1958, the ruthless and brilliant Hendrik Frensch Verwoerd.

Malan speaks to the nation – the white nation

To succeed in these aims, the nationalists needed to entrench their dominance over both the vast non-white population and a still-strong, largely English-speaking United Party (UP), which, although hardly a repository of liberal values, nevertheless recognised just how costly, impractical and ultimately dangerous a widening racial divide would be.

The NP also had to broaden its power base in the country at large and, most urgently, within the military, the police and the public service.

Opening moves

The new regime set about the business of 'Afrikanerisation' with a will, its first act the demotion of English-speaking General Evered Poole, wartime hero of the 6th SA Armoured Division's tough Italian campaign. He was now consigned to an insultingly minor post in Europe. Then, cleverly, it decreed that all public employees were obliged to be bilingual, a condition that sounded reasonable enough to the casual ear but which was, in fact, revolutionary. Many Afrikaners were fluent in both languages, most English-speakers were not, an imbalance that immediately led to wholesale replacements. There were also a number of retrenchments and outright sackings from key positions, and it wasn't long before senior and middle-ranking jobs, and in due course a large percentage of humbler ones as well, were firmly filled by people loyal to the National Party and the *volk*.

On the legislative front, the first salvo was fired in 1949 with the passage of the Prohibition of Mixed Marriages Act, perhaps an odd priority in view of the very few South Africans who had chosen to marry across the colour line, but a faithful reflection of the nationalists' obsession with ethnic 'purity' and their belief in the intellectual inferiority of non-white people. The measure, and the amendment of the existing Immorality Act outlawing any kind of sexual relationship between white and black, were described in parliament by Natives' Representative Sam Kahn (the only communist member) as 'the immoral offspring of an illicit union between racial superstition and biological ignorance'. As fate would have it, one of the first to be charged with immorality was a Dutch Reformed Church minister who had formed a liaison with his domestic worker. Irony aside, however, the two statutes, and especially the first, led to a great deal of disruption and heartache among those mixed couples who shared genuine personal commitment.

Bedrock laws

The government was now poised for its total onslaught on racial integration, but before it could begin to compartmentalise the country, it had to make up its mind just what race was and create the appropriate ethnic cubbyholes. This it did (in the broadest of ways; there would be refinements in the future) with the Population Registration Act, which recognised three main classifications: white, native and coloured. The first, it said in rather tortuous fashion, was 'a person who in appearance obviously is, or by general acceptance is, a white person, but does not include a person who, although in appearance obviously a white person, is by general acceptance and repute a coloured person'. Similarly, a native was defined as someone who in fact or by general acceptance and repute was a member of any aboriginal race or tribe of Africa, and a coloured as someone who 'is not a white person or native'.

In due course there would be other categories – Asian, Malay and so forth – but, quite apart from the morality of the exercise, those who interpreted the laws would soon come up against the hard practicalities. Race classification has no clear scientific basis, which forced the authorities to resort to a bizarre set of criteria (most degrading was probably the 'pencil test' to ascertain the curliness of a subject's hair). More functional, and destined to provide the cutting edge of the government's coercive control system, was the introduction of a card, issued to everyone on a national register, specifying the holder's name, sex, race and identity number.

The ground had now been cleared for the torrent of race laws deemed necessary to transform the country's human and social landscape. What use,

Malan asked parliament, would such laws as the mixed-marriages and immorality measures be 'if black and white continue to live together?' Segregation, he concluded, would have to be firmly entrenched.

First off the statute books was the Group Areas Act, which brought together all previous laws within one all-embracing legal formula that restricted each of the race groupings to its own residential and trading areas. Blacks were not the primary target of the legislation – they were already well regulated by existing statutes. But it did, immediately, force thousands of Indians and coloured folk out of mixed suburbs – described by the National Party as the 'deathbeds of the European race' – and out of their business premises.

Hard on the heels (and a natural extension) of Group Areas came the Reservation of Separate Amenities Act, which sought to provide each race group with its own public facilities – racially exclusive beaches, playgrounds, seating on buses, post office counters, lifts, entrances and so forth. This was the start of a whole system of law and regulation that would come to be known as 'petty apartheid'. The separate amenities, it was clearly understood, need not be equal in quality. After all, this was a time when the

'Petty' apartheid in action

chairman of the National Housing Commission could ask whether it was 'really necessary for a house to have a bathroom and waterborne sewerage? Are communal taps in native schemes such a hardship?'

Some Cape municipalities, heirs to a liberal tradition, simply refused to segregate their cities, but were eventually forced to do so.

Meanwhile, Jan Smuts had died. Known affectionately to people of colour as well as to white South Africans as the 'Oubaas' (the old boss), he had quietly passed away in September 1950, and when the funeral train rolled through the highveld countryside, people of all races lined the route to bid him farewell.

Whatever his ideological ambiguities – and they were many – Smuts was a man of many talents and of remarkable modesty, simple in his needs and tastes, intellectually brilliant, and respected by such great and disparate men as Winston Churchill and Mahatma Gandhi. He had also impressed the scientific world with his philosophy, his theories embracing issues as sweeping and fundamental as human history, climate and geography. In his book *Holism and Evolution* he gave expression to his unique vision of space, time and the human mind, and, at a less abstract level, he was generally recognised as one of the leading environmentalists of his time, harbouring a deep love for and profound knowledge of the natural world in all its forms.

Pledges, prayers and defiance

As one might expect, Malan's onslaught on human and civil rights triggered a reaction, though this was mild enough to start with and easily dealt with by the agencies of government. The non-white psyche in the early 1950s had been stunned, the liberal conscience overwhelmed, by the sheer magnitude of the changes. There simply wasn't the will, or indeed the means, to resist effectively. The white liberal mindset was summed up by Geoffrey Clayton, the respected

Archbishop of Cape Town (and a predecessor of the formidable Desmond Tutu), who, commenting on the segregation of education in June 1953, observed: 'In a country where there is as much colour prejudice as there is in South Africa, it is probable that a non-European boy or girl would not be happy in a European school … It would be impossible for the school authorities to ensure that he would be accepted by other children … When the child leaves school he would go out into a world where there is a widely accepted tradition of segregation.'

The regime's prime and, in its judgement, most dangerous enemy – a perception that echoed anxieties bordering on paranoia in other parts of the Western world (notably the USA, where Senator Joe McCarthy was launching his ferocious witch-hunts) – was the Communist Party of South Africa, which exerted a powerful influence within the trade union movement. The party was also developing an increasingly cosy relationship with both the ANC and the South African Indian Congress.

The CPSA, heedful of the looming threat, disbanded a few days before the passage of the Suppression of Communism Act in June 1950, later emerging with a minimally changed name – South African Communist Party (SACP) – but, faced with huge penalties for pursuing its egalitarian goals, it had to operate for the most part as a kind of secret society. Many of its cadres joined the African National Congress.

Nor were the ANC, the trade unions and other activist bodies neglected by a regime determined to stamp out the last vestiges of opposition. They were hounded into a state of near impotence by the draconian powers conferred on the police by the Criminal Law Amendment Act (1953), which made pretty well any protest, peaceful or otherwise, a punishable offence; and by an amended Riotous Assemblies Act, aimed largely at the unions and their right to strike.

The Defiance Campaign begins

Well before that, though, the extra-parliamentary opposition had begun to show the first semblance of a concerted approach, a process that the ANC's Walter Sisulu, a hitherto dedicated Africanist, had triggered after abandoning his exclusionism.

Early in 1952, while white South Africans were celebrating the 300th anniversary of Jan van Riebeeck's landing on the south-western Cape shores (April 1652), the ANC and its allies urged a throng of 50 000 in Fordsburg's Freedom Square to observe a 'national day of pledge and prayer'. On this occasion the ANC president, James Moroka, was especially outspoken in his condemnation of white misrule, pointing out that 'whatever page they [the whites] turn in the history of South Africa, they find it red with the blood of the fallen, with ill-will and insecurity …'

The rally was the starting point for what became known as the nationwide Defiance Campaign against discrimination in all its forms, its principal target the 'unjust laws which keep in perpetual subjection vast sections of the population'. Thousands of ordinary folk – blacks, Asians, coloureds – took part, drawing inspiration from Gandhi's early passive resistance

Walter Sisulu leads the Human Rights Day march

Men with a mission: James Moroka, Nelson Mandela and Yusuf Dadoo during the Defiance Campaign

The Making of a Nation

The Social Engineers: 1949–1960

campaigns, which, although peaceful enough (in intent, at least), had gone some way towards easing the lot of South Africa's Indians and which, much later, had helped to liberate India itself. A spokesman for the movement, a certain NR Mandela, described at the time as National Volunteer in Chief, stated that the campaign 'does not wish to destroy harmony. We ourselves will not tolerate violence,' but he also referred, ominously, to 'the next, more inclusive stage'.

Much of the activity was directed at 'petty apartheid', multitudes of non-whites challenging the system by entering forbidden areas without passes, joining Europeans-only queues, sitting on white benches, walking through white entrances, riding in white railway coaches, sunbathing on white beaches. But there were also labour strikes and, inevitably, outbreaks of arson and unrest, among the most serious those that flared in Kimberley and East London in November 1952, in which twenty-three blacks and two whites (one of them a nun) lost their lives.

The police, predictably, acted swiftly, raiding private homes and arresting key figures for 'promoting communism'. By October, more than 6 000 people were behind bars. On the face of it, the Defiance Campaign had been a failure, but in one important respect it succeeded very well indeed: it focused much-needed domestic and international attention on issues of profound importance. And it had earned the ANC a good 100 000 new members.

Nevertheless, the ANC was now leaderless and its structures in chaos, a crisis that plumbed the depths with the arrest and conviction of James Moroka. With remarkable lack of judgement, the defendant's lawyer had more or less placed his client at the mercy of the (white) court rather than fight the charges, and Moroka duly went back to his cell and into political oblivion. He was replaced by Albert Luthuli, an aristocrat and deeply religious man who was known to be a moderate; an advocate of political change achieved

Albert Luthuli: resistance leader and man of peace

through negotiation rather than confrontation, but who was now forced by circumstances – by the regime's unrelenting race oppression – to take an ever harder line. He was harassed by officialdom from the very moment of his elevation to the presidency of the ANC, then restricted to the Lower Tugela magisterial district (1954), arrested and tried for treason (1956) and, released for lack of evidence, went on to lead the protest against the 1960 Sharpeville massacre.

The juggernaut

Meanwhile, moves to redraw the map of South Africa along racial lines had begun. Prime mover in this monumental exercise, which lay at the very heart of nationalist ideology, was Hendrik Frensch Verwoerd, a Dutch-born, Rhodesian-educated politician of unusual intellect and dangerous vision.

Verwoerd became Minister of Native Affairs in 1951 and immediately set the ball rolling with the passage of the Bantu Authorities Act, which replaced

Hendrik Verwoerd and henchmen: a 'state within a state'

pass that blacks had been obliged to carry in the past. To make sure that no one could slip through the net, the holder's fingerprints were displayed in the book and filed away in a central registry.

Close on the heels of these ferocious control measures came the Prevention of Illegal Squatting Act, an especially sharp instrument of apartheid designed to cut out and remove the 'black spots' – those pockets of blacks who had been driven, principally by land hunger, into the country's designated 'white' areas.

Grand apartheid

All this set the stage for a vast, protracted programme of forced removals, a continuing exercise that would see whole communities uprooted from their often long-established and well-loved homes, many of the families to be deposited on alien and ungenerous patches of raw veld that would challenge even their most basic survival impulses.

Something, clearly, had to be done. Even the hardest-hearted nationalist realised that if 'grand apartheid' was to work, conditions in the overcrowded reserves must improve and, just as importantly, they must be governed properly. To this end, Verwoerd appointed Frederick Tomlinson, an academic, to head a commission of inquiry, which duly produced its report in 1954.

Tomlinson recommended the creation of self-governing black communities approximating to the existing reserves, but somewhat expanded and economically developed. They needed a lot of money, he said, and this should come from both government coffers and private industrial companies that would be drawn, by all sorts of financial enticements, into the deprived areas. Even so, he didn't think the new structures could possibly cope fully with mounting population pressures. Nor were they the answer to the regime's resettlement difficulties. There were just too many black people in the country, and many of

the somewhat pointless Natives Representative Council with a number of tribal and territorial bodies, to which some executive and judicial functions would be delegated. Only if society were restructured in this kind of way, said Verwoerd, 'could order be created out of the chaos into which the native problem has been allowed to drift'. These new councils, backed by the chiefs and headmen, would be accountable not to parliament but to an all-powerful Native Affairs Department. The measure prepared the ground for the later and far more comprehensive Promotion of Bantu Self-Government Act (1959), which created the infamous Bantustans.

A flood of legislation followed the 1951 statute, most notably the Native Laws Amendment Act (1952), which imposed tight restrictions on the movement of blacks outside the homelands, extended the pass system, placed a seventy-two-hour limit on the presence of 'unqualified' blacks in any urban area, and gave white local authorities the power to remove, forcibly, 'idle and undesirable natives'. The new law, which overnight criminalised tens of thousands of ordinary people, was backed up by the quaintly named Abolition of Passes Act, which, despite its title (a classic Orwellian one), simply substituted a detailed, ninety-six-page personal reference book for the simple them simply had to be regarded as residents of the towns and cities who were there to stay.

Verwoerd rejected the document, saying that no more land would be allocated, that the recommended expenditure was far too high, that white businesses would not be allowed into the reserves (though they'd be encouraged to set up shop on the borders) and that the tribal system of administration would be retained. Nevertheless, Tomlinson's basic ideas persisted, eventually evolving through a series of Bantustans into a system of semi-independent 'national states' (ten of them) and fully independent republics.

The town that died

The victims of the major apartheid laws were myriad, diverse and in many cases subject to profound personal hardship, often tragedy. At the everyday level there were few black city-dwellers who didn't suffer imprisonment for breaching the pass laws at some time during the three post-war decades. Indeed, a prison record soon became something of a badge of honour, worn by a multitude of decent folk who wanted nothing more 'criminal' than to work, live and move around freely.

In due course some terrible stories were to be told of mass relocations in the countryside. The assault that captured the headlines, though, was the destruction of Sophiatown, a suburb of Johannesburg deemed to be a black spot.

Sophiatown, let it be said, was something of a slum, dilapidated, ridden with crime, the overwhelmingly black community embracing some highly dubious elements. But it was also a place vibrant with creative talent, home to artists, writers, musicians, people with something meaningful to say. Moreover, this was one of the few parts of South Africa in which blacks enjoyed freehold rights to property.

Many people fought hard to rescue Sophiatown, none harder than Father Trevor Huddleston, an Anglican priest who had ministered to the residents of the townships since 1943 and who was to write movingly of the slum-clearance programme in his bestselling book *Naught for Your Comfort*.

On 9 February 1955, some 3 000 police, armed with automatic rifles and sub-machine guns, surrounded a rain-soaked Sophiatown as city officials began moving its residents – 110 families in the first batch – to their new homes in characterless Meadowlands, eleven miles away. As they left, anti-rodent squads closed in with cyanide gas pumps, and when they had finished, gangs of workers took over to demolish the houses. In time a trim little white suburb arose where Sophiatown had

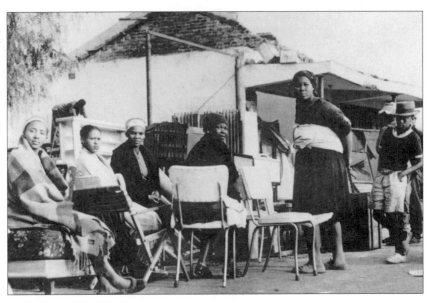

The women of Sophiatown outside their homes – just before the bulldozers arrive

The Congress of the People, Kliptown, Johannesburg

once stood. Cynically, the authorities chose to name it Triomf ('Victory').

In February 2006, survivors of the forced removal and their descendants were among those who celebrated the official restoration of the suburb's name. The wheel had turned full circle, and Triomf became Sophiatown once more.

Blueprint for liberty

At the end of June 1955, a British newspaper reported one of the most significant events in the annals of the liberation struggle. In an attempt to capture the atmosphere, it described a scene enlivened by 'African grandmothers wearing Congress skirts, Congress blouses and Congress doeks [head-scarves] … Young Indian wives with glistening saris and shawls embroidered in Congress colours; grey old African men with walking sticks and Congress armbands; young city workers with broad hats, bright American ties and narrow trousers; smooth Indian businessmen moving confidently among the crowds in well-cut suits; and a backcloth of anonymous faces, listening impassively to hours of speeches …'

The occasion was the Congress of the People, held in the dusty precincts of Johannesburg's Kliptown area and attended by more than 3 000 delegates representing a kaleidoscope of organisations ranging across the extra-parliamentary political spectrum. They had gathered to approve the Freedom Charter, a document which affirmed that South Africa belonged to all its inhabitants regardless of their race, and that no government could justly exercise authority except by the will of the people. It went on to call for the creation of a non-racial democracy, equal rights under and protection within the law, equal job and education opportunities, the redistribution of land, and the nationalisation of mines, banks and industries.

Left: Father Trevor Huddleston: fought long, hard and ultimately without success for the doomed Sophiatown community

The Freedom Charter, blueprint for a socialist future

The charter, heavily socialistic in tone and content, was seen at the time as a blueprint for the future, and was indeed to form the liberation movement's basic policy document in the long, hard decades ahead. In the end, though, much of it (and certainly the economic clauses), had to be abandoned. The eventual disintegration of Soviet-style communism and the hard realities of running a modern, competitive state in the capitalistic world of the 1990s consigned much of it to limbo.

Nevertheless, Kliptown was a watershed. Among the charter's chief signatories were the ANC, the SA Indian Congress, the SA Coloured People's Congress and the Congress of Democrats, a mainly white Marxist body largely comprising former members of the banned Communist Party.

Now, for the first time, there was unity of purpose – or at least the promise of unity.

Schools scandal

The year 1953 had seen the passage of one of apartheid's more far-reaching and, for the country's long-term future, most damaging pieces of legislation – the Bantu Education Act. Aimed principally at the 4 500 church mission schools, which the NP saw as subversive hot spots 'where dangerous, liberal ideas are fed by outsiders to untrained minds', the law brought the whole of black education under the direct control

Children of the Bantu Education Act

of the Native Affairs Department, whose chief, Hendrik Verwoerd, had already stated that the quality of black schooling had to be lowered in order to 'train and teach people in accordance with their opportunities in life'. These 'opportunities' in apartheid South Africa were more or less restricted to unskilled jobs in industry and commerce and menial ones in domestic service. Verwoerd asked: 'What is the use of teaching a Bantu child mathematics when it cannot use it in practice?' and went on to say that race relations could not be improved as long as the 'wrong education is given to natives', and that 'educated natives felt themselves superior to tribal Africans', which was a highly divisive attitude, and that people who believed in equality were not 'desirable teachers for natives'.

The noose tightened. Black teachers were deliberately paid a pittance (£2 a week), drastically reducing the number of bright young people who wanted to be trained for the classroom. And to counter the ANC's threat to set up 'alternative' centres of schooling, the new law forced their founders to register with the government. Those who failed to do so would be prosecuted for 'selling illicit education'.

Finally, blacks were to be excluded from the traditionally white universities; new tertiary institutions would be built in the homelands.

The new targets

On 15 January 1949, a mob from the Cato Manor squatter camp on the south-eastern fringes of Durban armed themselves with sticks and clubs and launched a savage attack on members of the local Indian community, singling out the traders for 'punishment' for the reported murder of a small black boy (who was later found alive and well). Their grievances, however, ran much deeper. Indian men retaliated; more than 140 people were killed and a thousand-plus injured.

The incident, the worst case of race rioting yet seen in the country, did much to persuade Indian leaders that, if their community was to enjoy any kind of stability and prosperity, they needed to cooperate with rather than stand apart from the black majority in their fight to improve non-white living conditions. The two groups, in any event, had much in common – both were being hounded by the apartheid government.

In fact, the latest round of persecution had begun well before regime change, with the Asiatic Land Tenure Act of 1946, which placed severe restrictions on Indian residential and trading rights. Both the Natal and Transvaal Indian Congresses had launched a two-year (though largely ineffectual) disobedience campaign, but the half-million strong Indian community now faced a much fiercer enemy, a government that viewed it as 'a strange and foreign element' that could not be comfortably fitted into the new order, and was intent on stopping all further immigration. It also proposed systematic repatriation, even of families who had lived in South Africa for generations. The first objective was to be fulfilled; the second proved too formidable, even for the nationalists.

Moves to create a common front culminated in a collective declaration – a document signed by

Dr Alfred Xuma of the ANC, Dr Yusuf Dadoo of the Transvaal Indian Congress and Dr GM Naicker of the Natal Indian Congress, committing the three bodies to the struggle against the government's race policies. This declaration, unsurprisingly, became known and respected as the Doctors' Pact.

Meanwhile, a bigger and much lengthier battle was being fought in parliament and the courts over the voting rights of the coloured people, rights that were entrenched in the Union constitution. The relevant clause, which represented a small but infuriatingly stubborn obstacle along the route to absolute political power, had been a priority target from the moment the National Party took office in 1948. The regime's stated intentions provoked a sharp reaction in both coloured and white activist circles.

In terms of the British parliament's South Africa Act of 1909, which created Union in the following year, any changes to the franchise arrangements needed a minimum two-thirds majority of both houses of parliament in Cape Town. The NP enjoyed nowhere near that margin in the 1950s.

DF Malan initially claimed that there was no real obstruction to his plans, declaring that South Africa's parliament had been the country's highest judicial authority since the Statute of Westminster in 1931, and that it could pass whatever laws it liked by a simple majority. In 1951, on his initiative, parliament enacted the Separate Registration of Voters Bill, removing coloureds from the voters' roll.

This measure was immediately challenged, most visibly in the streets, by the relatively low-key Franchise Action Committee and the largely white War Veterans Torch Commando, a conscience-driven movement of ex-servicemen led by the prime minister's namesake, Adolph 'Sailor' Malan. The latter's credentials as a legitimate spokesman for the white moral minority could hardly be questioned. During the war he had flown with the Royal Air Force, fighting in the skies over Dunkirk and in the Battle of Britain, and later rising to the rank of group captain (one of the RAF's youngest). Malan came back to South Africa a popular war hero, highly decorated for both his leadership qualities and the thirty-five enemy 'kills' (individual aerial victories) he had notched up. In 1951 he was wondering just what he had fought for. Included in the Torch Commando's campaign were mass rallies, one of which drew 45 000 protestors to the streets of Durban.

More worrying for the government, though, was the legal challenge. The Appellate Division of the Supreme Court in Bloemfontein held the Separate Registration of Voters Act to be unconstitutional and threw it out. DF Malan, angry but undeterred, then set in train a protracted, thoroughly cynical sequence of political and judicial acrobatic shows that began with a new bill confirming parliament as the Union's

Doctors Naicker, Xuma and Dadoo
sign the historic 'Doctors' Pact'

highest court. Lesser courts would now be exempt, he said, 'from the invidious necessity of becoming involved in constitutional issues'. But this, too, was declared invalid, and despite the government's complicated schemes to obtain the required two-thirds majority, the matter remained unresolved when the premier retired in 1954.

Malan's successor, Johannes Gerhardus Strijdom, then abandoned all scruples, bringing things to a conclusive end within a year by simply increasing the size and changing the composition of both the Senate (by the Senate Act of 1956) and the Appellate Division, and packing each with National Party loyalists. A resurrected Separate Registration of Voters Bill finally received the blessing of parliament and the courts. Its passage had taken five years.

The white conscience

By the end of the 1970s, the whole edifice of petty apartheid had begun to fall apart as racial inter-dependence, economic necessity, practical need and, often, sheer moral outrage chipped away at its edges. It was to be a further decade before the whites-only signs finally disappeared from beaches, park benches, train carriages and public foyers, but the process had begun.

In fact, some local authorities had never fully embraced the National Party's central doctrine. Cape Town's city council, for example, had not taken kindly to beach apartheid and, in fact, defied government's original instructions to erect notices, though it was eventually forced to do so.

But progress was slow. It wasn't until 1972 that Bloemfontein allowed non-white spectators into its main sports stadium, albeit in a separate section. In the same year many of the 800 white residents of the pretty little Transvaal village of Duiwelskloof, right-wing to the core, boycotted their hospital's anniversary celebrations because a local Indian doctor had not

been invited. Three years later, Cape Town opened its main theatre complex and concert hall to all races. And so it went, all over the country, though especially in the Western Cape: a great many whites rejected apartheid, most passively, a few actively. Official discrimination at the everyday level (though not the unofficial variety) finally began to slide into terminal decline in 1979, when the government relaxed the permit system on a wide range of shared amenities that included hospitals, libraries, cinemas, theatres, restaurants, fêtes and exhibitions.

The Torch Commando – mostly whites who had already fought against fascism – march in protest through Durban

Standing for justice: women of the Black Sash

Some fought hard against the system, both independently and as members of organised groups. Notable among the latter was the Black Sash, an association of dedicated women of all races opposed to segregation. The movement was launched in 1955 as the Women's Defence of the Constitution League in order, in the first instance, to resist the government's moves to disenfranchise the coloured people, but went on to stage high-profile protests and silent but highly photogenic 'stands' against discrimination and injustice. Their distinctive badge was a black sash worn over the right shoulder as a symbol of mourning for the loss of basic human rights.

It is probably unfair to single out any one person from the many white, coloured, black and Asian women who are remembered for their dedication and integrity, but Helen Joseph, national secretary of the doughty Federation of Women from the early 1950s, merits special mention, both for her relentless commitment and her stamina. In 1956 she helped spearhead the famous Women's March by thousands on the Union Buildings in Pretoria (her co-leaders, making up a racially representative quartet, were Lilian Ngoyi, Rahima Moosa and Sophie Williams), intent on presenting 7 000 individually signed anti-pass law petitions to Prime Minister Strijdom, who declined even to greet them from his office balcony. Joseph worked long and hard for what must have seemed at times to be a lost cause until the late 1980s. She had followed a painful road that, in 1962, had led to house arrest for a time (she was the first such detainee in South Africa).

The great march to the Union Buildings, Pretoria. The women were intent on presenting a petition signed by thousands; Premier Strijdom refused to see them

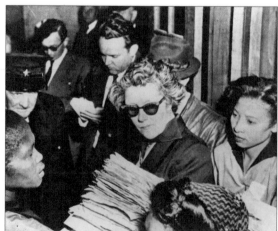

Lilian Ngoyi, Helen Joseph and Sophie Williams

At first, the dynamics of orthodox white opposition were orchestrated by the United Party, heir to Jan Smuts's rather ambiguous set of principles and, from the early 1950s, an increasingly spent political force. Smuts had been succeeded by his protégé JGN Strauss (though other contenders, notably Harry Lawrence, were really far more suitable), who lacked charisma and, indeed, caught as he was between the conservative and the progressive factions of the party, any sort of coherent race policy. The most Strauss could promise liberal whites and the great non-white masses was an undefined package of political rights after a long period of apprenticeship, and then only with the approval of the majority of white voters. He was eased out in 1956, to be replaced by Sir De Villiers Graaff, who presided over the UP's gradual demise during the next twenty-one years.

The central issue at this time was the UP's stance on national states, or Bantustans. The party officially favoured a racially defined federation in which political control remained with the white electorate, a position so close to that of the ruling National Party that the UP found it impossible to present itself as a convincing alternative government. In 1959, twelve of its more liberal parliamentary members broke away to form the Progressive Party, which rejected the basic concept of a racially divided society and later absorbed more members from the waning UP, changing its name successively to the Progressive Reform Party and then to the Progressive Federal Party, but always known familiarly as the 'Progs'. For thirteen years the Progs, sturdily supported by the super-rich Oppenheimer family, had just one representative in parliament, but this happened to be the gritty and gallant Helen Suzman, and the party exerted an influence far beyond its numbers. Suzman became the conscience of liberal white South Africa and bane of the establishment, her uncompromising stand on human rights, her sustained opposition to apartheid and her bitingly articulate

questions well publicised both locally and, increasingly, by the international media.

Mounting pressures

Four months after the Congress of the People produced its historic Freedom Charter in mid-1955, the police closed in, raiding the homes of more than 500 activists. It was the first assault in a campaign that would consign thousands to prison, see thousands more hamstrung by restriction orders and would culminate in the notorious, and in many ways farcical, Treason Trial.

Just before dawn on 5 December 1956, security forces arrested 140 people of all races in a countrywide swoop, transporting them by road, rail and air to Johannesburg's Old Fort prison. They were held there on allegations of treason, an offence that carried the death penalty. Among the detainees were a white parliamentarian; the wife of a former member of parliament (Sonia Bunting); the acting principal of the University of Fort Hare (the respected ZK Matthews); a Methodist clergyman; a sixty-five-year-old non-white pensioner; attorneys; journalists; trade union leaders; and, of course, officials of the extra-parliamentary political groups. Over the weeks and months that followed, other detainees arrived. The trial itself began in Johannesburg's Drill Hall in 1957 and dragged on. And on. The preparatory examination alone took a good two years to complete. Some defendants were never charged, others released for lack of evidence, and the dock became ever less crowded until, on 29 March 1961, when the sorry saga came to an end, only twenty-eight trialists were left. They included such prominent figures as Ahmed Kathrada, Helen Joseph, Lilian Ngoyi, Walter Sisulu and Nelson Mandela. All were acquitted.

The Treason Trial had taken five years to stumble to its dismissive conclusion. But however pointless the whole thing seemed, it did have an impact, especially

Treason Trialists pose for the camera. The accused were eventually whittled down to 28; none was convicted

The Making of a Nation

on international opinion. The global community now began to condemn outright what was happening in South Africa, the anti-apartheid movement given early impetus by a widely viewed BBC *Panorama* programme in June 1957 that featured JG Strijdom and a representative cross-section of activists, among them Chief Albert Luthuli. Strijdom denied that 'blacks as such' were unhappy about his race policy; opposition, he told the interviewer, was confined to 'detribalised Africans under the influence of communism'. But the premier made few friends in responding to accusations of ill-treatment. 'It is all a bunch of lies,' he said. 'There is here and there a little whipping and that sort of thing. You will find it anywhere in the world.'

Shortly afterwards, British arts, entertainment and sports personalities produced a manifesto deploring racial and religious discrimination in South Africa; among its signatories were Peggy Ashcroft, Peter Ustinov, Michael Redgrave, John Gielgud and Dr Julian Huxley. In November 1957, Eleanor Roosevelt, widow of the great American president, headed a list of 123 prominent figures who signed a 'declaration of conscience prohibiting apartheid'. Three years later, thirty-eight South African athletes winged their way to Rome. It was to be three decades before another such team would compete in the sporting world's premier celebration.

The movement splits

All through the 1950s there were sporadic outbreaks of urban unrest, most of them triggered by rising living costs and economic hardship. More often than not, the bus boycott was the favoured medium of protest. Especially notable was the boycott mounted by residents of the densely packed Johannesburg township of Alexandra, which started on 3 January 1957 and lasted three months. Thousands chose to walk up to thirty kilometres to and from work each day rather than use what they saw as a grossly overpriced public transport system. The ANC, whose support for the boycott had been lukewarm from the start, eventually called it off, much to the anger of its younger, more radical elements.

In fact, divisions between the ANC's leadership, which still advocated a multiracial and non-violent approach to the liberation struggle, and its hard-line Africanist faction were deepening by the month. For much of the decade the cracks were papered over. There were just too many arrests, detentions, bannings and threatening government statements for the disunity to become public knowledge. The ranks had to remain closed.

In May 1958, however, ANC leaders urgently instructed branches to implement the 'M-Plan', a contingency scheme drawn up during the 1952 Defiance Campaign that outlined arrangements for going underground. Its declared aim was 'To reorganise the ANC into house and block cells, and to enable it to work by word of mouth instead of by the printed word.' Nevertheless, this wasn't enough to prevent a split, especially now that so many of the movement's more sober-minded leaders had been taken out of the loop by the wave of detentions and by the Treason Trial.

Less than a year later, in April 1959, Robert Sobukwe and some 300 fellow radicals – those who rejected the Freedom Charter and its concessions

Africanist Robert Sobukwe

Sobukwe, founder of the breakaway, radical Pan-Africanist Congress, leads comrades to a mass protest – and to tragedy

to whites, coloureds and Indians – met in Soweto's Orlando township to form the Pan-Africanist Congress (PAC), a militant movement pledged 'to overthrow white domination' and 'strive for the establishment of an Africanist democratic society'.

Sobukwe, inspired by the heady promise of freedom that overlay much of 1950s colonial Africa, and especially by the pan-Africanist vision of Ghana's young firebrand Kwame Nkrumah, was the son of a manual labourer. He had grown up in the politicised Eastern Cape, was a prominent school sportsman (rugby and tennis) and an undergraduate activist at Fort Hare before making his voice heard at the ANC's 1949 annual conference. He was duly elected secretary of the Congress Youth League.

As a student, Sobukwe had called for the creation of 'a new Africa, an Africa reborn, an Africa rejuvenated, a young Africa'. Now, ten years later, his basic message remained much the same: he spoke of the 'liberation of Africa within our lifetime', expressing ideas that were to exert a profound influence on Black Consciousness leader Steve Biko. His rejection of all forms of paternalism – including the well-meaning white variety – and all obstacles to pure-black unity led to the loss of a teaching appointment. Sobukwe

was eminently employable, though, and for most of the decade he worked as a Zulu-language lecturer at the University of the Witwatersrand. He also edited the Zulu-language periodical *The Africanist*.

Shortly after its inaugural meeting, the PAC launched a concerted assault on apartheid, although its first effort, the so-called 'status campaign', which sought to enhance black dignity by banning such commonly used words as 'native' and the more insulting 'kaffir', failed to strike a chord.

The answer to this apathy, Sobukwe reasoned, was to mount a massive head-on attack on the hated pass laws by deliberately courting arrest in order simply to overburden the entire judicial system. This was something the ANC was already planning for 31 March 1960. The PAC decided to pip its rivals to the post by ten days.

The time was right: America and the European countries were talking about trade boycotts; British premier Harold Macmillan had just made his

Walter Sisulu burning his pass

The Making of a Nation

Township residents flee police bullets. The Sharpeville massacre was the turning point

watershed 'wind of change' speech to a startled South African parliament; the townships were tense.

Groups of protestors, heeding the PAC's call, began to gather at strategic points across the country.

Massacre at Sharpeville

On the sunny but chilly morning of 21 March, a crowd of black men and women began to close in on the police station at Sharpeville, a 'model' township near the Transvaal industrial centre of Vereeniging. Earlier, they had blocked roads in an attempt to prevent residents from going to work. Cars had been stoned.

By lunch time the seventy-five occupants of the station, most of them young, inexperienced Afrikaner policemen, were confronted by some 20 000 demonstrators, and their trigger fingers were itchy. Police reinforcements arrived, among them four Saracen armoured cars.

At about 1.15 p.m. a man was arrested; scuffles broke out, missiles were thrown and the police opened fire with .303 rifles and Sten guns. They continued to fire at the backs of the fleeing mob, sixty-nine of whom were killed, 186 wounded. The massacre made world headlines.

The killings were a turning point in the liberation struggle. Freedom, it was now abundantly clear, could not be achieved by peaceful means. And white South Africa could no longer regard itself as a paid-up member of the international community.

After March 1960, the country slid steadily into isolation.

The aftermath at Sharpeville

MAJOR EVENTS

Acts of Parliament: Population Registration; Group Areas; Suppression of Communism (1950). Bantu Authorities; the misnamed Abolition of Passes; Criminal Law Amendment (1951). Native Laws Amendment (influx control); Prevention of Illegal Squatting (1952). Separate Amenities; Bantu Education (1953). Promotion of Black Self-Government (1959). 1952: Defiance Campaign launched. 1954: JG Strijdom becomes prime minister. 1955: Freedom Charter adopted. Treason Trial begins. 1956: Coloured voters removed from common roll. 1958: Hendrik Verwoerd becomes prime minister. 1959: Robert Sobukwe forms Pan-Africanist Congress (PAC).

PEOPLE

The two presidents of the ANC in the 1950s are unusual and gifted men. Among other things, James Moroka (1891–1985) qualifies as a medical doctor at Glasgow University with financial help from an Afrikaner farmer and, in turn, later sponsors the studies of four white children. Albert Luthuli (1898–1967), a devout Christian, has no political ambitions; he becomes ANC leader more or less by accident when he attends a chaotic meeting out of respect for the seriously ailing John Dube, calls for order and is promptly elected to the top post. He goes on to serve as the personification of dignified resistance and to win the Nobel Peace Prize.

SCIENCE & TECHNOLOGY

Cape Town invalid and amateur astronomer RP de Kock is formally honoured for his 5 000-plus observations of 157 variable stars. A decade earlier he discovered a comet, which is named after him. South Africa produces its first home-grown car, the tiny two-seater Dart. It's a useful little runabout but rather ugly to look at, and it doesn't catch on. Sasol, the world's first and only viable oil-from-coal enterprise, is inaugurated (1950). A year later the giant Free State goldfields begin production and, in 1952, the first South African uranium plant comes on stream on the West Rand.

BOOKS

Literary luminary Nadine Gordimer publishes her first work, *The Soft Voice of the Serpent*, at the age of twenty-nine in 1952, followed a year later by the first of her many acclaimed novels, *The Lying Days*. Joy Packer, wife of the admiral in charge at Simon's Town, turns from fact to fiction with a string of bestsellers, including *Valley of the Vines* and *Nor the Moon by Night*.

Author Nadine Gordimer

MAGAZINES

One of Africa's most successful illustrated weeklies appears on the streets in 1951. *Drum* (initially called *The African Drum*) is the brainchild of Jim Bailey, son of magnate Sir Abe and aviation pioneer Lady Mary Bailey. Its content is imaginative and opinionated and it attracts a galaxy of talent, including Lewis Nkosi, photographers Peter Magubane, Jürgen Schadeberg and Alf Kumalo, and the noted writer, actor, poet

Drum: leader in the field

Athol Fugard, during a rehearsal of *The Blood Knot*, 1963

and broadcaster William 'Bloke' Modisane. The birth of one fine magazine coincides with the death of another. *Outspan*, which first appeared in 1927 and became something of a national institution in white South Africa, closes down in 1957.

MUSIC

Another *Drum* journalist with extra strings to his bow is Todd Matshikiza, who composes the music for South Africa's first and best jazz opera, *King Kong* (1959). Also among the period's jazz kings is Kippie 'Morolong' Moeketsi, whose gifts have been nurtured in Sophiatown, but whose familiarity with the gangster scene has stunted his career and nearly costs him his life. Moeketsi plays his saxophone and clarinet in brilliant company – with the Shantytown Sextet and the Jazz Pioneers, and with Abdullah Ibrahim (aka Dollar Brand).

STAGE & SCREEN

Local boys who make good include Johannesburg's Laurence Harvey (born Mischa Skikne), who makes his London West End debut in 1951 in *Hassan* and performs at the Old Vic before taking to the silver screen. His best remembered film roles are in the award-winning *Butterfield 8* with Elizabeth Taylor and *The Manchurian Candidate*. The domestic movie industry is invigorated by brilliant young film-maker Jamie Uys, who releases his first feature in 1950 and goes on to turn out a

succession of winners, among them gentle Boer–Brit satires in which he stars with Bob Courtney. Uys's first major dramatic work is *Dingaka* (with Stanley Baker), his most moving *Dirkie* and *Beautiful People*, his funniest the candid-camera *Funny People* and *The Gods Must Be Crazy*. Theatre-goers are electrified by Athol Fugard's first play, *No Good Friday* (1958), whose cast includes black players – a brave innovation at this time. A few years later, Fugard establishes his international reputation with *Blood Knot*, the inaugural play in a 'family trilogy' that deals with race classification. *Hello and Goodbye* and *Boesman and Lena* follow in due course.

SPORT

Highlights: Cricket – Dudley Nourse's gritty double century against England at Trent Bridge (he bats with a broken thumb). Rugby – the British Lions' sparkling and triumphant tour of South Africa (1955) and Tom van Vollenhoven's 80-metre break to spearhead St Helens to the UK League championship (he evades eleven tackles on the way). Golf – Gary Player's first British Open title in 1959 (he was eight strokes behind before the final round). Boxing – diminutive Jake Tuli's victory against Britain's Jerry Gardiner to clinch the Empire flyweight title (1954); and bantamweight Vic Toweel's memorable fight to win South Africa's first ever world title.

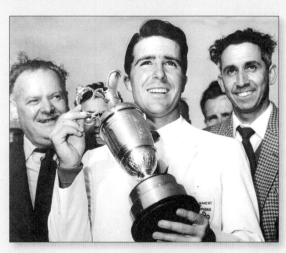

Young Gary Player starts his distinguished career

The Absurdities of Apartheid

During the early apartheid years there were laws, decrees and regulations by the hundred, each revealing enough in itself, perhaps, but the cold print doesn't really convey what was happening on the ground to ordinary people, each rule bringing its daily misery and, all too often, illuminating the farcical nature of the whole system. These are a few of the stories that appeared in newspapers during the first three decades of nationalist government:

- **White husbands change colour:** Under existing legislation, a woman always takes the race group of her husband. A new bill proposes that, where a white man is married to a native or coloured woman, he will be regarded in law as a native or coloured. (1952)
- **Riddle for the maid:** A native nurse-girl carrying a European baby gets into a non-European carriage at Johannesburg's Grosvenor Station and is told to remove herself. While she is explaining her difficulty, the train leaves without her but with the baby. A railway official states: 'All I can say is that the baby's mother should not have left it in the care of a native in the first place.' (1953)
- **Separating the milk:** It is proposed at the annual congress of the Free State Women's Agricultural Union that milk and cream sent to dairies by natives should not be mixed with that of European farmers. A delegate points out that milking is done by natives on all dairy farms. (1955)
- **No entry to church:** When a native reporter goes into a Dutch Reformed Church in Langlaagte one Sunday, the church authorities call the police. The editor of a magazine says that the reporter had been to several churches in Johannesburg recently. He had been turned out of some, including English churches. (1956)
- **Premises denied:** Mr Philemon Nokwe, who four months ago became the first native in the Transvaal to be called to the Bar, has been told he cannot take up chambers in His Majesty's Buildings, Johannesburg. He is informed of his exclusion by the Minister of Native Affairs, who advises him to 'explore the possibility of obtaining office space in one of the native residential areas'. This decision is regarded as a victory for a small group of advocates in the buildings who had complained that they would not be able to handle the law books in the library after Mr Nokwe had touched them, and that he would be entitled to take tea in the common room. (1956)
- **Colour-coded waitresses:** A warning has been issued to municipalities in the Pretoria area not to employ catering firms using white waitresses when non-European guests are being entertained. (1956)
- **Clean difference:** Apartheid in dry-cleaning has been introduced to Port Elizabeth. One firm has a white bag for the clothing of European customers and a grey bag for that of non-whites. (1958)
- **All-white All Blacks:** The head groundsman at New Zealand's Eden Park stadium has found the turf raised in one spot, as if above a grave, and a wooden cross inscribed with the words 'Here lies Racial Equality'. The 'grave' is taken to be an anonymous gesture against the decision of the New Zealand Rugby Union that the 1960 All Black team to tour South Africa will be all white. (1959)
- **Wrong husband:** A young Cape Town woman, pleading not guilty, tells the court that she found out her husband was classed as a Cape coloured only four months after their marriage, when she saw the marriage certificate for the first time. The certificate specified his race. She says her husband told her he was a German Jew, which accounted for his swarthy colouring. (1960)
- **Saving the 'correct' lives:** Members of the MOTH organisation in Greylingstad have been angered by the council's decision not to let the town's ambulance be used to transport seriously hurt Indian victims of road accidents. The town clerk says that the ambulance is for Europeans only, and had been donated by the MOTHs on that understanding. (1961)
- **Public embarrassment:** The Pretoria city council has banned a visiting Japanese swimming team from competing at the whites-only Hillcrest baths. The latest controversy is one of several that is being globally publicised and is causing embarrassment to a regime that is seeking to improve apartheid's image. Another issue attracting attention involves top Indian golfer Papwa Sewgolum, who has been refused permission to play in

Segregated petrol

the Natal Open. Note: Japanese are later to be granted 'honorary white' status by the government. (1962)

- **Tea-drinking condemned:** Referring to the presence of Mrs Albertina Sisulu, wife of Rivonia Trialist Walter Sisulu, at a diplomatic reception, the newspaper *Dagbreek* says: 'Thus originates the mixed gathering which ends in the mixed party of today. It is deliberately organised to undermine the pattern of living in South Africa. This is the motive behind the mixed tea-drinking of the Progressive Party.' (1964)

- **Mixed audiences chaos:** Mr Justice Steyn grants an order in the Supreme Court in Cape Town for the arrest of British singer Adam Faith. Mr Faith is not permitted by contract from performing in front of multiracial audiences, a condition he found unacceptable. Later, British singer Dusty Springfield also challenges the government's rulings. From now on, top artists may refuse to play before separate audiences, afraid their reputations will be harmed if they are seen as 'kowtowing to apartheid'. A month later, Community Development Minister PW Botha announces that sports promoters and organisers of public entertainment may apply for special permits for mixed-race events. (1965)

- **The cost of forced removals:** Mr Brian Bamford (UP, Wynberg) has calculated that 55 000 jobs would have to be found in the Transkei each year for natives removed from the Western Cape if the territory is to be made economically viable. He adds that the fantastic development that was possible in the Western Cape would not materialise if the 400 000 natives living there were to be expelled. Not only would a huge labour force be lost to the region, but a big consumer market would disappear too. (1966)

- **Rare performance:** Permission has been granted for Mr Jan Volkwyn, a coloured concert pianist, to appear with the Johannesburg Municipal Orchestra. It is granted on condition that he is not a regular member of the white orchestra, but would be appearing as a guest; he would appear in one item only; there would be no social mixing, and separate dressing and toilet facilities would be provided. (1966)

- **Mourners turned away:** Eight black men and women were yesterday barred by a Dutch Reformed Church minister from attending a funeral service for a white man. The man, thirty-six-year-old Dennis Hoft, was well liked by his black staff, each of whom had contributed fifty cents to buy a wreath, which was inscribed with the words 'God be with you until we meet again'. (1969)

- **Colour confusion:** The government's refusal to grant a top Japanese jockey a visa to race in two local meetings has created uncertainty around the country. In theory, Japanese are 'honorary whites'; in practice the position is far more complicated. Their official status in different circumstances is: For entry into South Africa, Asiatic; under the Population Registration Act, 'Other Asiatic'; under the Group Areas Act, white; under the Immorality Act, not known; under the Mixed Marriages Act, not specified. (1970)

There is less confusion about people of Chinese descent. Their privileges are being steadily whittled away under the apartheid laws. It takes only one complaint about their participation in an event, even from an anonymous person, for them to be banned. Recent examples of harassment include:

- The enforced withdrawal of thirteen-year-old Patricia Tam from the finals of a junior tennis tournament at Aliwal North.
- Port Elizabeth's Chinese community may no longer play miniature golf or use the skating rink at Humewood.
- A Taiwanese woman, Mrs Weiyien Wong Noether, wife of a German-born businessman, is detained at Jan Smuts Airport and then released a few hours later after being warned not to check in at a city hotel with her husband.
- The withdrawal of a Chinese girl, Ava Junkin, from

Rhodes University's Rag Queen contest after reports of a 'storm' brewing over her entry.

- The expulsion of eight Chinese toddlers from a crèche in a white suburb of Port Elizabeth.
- A Chinese woman married to a white man for thirty years is charged under the Immorality Act. (1970)
- **Painful wait:** A Johannesburg businessman reports that while a woman lay injured following a motor accident, the ambulance department refused to send assistance until her race had been established. (1970)

Entertainer Eartha Kitt: banned

- **Singer sanctioned:** Eartha Kitt, the internationally known American singing star on tour in South Africa, is barred from performing in the Bloemfontein city hall. (1971)
- **A sorry list:** A *Tribune* survey highlights some of the jarring features of 'petty apartheid' in the early 1970s. Some examples:
  - Coloured nurses may not attend to white hospital patients, while at home black nursemaids bathe white babies.
  - An Indian cancer expert is not allowed to lecture to white students.
  - A black man holding a master's degree in nuclear physics is offered a teaching post in a homeland high school at R55 a month.
  - Black schoolchildren must pay for textbooks; white pupils get theirs free from government.
  - Family life is held sacred for whites, while wives and children of black workers are officially referred to as 'superfluous appendages'.
- White and black people are not allowed to share a telephone party line.
- Indian barmen may not serve in a ladies' bar, but Indian waiters can serve women in hotel bedrooms.
- A black may not bequeath his house to his wife or children in a black urban area; when he dies, his land must be sold to the local authority. (1971)
- **Karate kid:** Mr Glen Popham, the thirty-five-year-old coloured man who captained the Springbok karate team against a British side and won a gold medal at the all-white South African Games in 1969, speaks of his fears and frustrations while he posed as a white to learn the sport. He trained at a white gymnasium, was entertained at club members' homes and at the homes of white families when on tours. He says, 'I felt awful when I went to friends' homes, because I could never return their hospitality.' (1971)
- **Medical misfit:** A coloured doctor is refused permission to treat his patients in an Oudtshoorn hospital because their ward is staffed by white nurses. (1972)
- **Municipal boycott:** At least four mayors of Reef towns will not attend Randburg's mayoral church service because the black mayor and mayoress of Soweto will be there. (1973)
- **Misdirected love:** Mrs Betsie Verwoerd, widow of the late prime minister, is quoted as saying that she objects to white children being cared for by blacks: if children were constantly left in the care of a servant, they could

Separate amenities

A beach constable moves black sunbathers off the rocks

only develop a love for their black 'mother'. She says that this leads to social integration, and from there it is only a short step to mixed marriages and the disappearance of whites as a race. (1973)

- **Diner's dilemma:** An international row has erupted over the ejection from a Durban hotel nightclub of a visiting black writer-photographer for the US Information Service, who was told he could dine but not dance on the premises. An official US protest was made, and it couldn't have come at a worse time. The new British government is hardening its attitude towards this country, and the United States, neutral until now, is driven to complain about an incident which to the rest of the world is incomprehensible. (1974)
- **Different noises:** The government has officially introduced 'earmuff' apartheid: employers will henceforth have to provide specially segregated anti-noise earmuffs for 'white, coloured, Indian and Bantu persons'. (1974)
- **A different kind of God:** Blacks have been barred from attending services in two Natal South Coast churches – because a Mr Smith of Amanzimtoti did not

like them walking past his gate on their way to worship. (1977)

- **Beach barriers:** A rigid crackdown on black people on Cape Peninsula beaches has stripped the Muizenberg Festival of its multiracial character. (1977)
- **Filling the prisons:** According to a University of Cape Town sociologist, the battery of pass laws resulted in 5.8 million prosecutions between 1966 and 1975. In a typical year, this would mean more than half a million arrests. (1978)
- **The colour of truth:** A forty-four-year-old white Sea Point woman has been ordered off whites-only buses, treated as a maid and has a broken marriage – all because a brain tumour and the appropriate drug therapy are making her skin turn progressively darker. She says she was shunned by friends, society, her husband and son. 'Now I know what apartheid is like,' she adds. (1978)
- **Parents' punishment:** The West Rand Administration is prosecuting six Sandton residents for allowing their domestic servants to have their children stay with them over Christmas. (1979)

Women are arrested for using a whites-only exit

INTO THE LAAGER
1960–1966

The early sixties are a time of dramatic change: colonialism has become a dirty word and infant nations throughout the Third World are celebrating their new freedoms. For white South Africans, these are threatening trends that push them ever further into the apartheid laager, leaving the liberation movement with just one option – armed struggle.

Thousands of people, led by Philip Kgosana, march from Langa and Nyanga
into central Cape Town in March 1960, in protest against police brutality

On 3 February 1960, Harold Macmillan, the aristocratic and deceptively languid British prime minister, faced a packed joint sitting of the South African parliament in Cape Town and, in quiet and measured tones, changed the course of colonial history for all time. A 'wind of change', he warned senators and members, was blowing through Africa. Britain would not sacrifice black African friendship by supporting race discrimination. It would not associate itself in any way with apartheid. South Africa must take care not to isolate itself from the global community.

The message had also been delivered elsewhere (in Ghana) a few days earlier, but no one had paid much attention. Now, in Cape Town, it was made crystal clear to politicians and public alike: Britain had decided to abandon her colonies; her future lay in Europe; the empire was about to be consigned to the history books; African colonial possessions would, ready or not, be set free to go their own way.

In fact, Africa was already changing, the process gathering momentum almost by the month. Ghana, formerly known as the Gold Coast, had been granted independence in 1956, and more colonies – Tanganyika, Kenya, Uganda, Nigeria, other British and Francophone territories – were lining up for liberty. In southern Africa, Roy Welensky's fragile Federation of the Rhodesias and Nyasaland, that most ill-fated of experiments in togetherness, was creaking its way towards dismemberment, and the Belgians were about to beat a hasty retreat from the Congo, leaving that vast, unprepared and unhappy country to tribal factions and hired mercenaries, to massive bloodshed and, in due course, to the mercies of a brutal kleptocrat.

Macmillan's perceived 'betrayal' shocked white South Africans, though why it should have done so remains a mystery: it had been quite clear for some time that the colonial order was on its way out.

Hendrik Verwoerd was among those who had correctly read the signs. South Africa, he knew, would have to go it alone, and in its own fashion. 'The Afrikaner,' he said, invoking the old myth, 'settled in a country which was bare. The Bantu, too, came to this country and settled certain portions.' In other words, apartness had been more or less built in from the very beginning.

Action and reaction

But Verwoerd and the National Party had more pressing problems at home. A month after Macmillan's seminal speech, the Sharpeville massacre hit the headlines, triggering rumours of a general uprising. Fresh in people's minds was the ambush and killing of a nine-man police patrol in Durban's Cato Manor area a few weeks earlier. A good number of panic-stricken whites rushed to buy arms, others made urgent inquiries about emigration. Albert Luthuli had called for a day of mourning; there was rioting in townships around Johannesburg. The government cancelled all military and police leave, declared a state of emergency and launched a massive wave of arrests, including that of PAC leader Robert Sobukwe. Altogether, 18 000 people were detained. Stock Exchange prices plummeted.

All this may seem to have been overreaction to a single if particularly bloody incident, but Sharpeville was by no means the only hot spot. On the very same

Goodbye to an era: Macmillan and Verwoerd

Verwoerd speaks to his constituency

day, some 5 000 'sons and daughters of the soil', most of them 'sons' from the hostels of Cape Town's strike-bound Langa township, surrounded the local police station. Stirred to mass protest against the pass laws by a twenty-three-year-old university student and peace activist named Philip Kgosana, they were asked how long they were prepared to remain 'a rightless, voteless and voiceless majority in our own fatherland'. Importantly, Kgosana told them to reject violence as the means to freedom because 'we are not leading corpses to a new Africa'. But that night the police moved in and the Cape Flats erupted into an orgy of rioting and arson.

Two days later, on 25 March, Kgosana, still urging peaceful action, led a 30 000-strong column on a long and remarkably good-humoured march from the distant Flats to the centre of Cape Town in protest against brutal police action. The authorities, faced with a crisis that could easily get out of hand, took the sensible option and promised a relaxation of the pass laws for at least a month. The concession was then extended to the rest of the country.

Nevertheless, the infection continued to spread, as Johannesburg, Durban and a dozen other centres flared sporadically, prompting security forces to wade into the crowds with teargas, batons and sometimes guns. On 8 April, the government banned the ANC and the PAC, forcing them underground. Their leaders had tried hard to follow the Gandhian path of non-violence, 'passive resistance' and civil disobedience. Now, outright insurrection seemed to be their only remaining option.

The short-lived crisis

The government's race policies and the methods it used to stamp out protest were roundly condemned by the April 1960 sitting of the UN General Assembly. Only South Africa itself, a barely tolerated member, voted against the resolution, and some key countries began to consider 'separate and collective action' to end apartheid. Even traditional allies were distancing themselves from what was rapidly becoming a pariah regime.

South Africa, though, would be a tough nut to crack; the National Party was determined to fulfil its stated mission, come what may. Verwoerd immediately set about uniting the *volk* in time-honoured fashion, drawing them further into the laager with a combination of pseudo-rational ideology and a certain odd but undeniable personal charisma.

The country was economically strong, well able to weather any storm stirred up by what his spokesman, referring to the newly independent states of Africa, once termed 'these young and ducktailed nations'. Admittedly, overseas investors had pulled out in their dozens after Sharpeville, but South Africa's gold reserves and those of a score of other commodities, some of them of crucial strategic importance in the Cold War era, provided a lot of muscle. Moreover, just to make sure of things, the government introduced strict controls on imports and on the export of capital. It also replaced the British sterling currency system with a decimalised local currency, the rand. The crisis, such as it was, passed.

Going it alone

White South Africans flocked to the referendum ballot boxes in October 1960 and, by a narrow majority, chose a republican form of government to replace their historic ties with Great Britain. The vote – 52 per cent

The 1960 referendum. *Right:* Helen Suzman campaigns against the formation of a republic. The white electorate voted – albeit narrowly – for republican status

for, 47 per cent against – almost exactly matched the comparative numbers of Afrikaners and English-speakers within the electorate.

Sheer pride in Afrikaner cultural identity, a fading but still painful hangover from British imperial excesses and dismal memories of the pre-war poor-white crisis had a lot to do with the result. But so did events in Africa to the north. Voters watched with a mixture of anxiety and complacency as mismanagement, corruption and the horrors of civil war engulfed great parts of the newly free continent. Nigeria, the Congo, Uganda and other infant countries were not coping well with post-colonial trauma. Indeed, some seemed to be on the brink of catastrophe, and practically no Afrikaner and very few English-speakers wanted to go down the egalitarian road they had chosen. White South Africans were safe and prosperous just where they were and, they felt, so were their fortunate black countrymen.

Despite the isolationist message delivered by the referendum, Verwoerd initially declared his intention to retain South Africa's membership of the Commonwealth, but he badly underestimated the

strength of anti-apartheid feeling within the Club, and at its 1961 London conference his fellow premiers made their views quite clear. Verwoerd had little option but to admit that he 'thought it better for South Africa and the Commonwealth to withdraw'.

On 31 May 1960, a rain-soaked but stoic crowd gathered on Pretoria's Church Square to hear their prime minister introduce CR Swart, the republic's first state president.

The armed struggle begins

Even before being banned, the liberation movement prepared to set up offices abroad. Oliver Tambo slipped across the Bechuanaland (Botswana) border and went on to head the ANC's external mission, which eventually established a lively civil presence in the Zambian capital Lusaka, and a largely military one in Tanzania.

But the immediate task was to recover lost ground on the home front, to reinvigorate a resistance movement shattered by wholesale arrest, imprisonment and curfew.

The fundamental question faced by an ANC leadership that had always regarded itself as both patriotic and principled was: Could the good fight for freedom, after decades of peaceful but wholly ineffectual protest, be fought without violence? The answer was a qualified 'no', and in June 1961, at a secret meeting of the national executive, Nelson Mandela's formal proposal that the movement switch to armed struggle was given the nod. Approval, however, was tacit: officially the ANC still subscribed to non-violence; unofficially it would turn a blind eye to acts of physical aggression.

Shortly afterwards, Mandela and a group of other like-thinking radicals, among them representatives of the SACP, formed Umkhonto we Sizwe ('Spear of the Nation'), the movement's armed wing, to undertake a campaign of targeted sabotage. The PAC's equivalent was Poqo, a word that means 'standing alone'. Poqo, however, was far more sinister in form and intent: an organism of secret and self-contained cells, its sole motivation was seemingly hatred for white people, and it dedicated itself to the business of murder. It operated for the most part in the Western Cape and Transkei and enjoyed little success. Its most publicised enterprise was an assault on a party of countryside campers sleeping beside a river; a woman, two young girls and two men were killed. Poqo's plans for a major insurrection – about which its moving spirit, Potlako Leballo, openly boasted – were easily thwarted by government's security arm.

On a much larger scale, and a lot more effective, were the activities of Umkhonto we Sizwe, or MK as it came to be known. Over the next eighteen months, the ANC's armed wing carried out more than 200 acts of sabotage against police stations, Bantu Administration centres, post offices, electrical substations, railway installations and the like – all 'hard' targets. MK tried hard to minimise the risk to civilian lives.

The big raid

The inevitable security crackdown came in March 1961, when Minister of Justice BJ Vorster gave notice that the government would legally 'limit the freedom of speech and movement of agitators'. Ironically, or perhaps deliberately, he made his announcement on the very day that Chief Albert Luthuli received the Nobel Peace Prize (officialdom, in untypically diplomatic mood, had unbent enough to allow the old man to travel overseas for the presentation). June saw the passage of the Sabotage Act, a measure that could be widely interpreted to detain or otherwise restrict anyone the regime disliked, and which was soon to be followed by the all-embracing General Law Amendment Act and its 'ninety-day' clause. The latter bestowed on every police officer the authority to detain, without warrant, any person suspected of 'political activities' for up to three months, and it was aimed directly at Umkhonto we Sizwe and Poqo.

Armed with its deadly new powers, the security machine went to work with a will, its campaign masterminded by two of the most

Pylons blown up by Umkhonto we Sizwe, the 'Spear of the Nation'

Some of the Rivonia Trialists: Nelson Mandela, Walter Sisulu, Govan Mbeki, Raymond Mhlaba, Elias Motsoaledi, Andrew Mlangeni, Ahmed Kathrada, Denis Goldberg

ruthless of the white supremacists. In their younger days, both Balthazar John Vorster and Hendrik van den Bergh, head of the Bureau of State Security (usually reduced to its revealing acronym, BOSS) had been active members of the Ossewabrandwag, the Nazi-type wartime underground movement; both were interned for the duration; each was now dedicated to the destruction of the resistance movement. The partnership proved lethally effective, its biggest coup accomplished on 11 July 1963, when a squad of detectives swooped on the Liliesleaf farmhouse in the northern Johannesburg suburb of Rivonia and arrested seventeen senior activists.

The ANC had purchased the property as a convenient hideaway and base of operations two years earlier, but its existence had eventually been revealed by a police undercover operative and the raid was perfectly timed. Almost the entire MK leadership was present. Among those taken into custody were Walter Sisulu, who was already wanted for skipping bail,

Govan Mbeki, Raymond Mhlaba and Ahmed Kathrada of the Transvaal Indian Congress, who was supposed to be under house arrest at the time.

A notable absentee was Mandela, already behind bars for relatively minor offences. He had managed to sneak across the northern border and, for a few months, strode the international stage with impunity. He had become a world figure, enhancing his celebrity and will-o'-the-wisp image in the few short, audacious weeks after his return to South Africa, but his luck had finally run out. On 5 August 1962, he was arrested and charged with incitement and illegally leaving the country. He drew a five-year prison sentence.

But police found one of Mandela's diaries at Liliesleaf, along with some notes on guerrilla warfare and revealing written recollections of his recent tour of independent African countries. This was altogether a more serious business than the merry dance he had led the authorities.

Meanwhile, a young student activist, Thabo Mbeki, son of the senior resistance leader Govan Mbeki, had

Mandela: the African Pimpernel

The man who was to become South Africa's first black president had been leading an eventful life since launching the armed struggle in 1961.

Indeed, the young Nelson Mandela's was an adventurous character, surprisingly frivolous in some ways. Not always considered a real political heavyweight by his senior peers, he was bright, charming, enthusiastic, a clever talker with a quick mind and a taste for fast cars and fast women, tending towards the flamboyant. He was also uncompromisingly loyal to and respectful of his close friends and colleagues, who fortunately included the level-headed Oliver Tambo, his former legal partner. Among his mentors, too, were Walter Sisulu and the impeccable Albert Luthuli, men with both feet on the ground. Mandela quickly matured in the immediate post-Sharpeville period.

During the two years that had elapsed since the massacre and clampdown. Mandela had been a fugitive from justice, travelling from safe house to friendly refuge around the country, often in disguise, chary of making contact with his lovely young wife Winnie and their children, speaking for the ANC from hidden places, an elusive figure whom the press had taken to calling the 'Black Pimpernel'. Dramatic stuff indeed, more so since he had spent six months of this time abroad, impressing British Labour politicians in London and eminent liberation leaders in Africa with his energy and ideas. He had

Above: Mandela in Johannesburg. *Below:* Learning about guerrilla warfare in Algiers

also attended the Pan-African Freedom Conference in Addis Ababa, staying on for a spell of training in guerrilla warfare before undergoing a further course in an Algerian camp.

But, inevitably, Mandela's luck ran out. On 5 August 1962 he was arrested and charged with incitement and illegally leaving the country. Sentenced to five years in prison, he became the captive of a regime that was about to round up the ANC leadership, try them and put most of them behind bars for decades.

sabotage, but flatly denied any conspiracy to launch an armed insurrection.

Mandela seized the opportunity to articulate his personal commitments and his vision for the future. Speaking from the dock, he told the court, and the world, that he had spent thirty years of his life 'knocking in vain, patiently, moderately and modestly at a closed and barred door … until today we have reached a stage where we have almost no rights at all'.

He ended with a moving plea for the creation of a non-racial South Africa. 'During my lifetime,' he declared, 'I have dedicated myself to the struggle of the African people. I have fought against white domination, and I have fought against black domination. I have cherished the ideal of a democratic and free country in which all persons live in harmony and with equal opportunities. It is an ideal which I hope to live for and

Yusuf Dadoo and Joe Slovo at a demonstration in London

also secretly left the country. He, however, had been detained by the authorities in Bulawayo, Southern Rhodesia's second city, and was able to continue on his way to exile, but only after the intervention of the British Labour Party. Tanzania's Julius Nyerere granted him asylum, and in due course he left Africa to study in the United Kingdom.

Trial of the century

Mandela joined Sisulu and others arrested during the Liliesleaf raid for the showcase 'Rivonia Trial', which began in the Pretoria Supreme Court in October 1963 and lasted seven well-publicised months. The ten accused admitted to some acts of

Afrikaner revolutionary

Advocate Bram Fischer, brilliant lawyer, grandson of

a colonial premier, and a lifelong communist, acted for the defence in the four-year Treason Trial and led the defence team in the later Rivonia Trial. He then went into hiding, was captured, charged under the Suppression of Communism Act, received a life sentence and, in 1967, was awarded the Lenin Peace Prize. He died six years later, lonely to the last: his family had been denied visiting rights, and were refused permission to attend his funeral.

achieve. But if necessary it is an ideal for which I am prepared to die.'

The defendants received life sentences. Mandela would spend the next twenty-seven years behind bars, but not just as another political prisoner. He was now a recognised leader of true stature.

Tightening the screws

With the resistance movement crushed, its leaders in jail, the majority of English-speaking voters content with their powerless but increasingly prosperous circumstances, the workforce relatively quiet, parliament well under control and the economy about to enter an unprecedented boom period, Afrikanerdom and its social engineers were moving towards the high summer of success. New capital, mainly from a flourishing Europe in search of stable investments, was pouring in despite growing international pressure to halt the progress of apartheid and dismantle its machinery. Especially supportive were a now fully recovered post-war Germany (which, happily for its conscience, was not yet a member of the United Nations) and a Gaullist France proud of its independent foreign policy and determined to weave its own network of international alliances.

The scene was set for fulfilment of the master plan – the creation of separate states in which black South Africans could enjoy political rights, or at least some of them, without jeopardising the security and well-being of the white minority.

But there were dilemmas. Most notably, the racial groupings were mutually dependent: blacks needed work, and the 'white' economy needed cheap labour. By now everyone, even the most diehard segregationist, accepted that a black workforce was a permanent, irremovable feature of the urban landscape. The ethnic omelette, it appeared, could not be unscrambled.

The two imperatives – segregation and interdependence – would seem to have been irreconcilable, but to assume so was to underestimate the regime's determination, its ingenuity and its downright cynicism. It simply made use of an arsenal of heavy weapons already on the statute books, most importantly the two Land Acts (1913 and 1936), an amended version of the Black Urban Areas Act (1945) and the ever handy pass laws, not to enforce total separation, but to control the size of the urban black population and thus contain all the perceived threats posed by a rapidly growing majority that would, if integrated, 'swamp' the ruling classes.

Together, the measures ensured, among other things, that no black persons could stay in a 'white' rural area unless they had been recruited by a farmer (a quota system made certain that the numbers were kept down).

The answer wasn't quite as neat when it came to the cities and towns, but Section 10 of the Urban Areas Act seemed to address the problem efficiently enough, or at least to maintain some sort of racial equilibrium. The crucial clause gave residential rights to just three classes of black people: those who had been born in the area, those who had worked continuously for ten years for the same employer, and those who had been in continuous residence for at least fifteen years. But – and it was a big but – anyone who was not able to claim birth rights could be 'endorsed out' if he committed a crime carrying a jail sentence of six months or longer. The work-seeker who did not qualify under Section 10 was allowed to stay in the area for just seventy-two hours, after which he could be arrested and deported.

The chequerboard

Permanent residential rights were thus tightly monitored and carefully tailored to add value to but not interfere with the white economy. The needs of the mines and factories could be filled for the most part by a shifting mass of migrant black labour, a 'temporary' army of workers packed into dreary and often unsafe single-sex

Inside a mineworkers' hostel: an appalling life

hostels for the duration of their seasonal contracts, after which they returned to their faraway homes. Some of the designated 'black' rural areas were just close enough to allow residents to commute on a daily basis, an arrangement that might entail a three-hour bus journey to get to work.

These were the lucky ones. South African society was fluid and a huge number of other black people, denied the opportunity to own property and at the mercy of a fickle labour market, were condemned to a jobless, poverty-stricken limbo.

Verwoerd and his social engineers were well aware of this, and they had their 'solution'. Eventually, ten quasi-independent national states, initially called Bantustans, would be carved out of otherwise unwanted land in terms of the Promotion of Black Self-Government

Act, each, according to the architects, a coherent territory that enjoyed a distinct cultural identity and whose inhabitants shared the same language, customs and traditional laws. Now, along with 'Bantustan', the word 'apartheid' was jettisoned in favour of the more positive-sounding 'separate development'.

But what was dreamt up by the ideologues in Pretoria had no basis in reality. The theory that gave an apparent moral force to the government's race programme sounded fine to some; the practicalities were very different. None of the designated homelands had a major town, and many consisted largely of degraded farmland that no white person would think of working for profit; the ethnic distinctions between the various 'nations' were largely imaginary: they didn't exist, and never had existed.

District Six: apartheid in action

Altogether, nearly two million black South Africans were 'relocated' during the 1960s. In addition, 600 000 Indian and coloured people and 40 000 whites (plus some Chinese) were moved in terms of the Group Areas Act. Among the most publicised of the mass removals was that of the District Six community on the fringes of central Cape Town.

District Six was a cosmopolitan little place inhabited by some 60 000 mostly coloured people. It hit the headlines in the mid-1960s, when it was declared a 'white' area and the demolition teams moved in. Over the next few years the residents were progressively removed, many taken off to their new homes in the developing, rather soulless town of Mitchell's Plain on the flat, desolate countryside east of the city.

Officialdom argued that the removals were part of a genuine upliftment programme, that District Six was chaotic, unhygienic and no longer tenable in terms of the Public Health Act. And indeed the place was overcrowded, crime-ridden, its buildings dilapidated. But it also had charm, a powerful community spirit and plenty of vibrant life, its narrow streets full of colour and movement, the air noisy with the cries of hawkers, argument and the laughter of children, fragrant with the scents of a myriad exotic spices. District Six had a soul. One former resident remembered that 'when we were evicted, we lost more than our home. We lost neighbours and friends whom we could depend on in times of sickness and other misfortune. The government gave us another home; it couldn't give us a sense of belonging.'

National Party apologists were careful to assure the world that the homelands were not dumping grounds, but nascent and viable states in their own right. Eric Louw, Foreign Minister in the late 1950s and early 1960s, had already explained to the UN General Assembly that they would 'progress along the road towards self-government and eventually form part of the South African commonwealth, together with the Union of South Africa, which will during the intervening period act as their guardian'. The programme, Louw continued, was in accordance with 'the trends and developments in the African continent', by which he meant the impending independence of a host of colonies, including the neighbouring British High Commission territories of Bechuanaland (Botswana), Basutoland (Lesotho) and Swaziland.

But when it came down to it, 'dumping grounds' were what the homelands became. The South African chequerboard was being laid out, and the civil authorities, hidebound by an inflexible separatist doctrine, were committed to shifting the human counters to fit the predetermined pattern. They did so with gusto.

The black spots were progressively eliminated as thousands of ordinary folk were deported because they were 'surplus to labour requirements'. Among them, according to an official statement of objectives, were 'the aged, the unfit, widows, women with dependent families who do not qualify for accommodation in European areas'. Other unwanted persons included 'Bantu on European farms who become superfluous as a result of age or disability', and 'doctors, attorneys, agents, traders, industrialists, etc. who are not regarded as essential for the European labour market'. Residents of towns and villages close to the homelands were shifted across the borders, or the borders simply redrawn to enclose them. Chunks of homeland and adjacent patches were consolidated in the interest of geographical neatness, thousands of homes bulldozed

and their occupants trucked away to new and unfamiliar places.

The Transkei region in the far south-east was probably the most credible element of this brave new world. It had enjoyed a modicum of self-rule in the past, a privilege conferred by the Glen Grey Act of 1894. Unluckiest were the black people of the Western Cape, which had been formally defined as a 'coloured labour preference area' and where, as a consequence, civic infrastructure for blacks – houses, schools, hospitals, electricity, proper sanitation – were minimal. Here, blacks were at the very end of the jobs queue, and tens of thousands were uprooted and sent back to their ancestral lands (which some had never seen) in the Ciskei and Transkei. Most of them simply trekked back, to create vast squatter camps on the windswept bleakness of the Cape Flats, entrenching a demon of deprivation that would continue to haunt city planners for decades.

Rhodesian rebel Ian Smith

End of an era

The complexities of a rapidly decolonising Africa arrived on the Republic's doorstep in 1965, the last full year of Hendrik Verwoerd's life.

On 11 November, Southern Rhodesia's white minority premier Ian Smith announced the colony's unilateral assumption of independence (the declaration would be known as UDI). Britain's Harold Wilson immediately imposed a range of economic sanctions, but turned down a demand from Africa's 'front-line states' to send in troops. An attempted invasion would be a logistical nightmare, and in any case, as Smith repeatedly pointed out, most white Rhodesians were of British stock with 'kith and kin' in the old country. Nevertheless, within days energetic steps had been taken in the councils of the world to isolate the troublesome colony and bring the rebel regime to its knees.

The death of Hendrik Verwoerd, architect of 'grand apartheid'

To Verwoerd and his cabinet, these were unwelcome developments that focused international attention rather too firmly on southern Africa's seemingly intractable race problems. He would much rather Smith had not taken the plunge, but still, rebel Rhodesia could possibly provide some sort of buffer to black nationalist infiltration from the north, and moreover, there was no way he could bring himself (nor would he be allowed by his constituency) to withhold support from his white neighbour. Nor, of course, could he afford to see economic sanctions succeed. South African government policy, he said, was 'to maintain ties of friendship with all neighbouring countries, whether white or black. This goodwill and these friendly relations remain unchanged. The Republic can therefore not take part in any form of boycott.'

It was a creed Verwoerd carried through to the last. Its practical core was an intention, eventually, to come to an accommodation with his neighbours in black Africa, something that he thought might well be within the bounds of possibility simply because his country was by far the strongest and richest on the continent, and it was in everyone's practical interests to coexist peacefully. He took the first small step on 3 September of the following year when he welcomed Chief Leabua Jonathan of Lesotho to the Union Buildings in Pretoria – the first ever meeting between a South African prime minister and the leader of an independent African state. A joint communiqué affirmed the principles of good neighbourliness and non-interference in the domestic affairs of other countries.

We shall never know how far along this road Hendrik Verwoerd would have travelled. He had already escaped death at the hands of a would-be assassin when a deranged white farmer shot him in the face at the 1960 Rand Easter Show. But now fate turned against him. On 6 September 1966, as he took his seat in parliament prior to making what was to be an important announcement (presumably on his plans to adopt a more genial foreign policy), a messenger walked across the floor and stabbed him to death. The killer, Dimitri Tsafendas, was later diagnosed a schizophrenic and adjudged unfit to stand trial.

MAJOR EVENTS

1960: British premier Macmillan delivers watershed 'wind of change' speech. Anti-Pass Law campaign launched; Sharpeville massacre shocks world; ANC and PAC banned. **1961:** South Africa leaves Commonwealth, assumes republican status. ANC forms military wing (Umkhonto we Sizwe), PAC forms Poqo. **1962:** Sabotage Act passed. **1963:** Liberation movement leaders arrested in Rivonia, Johannesburg. **1964:** Rivonia Trial: Nelson Mandela and others receive life sentences. **1965:** White Rhodesian leader Ian Smith declares colony's independence. **1966:** Hendrik Verwoerd assassinated; succeeded by BJ Vorster.

THE SWINGING SIXTIES

Middle-class South Africa responds to the revolution in morals, modes and social values that turns life upside down in the Western world. 'Flower power', 'hippie' and 'psychedelic' are among the decade's buzzwords; American society is fractured by massive and successful civil rights protests, later by mounting disillusion with the Vietnam War and campus riots. Gentler messages emanate from Britain, where the Beatles, Mary Quant and Carnaby Street define the mood of the times.

Miniskirts turn heads on Adderley Street, Cape Town

PEOPLE

Deaths at this time include that of Cissie Gool, who has been on a non-stop human rights campaign since 1930. For years she served as Cape Town's only woman city councillor. She also led passive resistance marches and was jailed and placed in solitary confinement. She obtains her law degree and is admitted as an advocate in the year before her death. Less well mourned is twenty-eight-year-old white schoolteacher John Harris, executed in 1965 for detonating a bomb on a platform at Johannesburg's main train station, killing one and injuring more than twenty others. Harris is a member of the African Resistance Movement and chairman of the South African Non-Racial Olympic Committee. He walks to his death singing 'We Shall Overcome'.

STAGE & SCREEN

The epic feature *Zulu*, about the valiant defence of Rorke's Drift, is a huge box office success. The part of Cetshwayo is competently filled by the king's direct descendant Mangosuthu Buthelezi; old photos show that the two are remarkable lookalikes. Starting to make her mark on the international stage is South African actress Yvonne Bryceland, whose performances in Athol Fugard's plays earn wide acclaim. André Huguenet, the highly respected pioneer of Afrikaans theatre and the only South African actor invited to appear at the 1951 Festival of Britain, dies destitute in 1961.

BOOKS

The young Wilbur Smith produces the first in a long and immensely lucrative string of blockbuster novels. *When the Lion Feeds* (1964) is a robust adventure story laced with a bit of sex, and it is banned by the local censors. Another bestseller is Credo Mutwa's *Indaba, My Children* (1966), which records, in a mix of folklore, praise song, fantasy and fact, a goodly chunk of African oral literature. Other literary luminaries of the time include Etienne le Roux, who publishes the first volume (*Sewe Dae by die Silbersteins*) of a brilliant trilogy and will go on to be remembered especially for his powerful

Magersfontein, O Magersfontein! Le Roux is a member of the Sestigers, a group of innovative young writers who are giving Afrikaans literature a refreshing new face. Among other members are Jan Rabie, Chris Barnard, André Brink, Abraham de Vries and poets Breyten Breytenbach (eventually imprisoned), Adam Small and Ingrid Jonker (who takes her own life, by drowning, in 1965). Popular English-speaking writers of the time are Robert Ardrey (an American-born Capetonian who becomes a kind of global guru on the subject of human origins), Geoffrey Jenkins (*A Twist of Sand*) and, virtually unknown because she wrote under so many pen names, Kathleen Lindsay, the most prolific author in the annals of English prose. Lindsay, who lives in Somerset West, turns out more than 900 lightweight novels during her literary career, typing (mostly at night) with two fingers. She also travels widely, runs her house, makes her own clothes and keeps thirty cats.

MUSIC & BALLET

Among the liveliest of the young and talented township music-makers is Lemmy 'Special' Mabaso, leading exponent of the joyous penny-whistle sound (featured in the ground-breaking 1959 jazz musical *King Kong*). Mabaso's reputation grows to the point where he is invited to appear at the Royal Command Performance in London. Meanwhile, South African operatic star Mimi Coertse has been receiving standing ovations on the global stage since her 1956 debut in Mozart's *The Magic Flute*. She is now ranked among the world's top four coloratura

A youthful Mimi Coertse: one of the world's top four

sopranos. Her ballet counterpart is Nadia Nerina, soloist with London's Sadler's Wells from 1952. Nerina has danced in all the major roles at Covent Garden and finally retires in 1966.

SPORT

Twelve-year-old South African prodigy Karen Muir swims to prominence when she breaks the world 110-yard (approximately 100-metre) backstroke record in Blackpool, England, in 1964, and goes on to set another seventeen world marks before she reaches the age of eighteen. Another youngster, cricketer Graeme Pollock, makes his first-class debut in 1960 at the age of sixteen. The normally stony-hearted racing fraternity is inspired by the saga of Sea Cottage, favourite for the 1966 Durban July Handicap. The horse is shot by a hidden gunman while on a training run and, lamed, is written off

Master strokemaker Graeme Pollock

– but he recovers to come in a brave fourth, win the Clairwood Handicap two weeks later and, in the following year, to share the July honours in the only dead heat in the race's history. South African golf, which has a generally honourable record, is shamed by the treatment meted out to Durban's Sewsunker 'Papwa' Sewgolum, who, although he has a bizarrely unorthodox style, becomes the first South African of colour to triumph on the international circuit (he is thrice winner of the Dutch Open). He features prominently in the SA Open and other domestic tournaments, but is cold-shouldered by the establishment (though not by Gary Player). On one occasion he receives his winner's trophy in the pouring rain while his white player-peers shelter in the clubhouse.

The Sounds of South Africa

Miriam Makeba: African Queen of Song

If anything gave the emerging nation a distinctive character, it was the music that was evolving in town and country. There were many strands, even – and perhaps especially – within the wider black culture. The various groups had ancient musical traditions, their peoples generally endowed with a natural aptitude for rhythm and multi-part harmony. But with rapid urbanisation in the early years of the twentieth century, a new, bouncy, anything-goes sound began to emanate from the townships of the industrial north, its popularity fed by the infant radio and recording industries. It was called *marabi*, and the early South African record companies, enticed by the expanding urban mass market, cheap performers and quick profits, exploited it to the full.

In due course, *marabi* and its successors became a lot more sophisticated as broadcasting and the gramophone exposed millions to the best of Dixie jazz, Louisiana blues and the big-band music of Ellington, Basie, Armstrong and other great artists. Talented local instrumentalists and composers who began to make a name for themselves included Abdullah Ibrahim (initially known as Dollar Brand), James Gwanga, Kippie Moeketsi and top trumpeter Hugh Masekela.

Meanwhile other forms were adding to the domestic mix, most notably perhaps that of the voice-only Zulu *mbube* 'choral band', which made its first big impact with Miriam Makeba's recording of 'Wimoweh' and cemented its integrity two decades on with Ladysmith Black Mambazo's splendid contribution to

Paul Simon's bestselling *Graceland* album. Then there was the penny whistle and home-made guitar kwela music of the streets, which originated in Johannesburg's Alexandra township in the 1940s and went on to gain enormous cross-cultural popularity. Over time, other, newer and mostly American sounds – rock, soul and reggae – were added to the heady township brew, eventually to produce what is loosely termed *mbaqanga*, but which had so many variations that there were probably as many distinctive styles as there were individual bands. They all, though, had something in common: they were fresh, innovative and exciting.

Jazz pianist Abdullah Ibrahim

Masekela: from Sophiatown to Manhattan

Mbaqanga is the name for African maize bread and, like the food, the music filled a void, a deep need in times of hardship and racial oppression. Oddly enough, few performers used it as a medium for political protest: it was played and listened to, from the beginning, for pure enjoyment.

Local music took to the stage with huge success on occasion. The first of what are probably the three most memorable musicals was *King Kong*, a jazz opera depicting the sorrows and joys of life in doomed Sophiatown before its demolition, the story revolving around renowned black boxer Ezekiel Dhlamini. Created by Stanley Glasser, its music was a blend of African, African-American and European styles, and when it reached London's West End in 1961 it caused something of a sensation. As impressive in their own way were Mbongeni Ngema's *Sarafina*, a lively production with vibrant Soweto as its backdrop, and *District Six: The Musical*, a record-breaking Cape show composed and written by David Kramer and Taliep Petersen.

Running parallel to all this were the purer jazz forms that enjoyed their heyday in the 1950s and 1960s (and suffered near terminal decline with the upheavals triggered by the Group Areas Act) and, quite different, the exuberant music of the coloured community, whose lively traditional celebrations owe something (in their parades, at least) to the American Deep South, but whose songs – the cheerful, sometimes racy *ghoemaliedjies* – are pure Cape. Distinctive, too, has been the canon of Afrikaans folk music, rooted in the nineteenth-century Boer struggle for recognition and often heartbreakingly poignant in its expression. The more commercial *boeremusiek* was a later arrival.

King Kong: a musical landmark

The youth take to the streets in Soweto, June 1976. The Soweto uprising was a turning point in the liberation struggle

CHAPTER 9

CRACKS IN THE WALL
1966–1978

*As the pressures mount,
the apartheid regime seeks to
make new friends in Africa.
But the ANC in exile and radical
young activists at home threaten the
very foundations of the state.*

With the dramatic death of Hendrik Verwoerd, a giant – superstar to some, the incarnation of evil to others – passed from the political scene. Nothing could again be quite the same for South Africans. Still, business seemed to be very much as usual in the weeks and months that followed.

Nobody really expected otherwise. Certainly no lurch to liberalism was anticipated. After all, the new man in charge once said: 'You can call such an anti-democratic system [as ours] a dictatorship if you like. In Italy it is called Fascism, in Germany National Socialism, in South Africa Christian Nationalism.' It was the kind of confident, in-your-face admission most whites wanted to hear. The National Party mandarins chose Balthazar John Vorster as their leader because of his loyalty to the *volk*, his commitment to policies laid down by the chief architect of 'separate development' and his crucial role in the suppression of black opposition within the country.

John Vorster in unusually amiable mood

Vorster, the former Minister of Justice, had neutralised resistance to apartheid largely through the agency of BOSS, an umbrella organisation under command of the tall, cadaverous police general Hendrik van den Bergh, who reported directly to the prime minister. BOSS enjoyed almost unrestricted authority to investigate and detain; was not obliged to account for the vast sums of money allocated to it; and had both the freedom and the resources to extend its operations to foreign parts – a competence that was soon to be exercised. Vorster had created a monster and, like Dr Frankenstein's, it would destroy him in the end.

To start with, though, there was an illusion that the future affairs of state might be handled in a slightly more relaxed way, that Afrikanerdom might be coming to terms with the realities of the twentieth century.

Dialogue and détente

BJ Vorster, a short, squat, unsmiling politician with none of his predecessor's presence, had thrust his way to the top as the hard man of the National Party, but one doesn't climb the peaks of power without being a pragmatist. He was well aware, as Verwoerd had been, that although all might be reasonably quiet on the domestic front, danger lurked beyond the borders. Soon after assuming office, he announced what was held to be a ground-breaking 'outward' programme, a policy of dialogue with black Africa. Its key ingredients were economic cooperation and the promotion of interdependence.

The initial omens were favourable. Within the southern subcontinent, South Africa seemed secure enough, ringed as it was by a *cordon sanitaire* of friendly, white-controlled states and thus hopefully insulated from the poison of revolutionary ideas. Portugal had thus far declined to join the general stampede to decolonise and remained in control, albeit tenuously, of Angola to the north-west and

Mozambique to the east. South West Africa could be regarded as the Republic's fifth province; Ian Smith's rebel Rhodesia was fragile but surviving; Lesotho, Botswana and Swaziland were too close, too small and too dependent to cause any trouble. There were potential enemies beyond this cordon, of course, but none, Vorster reckoned, that couldn't be seduced with soft words and promises of material benefit.

In the ensuing years Vorster made friendly contact with South Africa's near neighbours, with Malawi's Hastings Kamuzu Banda, who ranked among the most businesslike and dictatorial of the northerly African leaders, and with the Ivory Coast and Liberia in the far north. Even when Portugal abandoned her African possessions and the cordon began to crumble, Vorster persisted with his bridge-building approach, giving his immediate if rather grudging support, for instance, to the new Marxist regime in Mozambique.

But old friendships could not be allowed to stand in the way of regional tranquillity. As the 1970s progressed, Rhodesia began to emerge as a serious obstacle to détente, and the South African premier started the painful process of disengagement from his fellow whites across the Limpopo. The Republic's security forces, deployed in Rhodesia since 1967 – mainly to stop southward guerrilla incursions – were withdrawn from the escalating bush war and, in an unprecedented move, Vorster met with Zambia's Kenneth Kaunda to resolve a shared problem. The conference took place on the Victoria Falls Bridge that straddled the Rhodesia–Zambia border. Dialogue, it seemed, was working.

The bigger arena

Meanwhile, many of the leading ANC activists were in exile and busy establishing an international presence, notably in London, from where Oliver Tambo and the Umkhonto we Sizwe chief of staff, Lithuanian-born lawyer Joe Slovo, initially directed the movement's

The détente process: Vorster with Zambia's Kaunda

affairs. Offices had also been opened in Tanzania and, after Zambia became independent, in Lusaka, which was to serve as the ANC's external headquarters for the duration of the liberation struggle.

Things didn't go too well for the exiles at first. They had been expecting the massive moral, practical and funding support that had been more or less promised to the movement after Nelson Mandela's hugely successful odyssey in 1962, but nothing much materialised. The travails of newly won freedom were proving onerous for many infant African states; corruption, mismanagement and civil strife were tearing at the vitals of some; others, better placed, needed to stay on reasonably good terms with what was undeniably the continent's powerhouse in the far south.

There had been some guerrilla incursions, but they were poorly planned and quickly detected, and Vorster's security arm had handled them with almost dismissive ease. They were small affairs, usually involving brave little groups of no more than three or four persons, and sometimes even single individuals. On the only occasion on which a large-scale incursion was attempted – a head-on confrontation in 1967 – the insurgents were caught in the great sunlit spaces of Rhodesia's Hwange National Park and put to flight with the loss of seventy or so cadres. Many others were captured and consigned to Rhodesian jails.

However, the regime did have its Achilles heel. The long-defunct League of Nations had mandated the former German colony of South West Africa to the Union of South Africa as part of the 1919 Versailles dispensation, and now the League's successor wanted it back. Indeed, appalled by what the apartheid state was doing, both at home and in the disputed territory, the United Nations was demanding freedom for the huge tract of desert country that was now generally known as Namibia. In 1966, the world body declared South Africa's occupation illegal, and although the International Court of Justice had ruled in the Republic's favour, it eventually reversed its decision (in 1971). Finally, in 1974, the UN Security Council demanded South Africa's complete withdrawal.

On the face of it, Vorster, usually amenable to compromise providing it didn't endanger his country's security, had nothing much to gain from hanging on to the territory. It had little economic value apart from diamonds (these would continue to provide profit whatever the political arrangement, and offshore fossil fuels had yet to be discovered). Nor was it politically relevant any more: its seats in the Republic's parliament had once been crucial, but the National Party now enjoyed a very comfortable majority.

But Namibia lay on the way to Angola, which, in the mid-1970s, *did* present a real and present danger. Portugal, finally rid of the dictatorial Caetano regime, its economy creaking under the heavy burdens imposed by her poor and troubled colonies, pulled out of Africa

in the mid-1970s, leaving a power vacuum in Angola into which three liberation movements fought their way. Some major nations, most importantly the Cold War superpowers, had a stake in the outcome of the civil war and, although keeping their distance, set about creating proxies. The Soviet Union hired Castro's Cubans, and, at the urging of the US State Department, Pretoria agreed to intervene on behalf of the centrist, CIA-backed FNLA. This was a serious miscalculation, both militarily and politically. South African armoured columns pushed in from the south, reaching the outskirts of the Angolan capital, Luanda, but were abruptly halted by better armed and better equipped Marxist MPLA forces, supported on the ground by Cuban troops and, from a distance, by the Soviet Union.

It was at this point that the US Congress stepped in to reverse its own State Department's policy. America, it decided, could not afford to be associated with such profitless adventures in far-off lands, and the South Africans were abandoned at the height of their commitment. In a single disastrous stroke, Vorster had allowed the fruits of a patient, eight-year diplomatic offensive – détente – to disintegrate. South Africa was now seen to be the destabilising bully of the region; African distrust of Pretoria deepened; international attention focused sharply on the Republic's race policies.

The downhill road

As the decade progressed, the pressures mounted and the regime's international standing plummeted. In November 1977, the UN General Assembly banned arms exports to the Republic. France, a self-interested and friendly power up to the mid-1970s, stopped supplying military hardware; Britain followed suit in 1978; and the United States administration, tempering its anti-Soviet enthusiasms, prohibited the sale to South Africa of any products that could be used for military or police purposes. The spin-off was the rapid and successful development of a domestic arms industry, but loss of international credibility and friends coincided with the Arab oil crisis, a slump in the world economy, huge new import bills, a decline in investor confidence, rand devaluation and labour troubles.

And then there was sport, which occupied an especially sensitive spot in the collective white psyche. Sporting isolation, in fact, was one of the Anti-Apartheid Movement's chief weapons in a campaign of pressure and protest that had started in earnest after Sharpeville. Cricket became a casualty in 1968, when the South African game had reached peak quality. Basil D'Oliveira was a talented coloured sportsman who had learnt to bat in the narrow little streets of Cape Town's 'Malay Quarter', but, stifled by his country's race restrictions, migrated to Britain, earning selection to the English national squad after some stunning performances for his adopted county, Worcestershire. But his long-held dreams of one day taking the field at his beloved Newlands were shattered when he was refused entry to his homeland, initially as a sports correspondent and then, following his selection to the England squad, as a player. Justifying his churlish

Basil D'Oliveira: trigger for sporting isolation

decision, Vorster stated he simply couldn't allow the media and others to make political capital out of the issue or to use sportsmen 'as pawns in their game to bedevil relations, to create incidents and to undermine our way of life'.

Two seasons later, the national cricket side, rated among the finest in the history of the international game and including such giants as Eddie Barlow, the elegant Barry Richards, all-rounder Mike Procter, maestro Graeme Pollock and his pacy brother Peter, swept all before them in a home series against arch-rivals Australia. It was their last bow.

More dramatic, though slower, was the isolation of South African rugby. Dawie de Villiers's 1969 Springboks were given the hardest of times on their tour of the British Isles, when demonstrators turned out in force to wave placards, chant slogans, besiege stadiums, hurl smoke bombs onto some playing fields and scatter tintacks on others. For the first time ever,

Anti-apartheid demo in Swansea, Wales. Smoke bombs and booby-trapped playing fields send a powerful message

a visiting South African side failed to beat any of the Home Unions.

The white conscience

Meanwhile, the parliamentary opposition was also facing terminal decline. The United Party, once all-powerful child of the Smuts–Hertzog merger of the 1930s, had suffered a series of progressively debilitating election setbacks, the consequence of its failure to clarify its policies and, indeed, its basic principles.

The central issue was the concept of separate development – the national states, or Bantustans. The UP, embracing many shades of opinion and several cliques, officially favoured a kind of racially defined federation of territories in which political control would remain with white voters – a stance so close to that of the ruling party that it was well-nigh impossible to present itself as a convincing alternative government. As a result, its liberal wing was at serious odds with the party's general approach, or rather with its lack of any coherent approach to the most fundamental of national concerns.

A lone voice of dissent: Helen Suzman

Something of a watershed had been crossed as early as 1959, when twelve left-leaning UP members broke away to form the Progressive Party, whose sole parliamentary representative for the next thirteen years was the redoubtable Helen Suzman. Generously funded from the Oppenheimer family coffers, waspishly articulate, honoured around the world for her uncompromising stand on human rights, Suzman kept the flag of white liberalism flying high while the tired old UP disintegrated. Over the years, more members defected to the renamed Progressive Reform Party, which, after further realignment in 1977, became the Progressive Federal Party. By this time the UP was losing support to both right and left, and in that year its long-serving leader, Sir De Villiers Graaff, called it a day.

The moderate black voice

Black political opposition at home during the first part of the 1970s remained, for the time being, severely restricted, ill-organised and ineffectual. South Africa, after all, was approaching the status of a classic police state.

One major spokesman for legitimate black aspirations was Chief Mangosuthu Buthelezi, prince of the royal Zulu house, great-grandson of King Cetshwayo and autocratic head of the Inkatha cultural movement, whose membership was approaching the two million mark. The Zulu, numbering some seven million, most of them resident along the eastern coastal plain but with a strong presence in the great inland industrial centres, were and would remain South Africa's largest single linguistic group. And they had their own 'homeland' – KwaZulu, a fragmented area that lay for the most part between the Tugela River and the Mozambique border in the far north. Buthelezi's dreams embraced a unified and perhaps, one day, independent Zulu state, but for the time being he kept both his options and

Soweto: the crucible

Zulu nationalist Buthelezi in full flow

Throughout these years, discontent among the black majority, its freedoms denied and its leaders jailed or in exile, simmered dangerously. Something was bound to give, and in June 1976, it did.

On the sixteenth of that month, students gathered for a rally at Soweto's Orlando Stadium. The police were watching and, as the crowd grew, they lobbed gas canisters into its ranks. Then shots were fired, stones thrown, and what had begun as a peaceful march turned into a stampede.

News of the trouble quickly got around; barricades of burning tyres soon blocked the dusty streets, and by evening large parts of Soweto were in flames, gutted vehicles lay everywhere and hundreds had been killed, thousands injured.

Prime Minister Vorster had told his security forces to restore order 'at all costs', but the uprising lasted three days – and, more troubling for the government, it spread to some eighty other centres, initially to nearby townships and then to more distant battle-grounds. More than thirty people died in the unrest that swept Cape Town's Langa, Nyanga and Gugulethu areas, as many again in subsequent violence on the Cape Flats. Significantly, coloured students had joined in the protests.

The trigger for the Soweto uprising was a directive that Afrikaans be used as a teaching medium (together with English and a home language) at black secondary schools. The requirement, announced by the far-right Minister of Education and one-time chairman of the Broederbond, Andries Treurnicht, was received with fury and frustration by black pupils already bearing the burdensome load of disabilities and restrictions imposed by the Bantu Education Act.

There were, though, other and deeper roots to the crisis, among them the humiliations and hardships of race discrimination in all its forms, lack of citizenship, a pitiful shortage of civic amenities in the black

his eyes open, steering a tricky course between a regime he disliked and a Xhosa-dominated resistance movement he feared.

Buthelezi was a pragmatist, a man blessed with a quick mind and a strong will who vehemently rejected the government's separate development policy, believing in an integrated country governed on a non-racial basis as the first and most essential step towards securing the future. He stubbornly refused to negotiate KwaZulu's full autonomy, even though the territory was the most populous and economically developed of the ten homelands. Nevertheless, he rejected violence and condemned the ANC's militant methods as 'gross, indecent and offensive to every democratic norm', which endeared him to white South Africans. And his support for an anti-communist free enterprise system went down a treat in the Western world.

Rebellion: Soweto students take to the streets in massive protest against Afrikaans in schools

townships and restrictions on property ownership. The black majority had simply had enough. In an open letter to Vorster, Desmond Tutu, the outspoken Anglican bishop and future Nobel prize winner, had revealed his 'nightmarish fear that unless something drastic is done very soon, then bloodshed and violence are going to happen'. Tutu had warned: 'A people made desperate by despair and injustice and oppression will use desperate means,' and now his predictions were being fulfilled.

The Soweto uprising prompted a sea-change in resistance strategy. The revolution – for such it was – had been detonated by teenagers who, for the first time, had confidence in themselves as equals of youngsters anywhere. They bitterly resented the artificial barriers to personal advancement and drew both pride and inspiration from a new body of philosophical thought known as 'black consciousness'. However, their

demonstration and the rioting that followed were by no means spontaneous. They were part of a determined and fairly well-organised plan to undermine the social order and render the country ungovernable. The prime mover of the campaign was the Black Peoples' Convention, an umbrella body that gave some sort of cohesion to the various elements of the Black Consciousness Movement, whose chief evangelist in South Africa was a fiery young man called Steve Biko.

The martyrdom of Biko

Stephen Bantu Biko, born in 1947 and brought up in the Eastern Cape, had been expelled from the prestigious Lovedale High School for alleged anti-establishment activities (in fact, it was guilt by association: his brother had been arrested as a suspected member of Poqo, the PAC's military arm).

He eventually enrolled at Natal University's medical school, where he became deeply involved in the affairs of the local student body and those of the broader National Union of South African Students (NUSAS). Pretty soon, however, he rejected NUSAS as an irrelevant collection of liberal white do-gooders who did not and could not understand what it was like to be regarded as a second-class citizen of your own country. 'The integration that they [the well-meaning whites] talk about,' he said, 'is artificial. A one-way cause, with whites doing all the talking and blacks doing all the listening.' He despised those blacks who socialised with whites in order to 'boost their own egos' and as a result 'feel slightly superior to those blacks who do not get similar treatment … These campaigners are a danger to the community.'

Black consciousness, which borrowed much from the civil rights movement and African-American activism in the United States, focused sharply on the need for ethnic pride, self-confidence and cultural dignity, as well as on the absolute necessity for blacks to stand on their own feet and take control of their own destiny.

This kind of rhetoric was racially exclusive and would be out of place in today's world, but it was a valid enough assault on the white mindset of the day. It certainly appealed to a great many black people, and it both defined and reinforced a groundswell of popular sentiment that reached its critical point in the Soweto rebellion. It also set the pattern of race conflict for the next decade and more.

Biko, though, would not live to see much of the future. In mid-August 1977, he was arrested and detained

Steve Biko addressing the general students' council of the South African Students' Organisation (SASO) in 1971. His message: 'Be proud to be an African'

(though never formally charged) under Section 6 of the Terrorism Act. His jailers stripped him, placed him in leg irons and, over the next three weeks of interrogation, beat him so severely that one blow, the last, proved fatal, but not immediately. Government doctors monitoring his deteriorating condition urged hospital treatment, and so, still naked and shackled but now unconscious, Biko was bundled into the back of a police van and driven 1 500 kilometres to Pretoria, where he died, according to the family's legal counsel, 'a miserable and lonely death on a mat on the stone floor of a prison cell'.

Minister of Justice Jimmy Kruger shrugged off accusations of criminal mistreatment. Biko had been a troublesome prisoner, he said. Prison medical staff had found nothing wrong with him and his death 'leaves me cold'. An inquest absolved the police from blame: Major Harold Snyman, in charge of the four-man interrogation team, maintained that Biko had banged his head against the wall during a scuffle,

and officialdom chose to believe him. Much later, police guilt – and that of the attending doctors – was confirmed.

The volcano rumbles

Guerrilla incursions during these years were by and large dismal failures. The government's intelligence was just too good, informants were everywhere, the regime's control of society too tight. Nevertheless, hundreds, thousands of youngsters took the long and dangerous road to the sometimes equally hazardous training camps in Tanzania and elsewhere to learn about weapons and explosives, secrecy and sabotage, and about the socialist vision. They went because, for them, life in South Africa was insupportable, not only materially, but also because it offered neither dignity nor self-respect. As one captured infiltrator told his interrogators: 'I remember the humiliation to which my parents were subjected by whites in shops and other places where we encountered them, and the poverty.'

Far stronger than these external forces, though, were the internal pressures that were beginning to be exerted on the regime. These were many, various, generally unrelated, and in time they would prove to be irresistible. Even in the 1970s they were beginning to raise questions in hitherto confident conservative minds.

For a start, the low-grade war against insurgency was straining the state coffers. A compulsory one-year national service commitment for young white men had been introduced in 1967 and later lengthened to

Exiled newspaperman Donald Woods, friend of Biko and leading figure in the campaign to publicise his death

Bush training: Umkhonto we Sizwe cadres, based in Angola, learn about covert warfare

two years, an extension that contributed substantially to a fourfold increase in the defence budget and, moreover, alienated a great many white families.

Increasingly frustrated, too, was the private sector. Suffering the stifling effects of job reservation, it eventually dug its heels in. A 1972 proposal to further limit black access to the 'white' workplace, which would have prohibited employers from hiring, for example, a black receptionist or shop assistant, was abandoned in the face of stiff opposition.

In a very practical sense, indeed, big business seemed to be leading the way, most notably in the persons of Anton Rupert of the Rembrandt group and Anglo American's Harry Oppenheimer, one an Afrikaner, the other English-speaking, both of them giants of the corporate world. The two men got together in 1977 to form the Urban Foundation with the aim of opening as many avenues of advancement for non-whites as the law and prejudice would allow. Among the foundation's triumphs was the ground-breaking '99-year lease' scheme, which gave some black families a form of home ownership within officially 'white' areas.

Also significant were developments on the labour front. Blacks were excluded from the collective bargaining process, even though the shortage of skills was becoming critical; their advancement in the workplace was blocked and, to compound their woes, inflation threatened to outstrip wages. The consequence: serious industrial unrest in Durban when some 60 000 workers went on strike, similar incidents elsewhere. Labour leaders were arrested; twelve miners died in police action at Western Deep Levels near Johannesburg.

South African troops in Angola – Luanda, and victory, eluded them

Employers (notably, again, Anglo American) did their best to pre-empt further trouble by enlarging pay packets, but, clearly, an entirely new labour dispensation was needed. Two commissions of inquiry – the Riekert to investigate the use of black manpower and the Wiehahn to examine industrial relations – were appointed, and in due course recommended fundamental and far-reaching changes. Among these was the removal of practically every law that discriminated against black workers, a finding that would eventually lead to the abolition of influx control and the hated pass laws, and to the creation of a strong black trade union movement. The reports also urged that maximum use be made of all available skills.

Government accepted the main findings of the two reports, and by 1979 black unions were applying for formal recognition. Collective bargaining was now a fact of black economic life, and it would serve as one of the most powerful weapons in the fight against the system.

Social conditions had also been improving, albeit at a glacial pace. Government was well aware of the rumbling volcano, and new, properly designed townships were making their appearance. Admittedly the housing units were ugly, box-like little affairs, but many had sanitation, electricity and access to such amenities as clinics and sports fields. Moreover, the communities were also enjoying a degree of local autonomy, with largely elected councils and municipal budgets. But of course all this wasn't nearly enough. The backlog remained massive, and it was growing by the year as the black population spiralled (it had nearly doubled in the two decades between 1950 and 1970).

The Making of a Nation

Blurring the edges

A distressingly large number of liberally inclined white South Africans had left the country, most of them for new homes and careers in Britain and Australia. The exodus was especially marked after the passage of the 1968 Prohibition of Political Interference Act, and it injected a wealth of fresh talent and energy into anti-apartheid organisations. The young Peter Hain, moving spirit behind the sports boycott, was just one among many angry white exiles.

Nevertheless, a new and perhaps surprising kind of privileged liberalism began to flourish on the home front. Alan Paton had pricked the white conscience with his moving book *Cry, the Beloved Country* decades before, and playwright Athol Fugard was now helping to expose the raw underbelly of the social corpus with a succession of starkly realistic stage presentations that included *The Blood Knot* (1963), *Boesman and Lena* (1969), *Sizwe Banzi Is Dead* (1972) and the semi-documentary *Statements after an arrest under the Immorality Act* (1974). Nadine Gordimer continued to probe race and the human condition in her sparely written but oddly powerful novels.

There were others, perhaps even more influential – and remarkably, they were Afrikaners, collectively and loosely known as the Sestigers (sixtyists), heirs to the literary dynamic of those Dertigers (people of the thirties) who had proved Afrikaans a true language of poetry. Most disconcerting to the establishment was probably Etienne le Roux, who had won the prestigious Hertzog Prize in 1964 for his *Sewe Dae by die Silbersteins* (Seven Days with the Silbersteins), an ironic look at both fundamentalism and modern politics, and who went on to win the 1974 prize with *Magersfontein, O Magersfontein!*

Le Roux was much respected within the Afrikaner community. Even more so, arguably, was the venerable and venerated poet, playwright and essayist NP van Wyk Louw, doyen of the cultural mainstream, who

discomfited his conservative admirers by joining the new wave. Among other literary luminaries of the time were the prose writers Dolf van Niekerk, Abraham de Vries, the rising young star André Brink and the poets Adam Small, Ingrid Jonker and Breyten Breytenbach.

Breytenbach's impact was especially dramatic, and not just on the esoteric arts scene (he was a painter and prose-writer as well as a poet). Unwelcome in his home country, he spent most of the ten years after publishing his first volume in 1964 in Europe, working and gathering an impressive number of honours, but sneaked back into South Africa in 1975 on a false passport, was arrested, convicted under the Terrorism Act and imprisoned. During his seven years behind bars, he wrote five books of poetry and an English-language prose work, *Confessions of an Albino Terrorist* (1980).

All these and many others of various disciplines played an important role in blurring the ideological edges of white nationalism, helping to soften the

Poet and 'terrorist' Breyten Breytenbach, with his wife Yolande

mood of the dominant minority. The mood shift both reflected and created the new political climate. The establishment itself was beginning to split down the middle, for reasons that went beyond artistic pressure. Afrikanerdom's new moderates were embracing the modern age. Mostly young, mostly urban, they were collectively known as Verligtes, a catch-all phrase that meant 'the enlightened ones', and described all those NP supporters who wanted a modicum of reform. Their philosophical opponents were the Verkramptes, die-hard segregationists who were still in the majority and determined to ignore the realities of a changing world. There was furious debate within Afrikanerdom. The cracks were beginning to appear.

Lending powerful moral force to the reformist arguments were the churches, or at least many of them. Bishop Tutu and Cape Town's the Reverend Allan Boesak were the two non-white members of a triumvirate of clerics who kept the flames of protest burning brightly during the latter part of the apartheid era. The third, and most significant to the white psyche, was Christiaan Beyers Naudé, a Stellenbosch-educated one-time member of the Broederbond. He was also a minister of the Dutch Reformed Church and moderator of its Transvaal synod. An inter-denominational conference in 1961, to which the Afrikaner churches sent representatives, had concluded that apartheid was fundamentally unchristian, but Hendrik Verwoerd had smartly nipped such 'heresy' in the bud. He simply couldn't allow his regime's moral authority to be challenged by the very churchmen who had bestowed such authority in the first place. Naudé, however, remained absolutely and bravely loyal to the conference's conclusions, and in due course (1977) he was served with a five-year banning order.

Churchman-turned-rebel Beyers Naudé

The Info Scandal

These liberal encroachments on a still-monolithic system were fully reported by a press that had remained relatively free and commendably outspoken throughout the darkest days of repression. In the vanguard of investigative reporting was the *Rand Daily Mail*, later closed down after financial losses but with its integrity intact.

One of the print media's exposés was especially explosive. It reached deep down into the murky depths of government double-dealing, revealed a conspiracy at the highest levels and ended BJ Vorster's political career.

Dr Connie Mulder, Minister of Information and the Interior, was a fast-rising star in the National Party hierarchy and generally reckoned to be Vorster's heir apparent. He had approved a scheme put forward by his Secretary for Information, the young, flamboyant and equally ambitious Dr Eschel Rhoodie, who had impressed Hendrik van den Bergh, the sinister head of BOSS, as 'one of the most intelligent men I have ever met'.

The scheme was complicated, but essentially it involved pouring massive amounts of public money into what Rhoodie described as a worldwide programme of 'psychological and propaganda warfare'. Hundreds of secret 'projects' were dreamt up, some hare-brained, others promising, all

Grim faces before the fall: Vorster and Connie Mulder
contemplate the consequences of 'Muldergate'

underhand. One entailed the straightforward bribery of British parliamentarians on both sides of the House of Commons; others involved newspapers – the creation of an ostensibly independent South African daily, *The Citizen*, the launch of a right-wing paper in Norway (highly successful: the editor was able to form his own political party, which gained representation in the Norwegian legislature); the purchase of the *Washington Star* (the bid failed), and so on.

Vorster played no direct part in what soon became known as 'Muldergate', but he knew all about the programme and he kept quiet about it. When, towards the end of 1977, the Auditor-General reported misuse of funds within the Information Ministry, the floodgates of rumour, speculation and press comment opened, prompting the resignation of Mulder, Rhoodie, a raft of senior bureaucrats and of the prime minister himself, even though he had been officially exonerated.

Connie Mulder would eventually re-emerge as leader of a new, hard-line conservative political group. Vorster was moved upstairs, to the largely ceremonial state presidency, but his health was in decline and, as more and more revelations hit the headlines, he was obliged to resign that office as well.

Vorster was succeeded as premier by Pieter Willem Botha, a balding, bespectacled, short-tempered professional politician with the provocative habit of lecturing his listeners. He had clawed his way up the National Party ranks since becoming one of DF Malan's full-time organisers in 1948. By inclination, he was regarded as an unashamed segregationist, by nature a street-fighter. He liked to imply he was made in the classic Cape political mould, but was in fact a Free Stater, active in his teens and at the University of the OFS, moving to the Cape at the age of twenty (he did not graduate). Latterly, he had served as Vorster's Minister of Defence.

SPECTRUM 1966–1978

MAJOR EVENTS

1966: BJ Vorster succeeds HF Verwoerd as South African premier. **1967:** UN terminates South Africa's mandate over South West Africa (Namibia). **1969:** Steve Biko forms South African Students' Organisation. **1971:** Vorster launches détente initiative. **1975:** South African forces invade Angola, later withdrawing to establish a strong military presence throughout the northern area of South West Africa, which becomes known as the Operational Area during the ensuing fourteen-year bush war. **1976:** Soweto students stage uprising. **1977:** UN imposes arms embargo against South Africa; South African regime bans seventeen political organisations and two newspapers; Steve Biko dies in police custody. **1978:** Info Scandal: Vorster resigns.

PEOPLE

Visionary and PAC leader Robert Sobukwe dies from lung cancer in 1978. He has served a stretch in prison (at one point he found himself sewing mailbags in the company of Nelson Mandela). For the past years he has been restricted to the Kimberley area, during which time he qualifies as a lawyer. The era also sees the passing of leading black writer and *Drum* luminary Can Themba.

Among thousands prosecuted and persecuted by the regime is Mandela's attractive wife Winnie, who is placed under house arrest in 1970 after suffering seventeen months in solitary confinement. House arrest is an interlude. She will soon be sent back to prison.

A death that prompts a pause for remembrance, especially among veterans of the Second World War, is that of Perla Siedle Gibson, the beloved 'Lady in White' who sang to more than 1 000 troopships (in the busiest periods she would sing up to 250 songs a day) arriving at and leaving from Durban harbour during those grim years.

South Africa's Anneline Kriel, who will marry the 'Sun King' Sol Kerzner in due course, wins the 1974 Miss World title.

Miss World Anneline Kriel

DISASTERS

The historic little Cape settlement of Tulbagh suffers a devastating earthquake (6.5 on the Richter scale) in 1969. Most of its beautiful old buildings are destroyed, but in the years to come they will be meticulously restored to their pristine eighteenth-century condition.

MEDICINE

Professor Christiaan Barnard's cardiac team performs the world's first human heart transplant in 1967 at Cape Town's Groote Schuur Hospital. The organ, from a young woman killed in a car crash, is implanted into fifty-four-year-old Louis Washkansky, who survives for eighteen days before succumbing

Winnie Mandela behind bars

The Making of a Nation

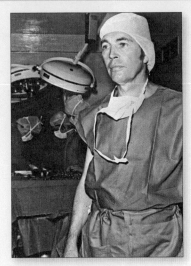

Christiaan Barnard performs the first human heart transplant

to pneumonia. Also at Groote Schuur, Susan Rosenkowitz gives birth in 1974 to six healthy babies, who will remain the world's only sextuplets until their sixth birthday. On that date, by remarkable coincidence, an Italian woman also produces six of the best.

SCIENCE & TECHNOLOGY

South Africa starts producing enriched uranium in the early 1970s – one of only four of the world's countries to do so, and by a cheaper process than the other three. The breakthrough will enable South Africa to build up a small arsenal of nuclear weapons. South African civil engineering also takes a step forward with the completion in 1972 of the Hendrik Verwoerd (now Gariep) Dam, the country's largest. The dam is part of the vast Orange River Project.

Airliners are rapidly replacing ships as the principal means of international travel. Unable to compete, the grand old Union-Castle Line, which has been plying honourably between Southampton and the Cape since 1900, ceases operation when the last of its mail ships, *Windsor Castle*, bids an emotional farewell to Capetonians in 1977.

ARTS & ENTERTAINMENT

Finally, decades after the rest of the world, South Africa gets its first television service (1976). There are thirty-seven hours of viewing per week, half in English, half in Afrikaans, with no commercial breaks. Most watched programmes are the local serials *The Villagers* and *Willem*.

Oswald Mtshali publishes *Sounds of a Cowhide Drum* (1971), which sells more copies than any other collection of South African verse. Another literary figure, Cape Town's Lawrence Green, dies in 1972, the year *A Taste of South-Easter*, one of his best known personal travelogues, appears on the shelves. Less noticeable – in fact, completely unnoticed – is the death of sixty-two-year-old artist Heidi Herzog, who paints exquisite floral pictures. Hers has been an especially moving story. She held a number of well-received exhibitions in pre-war Europe, but lost her husband and two children and, her spirit broken, eventually settled in South Africa. Her talents, though, went unrecognised, and she had been living in poverty (in domestic servants' quarters) in Durban and Johannesburg. Much later, her paintings will be highly sought after by collectors.

Welcome Msomi's smash hit *uMabatha*, a Zulu play based on Shakespeare's *Macbeth*, makes its debut in 1970. Msomi later takes it to New York, where it receives critical acclaim (and where Msomi eventually settles).

SPORT

Among highlights of the period: Yachting – the first Cape-to-Rio race is held in 1971; Knysna-built *Albatross II*, skippered by John Goodwin, is the overall winner. Rugby – the visiting 1974 Lions produce a memorable brand of the running game, trouncing the Springboks 3-0, with the last match (controversially) drawn. Bowls – the South African women's team wins the 1972 world championship; the men make a clean sweep of the 1978 event. Boxing – Arnie Taylor takes the world bantamweight title (1978) after being dropped to the canvas. He is saved by the bell and recovers to stop Mexico's Romeo Anaya in the fourteenth round. Golf – South Africa's Bobby Cole and Dale Hayes claim the 1974 pairs World Cup; black golfer Vincent Tshabalala shoots 69, 70, 66 and 67 to win the French Open. His career thereafter is plagued by back problems. Watersports – Shaun Tomson is officially rated the world's best surfer in 1975 and goes on to win the 1977 championship in Hawaii. Cricket – all-rounder Mike Procter, captaining Rhodesia, scores six consecutive first-class centuries (1971).

THE UNGOVERNABLE COUNTRY

1978–1989

Prime Minister PW Botha counters what he sees as a 'total onslaught' on his country with a 'total strategy'. The forces ranged against him, however, are now irresistible. The long-suffering majority has a greater goal in its sights – unconditional liberty.

Police clash with residents of Alexandra township

*T*he new prime minister, PW Botha, faced a daunting litany of problems when he took office towards the end of 1978, most pressing of which was the image of a party and government tainted by massive scandal. His immediate priority was to put as much distance as he could between himself and the Info Scandal cesspit. He promised a squeaky-clean administration, sacked his malignant security chief, Hendrik van den Bergh, on the very first day of his premiership, and dismantled the entire BOSS apparatus.

Van den Bergh, once ranked among the top three most powerful figures in Africa's most powerful state, disappeared into oblivion. Connie Mulder, Botha's rival for the top post, took a little longer to remove, but in due course a new commission of inquiry found that the one-time Minister of Information had been 'incompetent, lax and negligent', and he was expelled from both parliament and party.

Mulder would later return in different and, to Botha, threatening guise. More importantly, the now vacant leadership of the Transvaal NP was open for the taking by Dr Andries Treurnicht, a far-right hard man who would in due course split the party to form the Conservative Party, which, later in the decade, would become the official opposition.

Premier problems

Botha could now move on to bigger issues and confront both external and internal pressures that had been building up since the 1976 Soweto uprising.

The country's neighbours, especially, were beginning to be troublesome. The comfortable cordon of friendly, pliant states ringing South Africa – that buffer zone Vorster had been at such pains to construct – was no more. Mozambique and Angola were independent, Marxist and strategically well placed as launching pads for guerrilla assault; SWAPO insurgents were making their way southwards into the

The hectoring PW Botha: a political street-fighter

desert wastes of South West Africa (Namibia); the white rebel regime in Rhodesia, just to the north, was fast crumbling. And communism, that darkest of forces, was on the march, mounting what Botha termed a 'total onslaught' against 'the powers of order, Christian civilisation and the upliftment of the people'.

By this time, South Africa was the pariah of the world, increasingly isolated, its businessmen prey to a growing body of international sanctions, its sportsmen shunned. Foreign investment had dried up; companies were selling off assets and leaving; the temperature in the townships was rising; industrial unrest at home and incursions from abroad were constant threats. Above all, the entire apartheid structure was seen to be creaking at the seams.

PW Botha had few personal assets going for him apart from plenty of energy, a quick mind and a quicker tongue. An angry man, heir to the bitterest memories of embattled Afrikanerdom (his mother and two of his siblings had died in a British concentration camp; his father had been captured and imprisoned on a faraway island), he had come through the political ranks the hard way, as a professional republican activist who preferred confrontation to civilised debate. An admonishing finger, much like an irritable headmaster's, quickly became part of his public persona, a delight to cartoonists generally and to brilliant satirist Pieter-Dirk Uys in particular.

Yet Botha, for all his bombast, was a realist. He saw that the kind of apartheid conceived by DF Malan and executed at immense cost by Hendrik Verwoerd was simply unworkable. It always had been, of course, but now its fault lines were clearly visible. We must, Botha told white South Africa, 'adapt or die', remove 'unnecessary discrimination', reject race domination, provide equal rights and opportunities for all, initiate a 'total strategy' to counter the 'total onslaught'.

The new strategy

There was a considerable amount of quiet but authoritative support for a new dispensation. Botha's own armed forces were telling him that the status quo was militarily indefensible. Significant, too, were the pressures being exerted by big business. Afrikaner capitalism had emerged as a telling force in the economy – a far cry from its origins in the depressed years between the two World Wars, when it had served simply as a counter to threats from English-speaking exploitation and low-paid black workers. It was now powerful, almost dominant. Insurance giant Sanlam had become the country's second largest corporate entity (after Anglo American), and it wanted an end to instability and a free flow of contented black labour.

Botha's approach to the external dangers was two-pronged – a stick-and-carrot policy that would both intimidate and seduce potential enemies. The carrot was a proposed 'constellation of southern African states' composed of neighbouring countries and the quasi-independent homelands, which in practice would, through a combination of bribery and threat, be persuaded to keep the ANC out. The 'stick' would be a programme of regional destabilisation that entailed South Africa's secret support for home-grown resistance movements in both Mozambique and Angola.

The policy seemed to work well enough, especially in regard to Mozambique. Botha had quickly come to terms with the country's Marxist leader, Samora Machel, and later (in 1984) cemented the relationship with the signing of an agreement – the Nkomati Accord – that guaranteed each party would respect the other's integrity and ban hostile elements from its territory. The accord proved a severe setback for the ANC.

More complex were the challenges on the domestic front. Again, there were two basic objectives, both part

Entente cordiale: Botha with Mozambique's Machel

of a comprehensive 'twelve-point plan' that Botha unveiled to a conference of some 250 top businessmen at the Carlton Centre in Johannesburg, in 1979.

Central to the scheme was a stronger and richer network of 'national states' (homelands), two of which had already been granted what was deemed to be full independence (Transkei in 1976; Bophuthatswana in 1977). Two others – Venda and Ciskei – were in the process of a status upgrade. In these self-governing ethnic states, it was hoped, a prosperous and stable middle class would evolve.

At the same time, petty apartheid, which was proving so destructive to both domestic morale and the country's international standing, would disappear from the South African scene. This was the second part of the overall strategy, and it envisaged the removal of offensive whites-only signs, a relaxation of laws that restricted the hiring of labour and non-white ownership of property, as well as social integration. All this would, again, encourage the growth of a grateful black middle class that, although denied the status of citizenship, would perceive its interests to be identical with those of the ruling white establishment, cherish stability and, by its very nature, reject Marxist influences.

In short, Botha intended to soften the edges of the apartheid system, giving it better functional value and a more respectable face while leaving the basic ideology – separate development – intact.

The fiendish plan

All these developments, Botha said, needed an appropriate framework, a new constitution to replace the Westminster system of democracy inherited seventy years before from the old imperial power. Conditions in multicultural, evolving South African society were, after all, very different from those in the advanced countries of the West. To devise such a constitution, Botha abolished the upper parliamentary house, the Senate, and replaced it with a President's

	YES / JA	NEE / NO
PORT ELIZABETH	60661	25901
KROONSTAD	55486	32321
DURBAN	123783	44442
GERMISTON	113600	60241
ROODEPOORT	105307	80238
GEORGE	31256	11426
PIETERSBURG	31403	34827
PIETERMARITZBURG	50519	20060
BLOEMFONTEIN	52019	26960
JOHANNESBURG	194396	85554
KIMBERLEY	34815	17898
OOS LONDEN	53202	15087
KAAPSTAD	221511	71456
BEAUFORT WES	22502	7733
PRETORIA	209763	157433
TOTAL / TOTAAL	1360223	691577
% YES / JA		
% NO / NEE		
REJECTED VOTES VERWERPTE STEMME	10669	

Whites vote 'yes' for a flawed constitution

Council of nominated coloureds and Indians, as well as white members (but no blacks).

The council sat for two years, and when it finally rose, it recommended a fiendishly complicated plan to accommodate the democratic aspirations of three of the four main ethnic groups. The fourth and largest, the black majority, was not to be part of the central political process. Blacks were technically citizens of the various homelands, which had their own constitutions, and would be able to exercise their franchise only in their 'tribal' or 'traditional' lands. The fact that millions of black people had been born and spent their entire lives hundreds of kilometres from their so-called homelands, areas that many had never even set foot in, was of no consequence.

Major elements of the proposed new constitution included abolition of the post of prime minister in favour of an executive president, who presided over a non-racial cabinet that would handle 'general affairs' – matters that affected white, coloured and

Indian South Africans. In addition there would be three ministers' councils dealing with each group's 'own affairs', or matters affecting its particular group. The legislature would consist of a three-chamber parliament comprising a 178-seat House of Assembly for whites, an 85-seat House of Representatives for the coloured community, and a 45-seat House of Delegates for Indians.

The proposals did indeed offer the latter two segments of South African society a role in the governing of their country, but in practice real power would remain in white hands – a fatal flaw.

Predictably, white voters returned a massive 'yes' response in the referendum on the proposals. In due course, coloured and Indian leaders tested their acceptability in less formal fashion and came up with the politically correct answers. Alan Hendrickse of the coloured Labour Party and the hierarchy of the recognised Indian groups decided to cooperate in a process that promised at least some political progress. Only a minority of their constituents seemed to agree with them.

Changing times

The cumbersome new constitutional arrangement, whatever its failings, certainly changed South Africa's political landscape and, predictably, provoked an abrupt backlash. More accurately, it prompted a variety of reactions that served mainly to create plenty of confusion and some drama.

Those whites on the right of the spectrum were drawn into one or other of the two main minority groups, namely the far-right Herstigte Nasionale Party (HNP), founded by the quietly spoken little lawyer Albert Hertzog after he lost his place in the Vorster cabinet and later headed by Jaap Marais, or the newly formed and much more energetic Conservative Party (CP). The latter had been launched in 1982 by Andries Treurnicht to fight a 'dangerous drift to the left'. Its

Andries Treurnicht, leader of the Conservative Party

leadership included ex-ministers Ferdi Hartzenberg and Connie Mulder of 'Muldergate' fame, and there were sixteen dissident former Nationalist MPs in its ranks.

Some whites, though, perceived even the CP to be too compromising on the central issue of

Eugene Terre'Blanche, leader of the far-right AWB

Archie Gumede, one of the leaders of the UDF, surrogate for the banned and exiled ANC

race supremacy, and they gathered together in a variety of interlinked neo-Nazi groups, the noisiest of which was the Afrikaner Weerstandsbeweging (AWB), a 'cultural association' founded by the big, bearded, buffoonish but oratorically skilled Eugene Terre'Blanche (familiarly known as ET). Terre'Blanche's brainchild had been born nearly a decade earlier (in 1973) in a garage in Heidelberg, Transvaal, and it was attracting a surprising and, at the time, worrying amount of support in the country's northern areas. The AWB, a throwback to a much earlier and simpler era, sought to protect Afrikaner cultural identity against encroaching foreign influences, and it lobbied strongly, occasionally violently, for the creation of a *Blanke Volkstaat* (independent white state). It also enflamed the xenophobic passions of its supporters with emotive speeches, military-type uniforms, ceremony and symbols that came very close to those of the Third Reich. Not even this was enough for the *extreme* extremists, for those few fanatics who joined the Blanke Bevrydingsbeweging (White Liberation Movement).

To the left of Botha's NP during the 1980s stood a polyglot collection of groups ranging from the mildly reformist to the far-left radical.

The major players within parliament were the Progressives (who lost their role as official opposition to the Conservative Party in 1987) and the rump of the old UP, now renamed the New Republic Party, a tired body of men and women who finally gave up the ghost, also in 1987. The Indian and coloured assemblies had their several, variously shaded groupings.

Outside parliament, the biggest and most effective of the legally recognised movements was the United Democratic Front (UDF), an umbrella body of around 400 affiliated civic, church, sports, trade union and other organisations formed in Mitchell's Plain, Cape Town, in 1983 specifically to oppose Botha's three-chamber system of government. The UDF failed – was bound to fail – in its immediate objective, but, importantly, survived and grew to take over the ANC's once legitimate internal role (it identified with the ANC, and in fact was in some important respects the surrogate of the ANC) and which became the principal thorn in the regime's flesh during most of what turned

Future Finance Minister: Trevor Manuel
at a UDF press conference, 1984

out to be a turbulent and politically critical decade. The movement was eventually banned.

The UDF's ANC and communist affiliations were plain enough to see. The admirable Albertina Sisulu and veteran activist Archie Gumede served as its joint presidents. Albertina, wife of Walter, had campaigned long and vigorously against the Bantu Education Act and suffered a succession of banning orders and detentions from the 1960s onwards. Gumede had been an ANC stalwart since the 1940s, and was to become the telling voice of the Release Mandela Committee. Also serving or otherwise associated with the UDF were Mandela himself, still languishing in prison but now very much an icon – no, *the* icon – of the liberation movement, and Oscar Mpetha, leader of the ANC in the Western Cape and champion of Cape Town's strife-torn Crossroads squatter community. Mpetha was also incarcerated in terms of the

Suppression of Communism Act and, in 1985, became Robben Island's oldest inmate at the age of seventy-six. Among political colleagues and fellow Islanders were Mosiuoa 'Terror' Lekota (the nickname referred to his prowess on the football field) and Popo Molefe, later to become head of the ANC's Election Commission and first premier of North West province.

Other leading UDF lights included Allan Boesak, president of the World Alliance of Reformed Churches, Afrikaner churchman Beyers Naudé, activist Helen Joseph and Hassan Howa of the influential South African Council on Sport.

The movement subscribed to the non-racial Freedom Charter and rejected violence – a stance that, in 1984, earned it implicit moral backing from an unlikely source. In April of that year, the mother church of the NGK, largest of the Dutch Reformed churches, declared that there was no biblical justification for apartheid and 'no such thing as white supremacy or black inferiority'. It was the task of the church, said moderator Johan Heyns, to protest against unjust laws and for its members to 'confess their participation in apartheid with humility and sorrow'. Times were indeed a-changing.

The ANC in exile

On 2 June 1980, guerrillas mounted an efficiently synchronised attack on Sasol and Natref installations in Sasolburg, on the northern Orange Free State border. Eight huge oil storage tanks were destroyed in the explosions.

For the ANC's military wing it was a signal success, but, in truth, one of the very few it could celebrate during the first half of the decade. Money wasn't the problem, nor were weapons; quantities of both were flowing in. But neither was proving much of a help against an intelligence and security service that seemed to know all about a planned incursion even before it had been launched; that had managed to penetrate the

The big strike – Sasolburg oil plant on fire

Bureau (CCB) and other sinister elements of the South African security forces. In 1982, white dissident and labour leader Neil Aggett was found hanged in his prison cell after being held in solitary confinement, deprived of sleep and subjected to more than sixty hours of non-stop interrogation. But most of the victims were black. Among the most shocking murders was that of the so-called Cradock Four in the Eastern Cape.

The armed struggle became even harder to wage after Botha's surprisingly successful neutrality pact (the Nkomati Accord) with Mozambique's Samora Machel and the various agreements he concluded with other neighbouring governments, though these did not stop the South African security forces from launching cross-border strikes. Sticks as well as carrots were still part of the 'total strategy', and large-scale raids were mounted on a camp in Angola, where more than 600 people died, and on ANC bases in Botswana and Lesotho.

ANC training camps; that seized infiltrators almost as soon as they crossed into South Africa; and that was not shy of murdering sympathisers and targeting associations both within and outside the Republic.

Among the more shocking of the killings was that of Ruth First, activist, journalist and wife of senior ANC and SACP luminary Joe Slovo. First had helped found the Congress of Democrats in 1953, was later detained in solitary confinement under the notorious ninety-day clause (she attempted suicide while in prison) and, on her release, worked in London, editing a number of influential works (including Nelson Mandela's *No Easy Walk to Freedom*) and writing her own, among them a well-received biography of author and feminist Olive Schreiner. In 1977, First took up a professorship at the Eduardo Mondlane University in Maputo, Mozambique. When she opened a letter one morning four years later, it exploded in her face, bringing to a tragic end what had been a dedicated if rather lonely life.

There were other, less well-publicised deaths at the hands of the bizarrely named Civil Cooperation

Ruth First – murdered by post

The doomed 'Cradock Four': Sicelo Mhlauli, Sparrow Mkhonto, Fort Calata and Matthew Goniwe.
A group of security policemen later admitted to killing them

Moreover, there were difficulties in the ANC's own ranks, notably with depressed and mutinous cadres in the northern Angolan camps, especially after a failed operation conducted jointly with Angolan government forces against Jonas Savimbi's pro-South African rebel movement, UNITA. The dissidents, quite contrary to Oliver Tambo's wishes (his internal security arm acted independently), were 'disciplined' with unusual severity, a reaction that was later to damage the movement's image.

For the ANC, though, there were some lights in the darkness, the brightest of them in the persons of two outstanding figures who were making their presence felt.

Martin Thembisile 'Chris' Hani, aged thirty-seven in 1980, was cast in the mould of popular hero, clever, articulate, a charming leader of men who radiated charisma. He had been born in the Transkei and brought up a devout Christian, but embraced Marxist ideology while a student at Fort Hare University, where he also learnt to love the classics. In 1957 he joined the ANC and left the country six years later for military training in the Soviet Union, returning to Africa to fight in the Rhodesian bush war. From the mid-1970s he was based in Lesotho as organiser of the ANC's structures in the Eastern Cape. He was a senior member of the SACP, as well as of the ANC. In 1987 he became MK's chief of staff. He remained the idol of thousands of young black South Africans until his untimely death in 1993.

A year older, quieter, rather more elegant and beautifully mannered was Thabo Mbeki, a man with

Chris Hani, hero to the youth

Thabo Mbeki: diplomat supreme and future president

a fine feel for diplomacy and intellectual debate. He had gained a master's degree in economics at Sussex University, England, and in the late 1960s was based in the ANC's London office, from where he helped organise anti-apartheid rallies and campaigned for international support for the cause. He also completed a spell of military training in the Soviet Union before transferring to Lusaka, Zambia, where he served for a time with the movement's revolutionary council and eventually took his place on its national executive.

The international scene

The 1980s were the era of Ronald Reagan in America and Margaret Thatcher in Britain, two global leaders who thought very much alike and, moreover, formed a warm personal friendship. To these powerful politicians, there was only one enemy to be feared, fought and, if possible, conquered – the Soviet Union, author and executor of the communist menace and, to Reagan, the ultimate Evil Empire.

The apartheid regime drew a measure of comfort and support from this superpower confrontation. Whatever its moral faults, white South Africa professed to be a bastion against communist encroachment and, in a technical sense, it had both the will and the means to serve as such. The Republic was very much the powerhouse of Africa, its economy dwarfing those of all the other sub-Saharan countries combined. It produced about half the world's gold, and had the largest known reserves of platinum, high-grade chromium, manganese, vanadium, fluorspar and andalusite. Great quantities of iron ore, copper, uranium, zinc, cobalt, nickel, phosphates and about fifty other metals and minerals, some of them strategically important, lay beneath the sun-soaked soil of the great interior plateau. Immense quantities of diamonds were mined from the kimberlite pipes of the Northern Cape and, more productively, from the alluvial gravels of the sandy western seaboard.

And then there was coal, about fifty-eight billion tons of it, which provided the country with its electricity and supported a uniquely viable synfuel industry.

South Africa accounted for 64 per cent of the continent's power generation; 25 per cent of its gross product; 40 per cent of its industrial output; and 60 per cent of its steel production. South Africans drove nearly half of Africa's vehicles and used 36 per cent of its telephones. In global terms the Republic may have been a somewhat minor player (its GNP was roughly the same as that of the US state of Maryland), but in Africa it was a giant.

International sanctions were damaging the country, of course, but their overall effect was patchy, their application half-hearted (many of the world's most important traders had declined to toe the line) and their consequences ethically dubious. Neighbouring states, as well as the ordinary people of the country, depended on a healthy South African body economic.

Moreover, sanctions were nudging South Africa towards near-complete self-sufficiency, especially in the realm of military hardware. Local weapons and equipment-manufacturing plants, coordinated by the government-owned Armaments Corporation (ARMSCOR), were rolling off production lines and they were of surprisingly high technical quality. Among them were rifles (the excellent R4), multi-purpose machine guns, the high-precision G5 155-mm field gun and its mobile equivalent, the G6; the Olifant tank; armoured vehicles of various sorts; innovative communications systems; the advanced frequency-tapping two-way radio; a combat helicopter and jet aircraft (an adapted version of the French Mirage).

And, helped by Israel, South Africa was developing a nuclear capability.

For all practical purposes, the Republic was one of the West's more solid Cold War assets, and President Reagan showed his colours in his first year in office when he described South Africa as a 'a friendly country, a wartime ally', and then adopted a fence-sitting policy that became known as 'constructive engagement'. Neither of the two Western conservative leaders wanted to see their southern friend brought low, but both had powerful anti-apartheid forces ranged against them at home (Congress and the African-American lobby in the US; immense popular sympathy for the liberation cause in the UK).

Botha's government, though, didn't make it easy for its overseas friends with its raids into neighbouring territories and its all too visible policing methods at home.

The price of progress

By the mid-1980s, apartheid, or at least Botha's 'unnecessary discrimination', was already crumbling under pressure from political and market forces. Even before his constitutional changes were in place, nearly 800 obsolete discriminatory laws had been removed from the statute books, followed during the first session of the new tricameral parliament by the demise of the Mixed Marriages Act and the key Section 16 of the Immorality Act, which prohibited sexual relations across the colour line.

Job reservation had long been subject to natural erosion and now, with the help of the private sector and the new black trade unions, it had entered its twilight years. The doors to genuine black advancement in the workplace were being prised open; the influx and pass laws were about to be legislated out of existence (1986); black people could virtually buy their own homes in terms of the new long-lease arrangement (few in fact chose to do so); and black-run municipalities were being created (admittedly with little enthusiasm from the residents).

The fundamentals of race separation, however, remained intact, preserved and extended in the evolving homeland system and the ideology that lay behind it. And that system, quite apart from the hostility it was generating both at home and abroad, was costing the regime dearly in terms of sheer hard cash. Botha's treasury was having to pay for not just one administration, but eleven: the national government and its cumbersome threefold parliament and public service, plus the governments and administrations of the four 'independent' republics and the six semi-independent national states, all with their chief ministers, cabinets, bureaucracies, official limousines, expense accounts, status symbols, and an even more costly lack of administrative skill and integrity. In the latter half of the decade, 'grand apartheid' and its gravy train were absorbing a full quarter of South Africa's gross national product and more than half its annual budget.

This kind of financial profligacy helped deepen a mid-decade recession that had already begun, originally triggered by value declines in commodity exports, a falling gold price, a devaluing rand and politically inspired loss of investor confidence. Intensifying international pressure, exerted through economic sanctions, diplomatic isolation and boycotts in the arts, entertainment and sport realms, had also contributed to the sorry mess. And, always, there was urban unrest, a familiar feature of township life in the post-Sharpeville years but, from 1984 onwards, reaching critical proportions. Riots, stonings, massive funeral rallies and the mob killings of suspected collaborators, many by the frightful 'necklace' method, had become an almost daily occurrence. So too had harsh police reaction, often overreaction, as security squads made free use of their quirts and batons, teargas canisters, rubber bullets, birdshot and, occasionally, as the violence escalated, automatic weapons.

Township in flames. Violence nudged the moderates on both sides closer to dialogue

The Making of a Nation

'The Arch' – Desmond Tutu, prickly thorn in the establishment's flesh

Running parallel to all this were massive school and worker stayaways, the latter engineered by the National Union of Mineworkers (NUM) and the newly formed (1985) umbrella Council of South African Trade Unions (COSATU).

A country in chaos

On the face of it, the township troubles appeared to be spontaneous expressions of anger by radical and mostly youthful sections of a deprived and humiliated urban populace, but there was a coherent element here. The outbursts were certainly encouraged (if not actually orchestrated) by the ANC in line with its call, broadcast from Addis Ababa, to 'render South Africa ungovernable'.

The violence presented moderates, and especially serious members of the Christian and other religious faiths, with a profound moral dilemma: they were committed to the struggle against apartheid, but how to reconcile the scriptural message of peace with the bloodshed that was flowing from that struggle? It was

a difficult, perhaps impossible question to answer. The best they could produce was a compromise, the so-called Kairos Document, prepared by some 150 clerics from sixteen denominations and published towards the end of 1985. In it they expressed support for civil disobedience and implicitly rejected violence, an approach already adopted by Desmond Tutu, now head of the South African Council of Churches. The vivacious little bishop had been awarded the 1984 Nobel Peace Prize for his stand against injustice and he was now a global figure, familiar to televiewers around the world.

Tutu had also made known his approval of international sanctions, which earned him the hostility of large numbers of whites (even liberal ones), as well as some non-whites. Their dislike, though, was not unqualified: Tutu was well-nigh universally respected for his integrity and for his moral as well as physical bravery, notably after 1986 when, standing virtually alone, he faced down a lynch mob to rescue its intended victim.

The two Bothas, Foreign Affairs Minister Pik
and president PW, in grim mood

On 25 July 1985, President Botha declared a
state of emergency in thirty-four of South Africa's
260 magisterial districts, and troops moved into
the townships to restore some sort of order.

Facing the Rubicon

Botha's emergency measures were a failure. The violence
continued and the regime's 'reform' initiative stuttered,
then foundered on the rock of sheer necessity. Security
rather than change was now the central issue.

The government had to act quickly and decisively
to recover lost ground, not only at home but in the
wider world arena, where the Republic's standing had
reached an all-time low. So, in July 1985, Botha let it be
known through Foreign Minister Pik Botha that he
would announce a brand new programme, indeed a
radical change of direction, at the forthcoming
National Party congress in Durban.

It was billed as a seminal event, a decisive revelation
that would take the country forward on a journey
towards peace and unity and from which there would

be no turning back. Press and public waited with keen
anticipation; television crews from around the world
prepared to provide prime-time coverage; newspapers
took to calling the great moment 'South Africa's
Rubicon', an allusion to Julius Caesar's irreversible
river-crossing on his way to power and glory.

But at the last moment Botha took fright, and
instead of promising a hope-filled future, a New
Jerusalem, he merely wagged an index finger at his
audience and told the international community 'not
to push us too far'. The real enemies, he complained,
remained the communist menace and the spectre of
revolution. He would continue the reform process,
but he would not give in to 'hostile pressure and
agitation from abroad'.

The letdown was sudden, complete and catastrophic.
The value of the rand fell so far and so fast that
government temporarily shut down the money markets
and the stock exchange and sought (without success)
to persuade international banks to reschedule South
Africa's debts. Foreign debt repayments were frozen.

Worse still, the country was again plunged into a
frenzied maelstrom of violence and counter-violence.
South Africa was indeed becoming 'ungovernable' as
township gangs rampaged without any control save
that extended, with varying degrees of success, by
'street committees', which, since all the more
competent local leaders had been rounded up by the
police, were often run by ordinary thugs. Inevitably,
the anarchy – the banditry, the assaults, the kangaroo
courts and everything else that goes with anarchy
– provoked a savage backlash from the older, more
conservative township elements, who became known
as the 'vigilantes'. But their no-holds-barred warfare
with the 'comrades' served only to deepen the crisis.

The critical year

It was in this volatile context that white conservatives
showed they were still a force to be reckoned with.

Admittedly the NP had moved even further to the right in the 'reformist' years of the early 1980s – Botha was now assuring the electorate, during the run-up to the 1987 polls, that there was little prospect of progress while the violence lasted, that he would not negotiate with people who used the limpet mine, the petrol bomb and the 'necklace' as instruments to bring about change. But this wasn't enough. He was talking to a seriously worried white constituency who now, more than ever, looked to the laager for security. Andries Treurnicht's Conservative Party, hitherto written off by the English-language press, was now posing a distant but very real threat to the NP's political dominance. In the event, the CP gained twenty-two parliamentary seats in the election, came close to winning a dozen more and would have put up an even better show had right-wing support not been split. For the first time since the National Party took control in 1948, the government found itself standing to the left of the official parliamentary opposition.

Chaos in KTC township, Cape Town, 1986

State of emergency: troops in the townships

Dark days indeed, it seemed, but the signs were not entirely unpropitious. What the vote had also provoked within white South Africa was a discernible move to the left. Reform-minded independents had put up a surprisingly good fight against their NP opponents and, most revealingly, there was clearly an element within the National Party itself that was both progressive and numerically significant.

Moreover, there was also movement behind the scenes with attempts – tentative as they were at this stage – to start a dialogue that would one day bridge the great racial divide.

First contacts

If nothing else, PW Botha was a realist, and however much he blustered in the public forum, he knew he had to connect, somehow, and on a meaningful level, with the liberation movement. The difficulty, though, was that no one outside prison could legally represent the country's majority. The movement's clear and undisputed leader had been behind bars for the past quarter-century and was now sitting in Pollsmoor Prison, a few minutes' drive from Tuynhuis, the presidential residence in Cape Town.

Nelson Mandela had been through a rough time, especially in the early years of his incarceration on Robben Island. But by the 1980s, isolation, humiliation and hardship had transformed the man and his image, immensely raising the stature of both. Mandela had shown himself to be a visionary leader at his trial in 1963, an idealist who believed with all his heart in the dignity of the common man and the universal right to equality of opportunity. Nothing had happened in the intervening period to diminish either his passion or his reputation. Indeed, successive National Party governments, by the very act of removing him from public discourse, had helped elevate him to iconic status, a distant and revered figure unblemished by the mistakes and often questionable methods of the activists.

He was also the man who had said, twenty years before, that the black majority would accept a gradual transition to full democracy, a stance that seemed a lot more comforting to an embattled Afrikanerdom now facing the prospect of outright revolution.

In fact, approaches had already been made as far back as the early 1980s to the world's best known political prisoner. Botha had offered to release Mandela on condition he agreed to retire to his Transkei homeland and keep quiet. The proposal was, of course, turned down. A later approach by a visiting European intermediary, arranged through Progressive MP Helen Suzman, seemed to bring the two sides a shade closer together: Botha had insisted that Mandela renounce violence as a precondition to talks; Mandela let it be known, in a letter smuggled out of prison and read by his daughter, Zinzi, to a large Soweto gathering, that violence would cease only when the ANC was legalised. The parties seemed to be locked in an unbreakable stalemate, but they were still talking.

Contact was resumed in 1985, though it was of a very different kind. The principal meeting was between the executive committee of the ANC in exile, which included both Oliver Tambo and Thabo Mbeki, and a fifty-strong, mainly Afrikaans-speaking group of white businessmen, academics and professionals led by the articulate Progressive politician, Frederik van Zyl Slabbert. The venue was Dakar, Senegal.

Members of the white delegation publicly disclaimed support for the ANC but recognised the vital need to begin a dialogue. Botha condemned them as 'political terrorists' mainly to appease restive right-wing elements at home. The ANC delegation expressed admiration of its guests for breaking ranks with the ruling establishment.

It wasn't much, but it was a start, and Botha did follow it up. He gave the go-ahead for another, much less formal meeting, this time in England, between business leaders and top ANC figures led by Mbeki. Of the senior NP members, only FW de Klerk, the

After Dakar: Mbeki with the liberal-minded Frederik van Zyl Slabbert

deeply conservative Frederik Willem de Klerk.

In the last few weeks of his tenure, Botha had clung grimly to the presidency over the protests of a growing body of party members who had come to believe that both the 'total strategy' and, indeed, apartheid itself had passed well beyond their sell-by date. This was, after all, a very different world from the one that Botha had confronted when he assumed office a decade before. The Berlin Wall was coming down and the Soviet empire crumbling, bringing an end to both the Cold War and the old international order. Competition between superpowers no longer dictated strategic policies and the interrelationships of national states. Neither the South African regime nor the liberation movement could remain immune from these new and powerful winds of change. It was a time for compromise.

reputedly hard-line leader of the Transvaal NP, was in the know; neither side wanted any kind of publicity; each was feeling its way through the political minefield ahead. But the talks were invaluable. Botha's thinking was seen to be surprisingly positive, and the apartheid regime now knew it was dealing with reasonable, clever, highly civilised people.

How matters would have progressed beyond these early, informal discussions remains one of the big 'ifs' of the liberation story. Perhaps Botha's other self, the angry old hawk who had spent his life on the battlements of white supremacy, would have called a halt to the whole risk-laden process. Perhaps not. Early in 1989 he suffered a mild stroke and resigned as both National Party leader and, much more reluctantly, as state president.

The moment of truth

Botha's departure was not without controversy. Unexpectedly, the party caucus voted to replace him not with the moderate and personable Pik Botha, Minister of Foreign Affairs and an early front-runner for the top post, but with the largely unknown but apparently

The 1989 general election confirmed that white sentiment had polarised: the National Party, still controlled (but barely) by its traditional conservative wing, launched a last-ditch 'smear and fear' campaign to evoke all the old prejudices and anxieties and thus stampede voters back into the laager, but it had lost too much ground, both to the right and to an expanding body of level-headed opinion which argued that the country was heading for all-out anarchy.

When De Klerk entered the presidential suite in August 1989, he was immediately reminded how severe, indeed irresistible, were the pressures to release Nelson Mandela and come to a lasting accommodation with the black majority.

MAJOR EVENTS

1978: PW Botha replaces Vorster as South African premier. **1979:** Botha launches 'total strategy'. Black trade union movement gets the go-ahead. **1981:** Around 800 minor apartheid laws scrapped. **1983:** United Democratic Front launched. **1984:** Botha implements new (tricameral) South African constitution. **1985:** State of emergency declared. **1986:** South African military mounts raids into neighbouring countries. **1987:** NP wins elections but loses ground to both right and left. Independent white delegation meets with ANC in Dakar, Senegal. **1988:** Botha suffers mild stroke. **1989:** FW de Klerk replaces Botha as South African president.

PEOPLE

Mozambique's President Samora Machel is killed when his Russian-piloted aircraft crashes in a remote area of the Eastern Transvaal when it mysteriously strays off course (1986). Another enduring aviation puzzle is the loss of SAA's Boeing 747 airliner *Helderberg* (1987), which plunges into the sea off the island of Mauritius with the loss of everyone on board. Sinister rumours about its cargo circulate.

Among the most bizarre episodes of the period is the 'invasion' of another Indian Ocean island state, the Seychelles, by forty-four mercenaries led by Colonel 'Mad Mike' Hoare of Congo fame. They arrive on a purported sporting and drinking holiday, shoot up the airport, hijack an Air India airliner and are eventually rounded up. Hoare goes to prison.

A Tzaneen woman, Pat Anthony, makes medical history when she becomes a surrogate mother for her own daughter and gives birth to her own grandchildren (1987).

Distinguished South Africans of the decade include molecular scientist Aaron Klug, who receives the 1980 Nobel Prize for chemistry. Making waves in the hospitality and entertainment world are Sol Kerzner and his gigantic Sun City enterprise, a glittering pleasure ground set in the bleakness of the 'independent' republic of Bophuthatswana. It is the first of his several casino–hotel complexes that will transform South Africa's tourism industry.

STAGE & SCREEN

Actors Janet Suzman and John Kani challenge South Africa's race laws when they take the lead parts in a 1987 production of Shakespeare's *Othello* at the Market Theatre, Johannesburg. A different kind of artist with a message is Mbongeni Ngema, whose hit musical *Sarafina*, set in Soweto, is staged in New York and later filmed. Other local stage productions include *Woza Albert!*, adjudged 1983 Play of the Year by London's *City Limits* magazine, and *District Six: The Musical*, created by Capetonians David Kramer and Taliep Petersen (1987), the longest-running show in South Africa's theatrical annals.

Other bright moments are provided by satirist Pieter-Dirk Uys, who directs his biting wit at the conservative white establishment generally and the finger-wagging PW Botha in particular; Joseph Shabalala and Ladysmith Black Mambazo (among their successes is their collaboration with Paul Simon to produce the popular *Graceland* album); and 'white Zulu' Johnny Clegg. Clegg's Juluka group has already toured Europe (and especially France) with panache; his new Savuka band promises even greater things. Most popular local screen production of the period is Jamie Uys's *The Gods Must be Crazy*. It's also the top-grossing non-Hollywood movie of 1986.

Pieter-Dirk Uys as Captain PW Botha of the SA *Bothatanic*

SPORT

Rugby: The Springboks visit New Zealand for the last and arguably most dramatic time prior to isolation (1981) and play good rugby (they lose the series by the narrowest of margins). But the tour will be remembered for the violence of the anti-apartheid protests and for the telegenic aerial flour-bombing of the players during the final test match.

Cricket: Fifteen rebel English cricketers, including Graham Gooch and Geoff Boycott, are banned from representing their country for three years after touring South Africa in defiance of sporting sanctions.

Athletics: The mid-1980s belong to Zola Budd, the teenage barefoot track star from the Free State, who shatters Mary Decker's world

Gerrie Coetzee, first local to hold a world
heavyweight title, fells the US's Leon Spinks

Zola Budd, running barefoot, moments
before she tripped Mary Decker (right)

5 000-metre mark, applies for and gets British citizenship in record time (two weeks), and represents the UK at the Los Angeles Olympics. Disastrously, Budd's flying heels bring Decker crashing to the ground and the South African trails home far down the field. Better luck attends South Africa's Sydney Maree, who wins the 1981 Fifth Avenue mile in New York, and Wally Hayward, who becomes the oldest person to complete the Comrades Marathon: in 1988, aged seventy-nine, and again in 1989.

Swimming: At the other end of the age spectrum is twelve-year-old South African Kevin Anderson, the youngest swimmer to conquer the English Channel. He holds that record for just one day.

Motor sport: Jody Scheckter wins the 1977 Formula 1 championship, the first and to date only South African to do so. In that year, he buys his first personal car, a second-hand Rolls-Royce. Not to be outshone, South Africa's Désirée Wilson becomes the first woman driver to win a Formula 1 race when she crosses the finishing line at Brand's Hatch, England (1979). Shortly afterwards she wins the 1 000-kilometre Monza Endurance Classic.

Boxing: Gerrie Coetzee becomes South Africa's first world heavyweight champion (1983); stylish Brian Mitchell claims the WBA junior lightweight title.

Tennis: Kevin Curren reaches the 1985 Wimbledon men's singles final, but goes down to seventeen-year-old German rising star Boris Becker.

Free at last! Nelson Mandela, hand in hand with his wife Winnie, walks out of Victor Verster Prison after twenty-seven years of imprisonment

CHAPTER 11

THE ROAD TO FREEDOM
1989–1994

Finally, the two sides
make contact, tentatively at first,
but with growing confidence that,
against all predictions, they can devise
the miracle of racial reconciliation.
Standing tall at centre stage
is a giant of his time —
Nelson Rolihlahla Mandela.

On 11 February 1990, Nelson Mandela, grey-haired, wearing a new charcoal-coloured suit and looking very much the statesman, walked to freedom through the gates of Victor Verster Prison near Paarl, north-east of Cape Town. His appearance, with his wife Winnie at his side, was greeted with joy by the black people of South Africa, and with a mix of profound relief, hope and not a little anxiety by the rest of the country.

Mandela had been incarcerated on Robben Island since the bleak winter day in 1964 when he was ferried across the narrow strait that separates the former leper colony from the Cape mainland and consigned, the authorities hoped, to oblivion. They gave him a canvas jacket, a jersey and a pair of shorts to wear – the latter, he recalled, was to remind black prisoners that they were 'boys' – and placed him in a two-by-three-metre cell equipped with a thin mattress and two thin blankets. The cell was damp, the air bitterly cold. He slept with his clothes on.

The prison and its routines, Mandela later wrote in his acclaimed autobiography *Long Walk to Freedom*, were designed to break the spirit, destroy the resolve, exploit every weakness, negate individuality and so eliminate 'that spark which makes us human'. Inmates enjoyed what he wryly remembered as a 'balanced' diet, the food hovering between the unpalatable and the inedible. And they were worked hard during their first thirteen years in the island's limestone quarry, although Mandela found the labour invigorating rather than painful. The hardest of all to bear was separation from family and, indeed, lack of contact with or any

Nelson Mandela and Walter Sisulu, secretly photographed on Robben Island in 1966

The Making of a Nation

news from the outside world. Category D prisoners (the initial ranking) were allowed one letter and one visitor every six months, and even these often failed to arrive. Newspapers were sheer gold; the rules forbade prisoners access to them, but an old copy could occasionally be scavenged from a rubbish bin and the reports laboriously copied out on scraps of paper and clandestinely circulated.

That Mandela survived the challenges, eventually to re-emerge with mind and body intact, his vision clearer and his resolution stronger than ever, were minor miracles that he put down to the companionship and sense of community among the inmates. He was seldom alone, except during spells of enforced isolation. Three- or four-day periods of solitary confinement, silence and starvation were frequently inflicted for any one of a wide range of trivial 'offences'. He drew strength from close friends among his fellow prisoners, among them Walter Sisulu, Ahmed Kathrada and, later, Mac Maharaj, and from their collective sense of purpose. The struggle continued, even if the arena was now miniscule.

Time passed in surreal fashion. 'The minutes,' recalled Kathrada, 'can seem like years and the years go by like minutes.' But, like prisoners everywhere, they organised themselves, analysing the past and planning for a distant future, the senior ANC inmates forming a fraternity they called the High Organ. A wider disciplinary group, which included the more radical PAC prisoners, came to be known as The University.

And, for Mandela, there were highlights: small victories in the perennial battle with the prison governor for better clothing, better food, better conditions; occasional minor legal triumphs (he had agreed to represent some of the island's common-law prisoners in their appeals); visits from his lawyer, from the Progressive parliamentarian Helen Suzman, from his wife Winnie. Some rare bits of news from the broader world gave him surprisingly powerful jolts of satisfaction: word of the mid-sixties ANC armed

incursions across the Zambezi River into rebel Rhodesia, for example, filtered through, and although the cadres had been overwhelmed by bigger and better organised forces, he felt they had at least shown that the liberation movement was alive and kicking.

Better times

Life for the Islanders gradually improved as the struggle in the townships intensified and as the regime began to realise that neither the country nor the international community had forgotten Mandela and his colleagues. Moreover, throughout these years Mandela had shown himself to the authorities as both a leader of men and someone to be respected, admired, even liked. He saw no sense in fighting the prison system on principle, antagonising his jailers for no good reason. He would lead a go-slow strike, make formal representations, complain when such moves promised to pay dividends, but for the rest he tried to get on with the prison staff. Even those warders with a sadistic streak had an all-too human side to them, and maintaining friendly relations brought small but real rewards. It was the kind of positive approach that Mandela retained throughout the dark years and later took with him into the councils of the great.

By the mid-1970s, the quarry had become a thing of the past; the political prisoners had time to study (several completed degree courses), to enjoy sport and cinema shows, to think, to debate. During these later years on Robben Island, Mandela became a passionate gardener (he grew vegetables for both inmates and staff) and a keen, if modestly skilled, tennis player.

Debates would sometimes become violent quarrels between the factions, most dangerously after the arrival, following the 1976 students' uprising, of a group of young, aggressively militant members of Steve Biko's Black Consciousness Movement. Initially the youngsters tended to dismiss Mandela as a has-been from a bygone era, old, out of touch and

In time, conditions became easier:
Mandela working in the garden, 1977

irrelevant, but in due course he earned their respect. He remained the leader.

Glimmers of hope

The first gate along the long road to freedom opened slightly one day in March 1982 when Mandela and three close colleagues – Walter Sisulu, Raymond Mhlaba and Andrew Mlangeni (Ahmed Kathrada would follow) – were suddenly, without warning, transferred to the large Pollsmoor prison complex in the centre of the Peninsula just to the south of Cape Town. They left Robben Island in the late afternoon, and, as the old man gazed back through the fading light, he was surprised to feel a twinge of sadness. Bleak though the island's precincts were, they had served as home for almost two decades.

By now the regime recognised Mandela as a key figure in the political equation. The liberation struggle, reborn in 1976, was intensifying, alarmingly so, and the government was reacting with predictable brutality. The South African Defence Force had raided the ANC's Maputo offices in 1981, killing thirteen people; a year later its Maseru (Lesotho) premises were targeted (death toll: forty-two). Activist Ruth First, wife of senior ANC, MK and Communist Party leader Joe Slovo, was murdered in December 1982. MK had also been busy, attacking the Koeberg nuclear plant outside Cape Town, together with several other installations around the country. In 1983 it exploded its first car bomb outside Military Intelligence headquarters in central Pretoria, killing nineteen and injuring more than 200. The confrontation contained the seeds of an all-out civil war; both sides needed to explore their options.

Pollsmoor was an entirely new world, a different environment. The four prisoners were housed in a spacious (fourteen-by-ten-metre) third-floor room furnished with comfortable beds, clean sheets and blankets. Next door were proper bathroom and toilet facilities. The outside area comprised a long L-shaped terrace bounded by a high wall over which Mandela could glimpse the top of the lovely Constantiaberg mountains – a tantalising view of what he whimsically thought of as 'the tip of an

The campaign to free Mandela
continued throughout the years

iceberg that was the rest of the world'. And there were pleasures nearer at hand, on the rooftop, where he would create a fine garden.

First contacts

There had been feelers even before Mandela was transferred to Pollsmoor. Jimmy Kruger, Minister of Police and Prisons (and of Justice) had made two informal visits in 1976, though his principal objective was Mandela's blessing on the launch of an 'independent' Transkei homeland (he offered a substantial sentence reduction as a bribe, which showed just how little he knew of his prisoner). Now, in the mid-1980s, PW Botha needed to make good on his public promises of political progress.

As a start, two prominent Westerners, the amiable European Lord Nicholas Bethell and the American law professor Samuel Dash, were allowed an interview, their path to Pollsmoor smoothed by the new Minister of Justice, Kobie Coetsee, who seemed to Mandela to belong to a new, enlightened breed of Afrikaner politician. Both visitors wanted to know whether the ANC would make concessions if the government agreed to dismantle its 'petty apartheid' structures. To these inquiries, Mandela responded with characteristic patience. It was not the black man's ambition, he explained, to marry into the white community, swim in white pools, sit on white park benches. Black people wanted full equality, and although it was highly unlikely they could defeat the regime on the battlefield, they were certainly able to make life very difficult, even intolerable, for white South Africans.

Botha made his first formal move to bring Mandela on board at the end of January 1985, when he offered publicly to grant amnesty to all political prisoners, provided only that they renounced violence. This, clearly, was an attempt to split the ANC by alienating the imprisoned group from an external leadership committed to the armed struggle.

Mandela's reaction was unequivocal, delivered at a mass rally in Soweto by his daughter Zinzi. The exiled Oliver Tambo, he said, had been his beloved friend and comrade for fifty years and he was not about to betray him now. 'I am not a violent man,' he continued. 'I cherish my freedom, but too many people have died since I went to prison. What freedom is being offered to me when I may be arrested for a pass offence, when I have to ask permission to live in an urban area? Only free men can negotiate. Prisoners cannot enter into contracts. Your [the people's] freedom and mine cannot be separate. I shall return.'

Meanwhile, prison life was becoming ever more comfortable. The political ice, too, began to melt, notably after Mandela returned to Pollsmoor following a successful prostate operation at a private hospital in Cape Town. While convalescing in his private ward, he had received a surprisingly amiable visit from Justice Minister Kobie Coetsee, who popped in 'as if he were calling on an old friend who was laid up for a few days. I was amazed. It was an olive branch.'

Back at Pollsmoor, Mandela moved into new quarters, a three-roomed private suite with access to the rooftop garden. He described his surrounds as 'palatial'. He missed the companionship of his fellow prisoners, though not their watchful scrutiny. Peaceful political solutions were now vital; township unrest and police counteraction were propelling the country into the kind of nightmarish situation feared by all men of goodwill; his new solitude would allow him to negotiate without interference. Ideally, of course, the initiative should have come from the ANC in Lusaka, but communication was difficult, collective decisions virtually impossible, and Mandela was the man on the spot. And, if it came to the push, the ANC could always distance itself from any agreements he made and claim that he was simply a time-expired old man isolated from the mainstream.

Inching closer

A splendid opportunity had been lost when the Commonwealth Eminent Persons' mission was aborted in May 1986 following the SADF raids into Botswana, Zambia and Zimbabwe. Nevertheless, Mandela did manage to meet the group and to lay out his position. He was, he told the mission, a nationalist, not a communist, and, more important, he indicated that if Botha pulled his troops out of the townships, the ANC might suspend the armed struggle. This was transmitted both to Oliver Tambo in Lusaka and to Prime Minister Botha.

Not too long afterwards, Mandela was driven to a secret meeting with Kobie Coetsee at the latter's Cape Town residence. The process seemed to be progressing, and an encouraged Mandela looked forward to a face-to-face meeting with PW Botha himself.

However, unbelievably in the context of the deteriorating public-order situation, months passed without further word. Not that the long, fallow period was without incident, at least on the personal front. Around Christmas 1986, Pollsmoor's governor, Gawie Marx, invited Mandela for a drive around Cape Town, and the two men explored the byways at leisure, a singular joy to someone who had been locked up for so long. There were no guards, and when Marx stopped for refreshments at a corner shop, his 'prisoner', alone in the quiet street, felt an almost irresistible impulse to run away, and keep running. But he didn't.

Eventually, well into 1987, Mandela saw Coetsee again, several times, and was persuaded to meet with a special government task team to hammer out some of the ground rules for a serious dialogue, though his agreement was given somewhat reluctantly. One of the men he would be dealing with was Niel Barnard, head of the National Intelligence Service, successor to the Bureau of State Security. Moreover, Mandela's Pollsmoor colleagues were none too keen on what could be interpreted as 'collaboration'. Oliver Tambo, in far-off Lusaka, thought the intention was laudable enough, but dangerous: the ANC could be falling into some sort of trap. But the last thing Mandela needed at that point was an alienated Botha, and when it came down to it, all he really wanted was to get the regime and the liberation movement talking to each other.

The first of the working group's weekly forums – deliberations that probed the basics and pinpointed the differences between the two sides – was held in Pollsmoor's well-appointed officers' club. The

Representing the ANC from afar: Oliver Tambo in Maputo, 1986

The Making of a Nation

immediate issue was the armed struggle: each wanted the other to renounce violence as a precondition for dialogue. The regime's representatives argued that they simply could not announce the start of serious negotiations without a concession from the ANC; Mandela told them that it wasn't his job to pull the regime out of a hole it had dug for itself. But he did put their minds at rest on a number of sensitive points. The ANC and Communist Party were separate entities, he explained (though he would not break with the SACP, a long-time ally); the ANC was not wedded to a purely socialist agenda despite what the Freedom Charter said about the nationalisation of banks and industries; South Africa would belong to *all* its people; the majority would need the involvement of the minority; the future of the white community was secure. These were reassuring words indeed.

Meanwhile, the external ANC continued to show a stern face to the watching world. It had declared that meaningful talks were conditional on the release of political prisoners. On the movement's seventy-fifth birthday in 1987, which was celebrated in Tanzania, Oliver Tambo told the gathering that the armed struggle would go on intensifying until the regime decided to dismantle apartheid.

Talking with the enemy

It was time for Nelson Mandela to move to even more congenial quarters. His now universally recognised stature demanded this, and so did his health. Tuberculosis had been diagnosed, his lungs were full of water and he was obliged to spend six weeks in Tygerberg Hospital north-east of Cape Town. He was the hospital's first black patient and became hugely popular with the staff. He won the hearts of both white and coloured nurses, who spoilt him shamelessly. At one point they invited him to a party, and when his security detail told him to stay where he was, the youngsters moved the festivities to his room.

His convalescence at a happy end, Mandela was driven from hospital to the Victor Verster 'model prison' in the beautiful winelands of the Cape hinterland, his new home the three-bedroomed house previously occupied by the head of the prison.

Here, there was real comfort. Warrant Officer Swart, a superb cook, was assigned to look after him, and did so splendidly over the next few months, preparing gourmet meals for a succession of comrades who called in after the authorities eased the restrictions. The two men – the ageing black statesman and his young Afrikaans-speaking companion – got along famously, arguing only once, when Mandela insisted on making his own bed, a chore he had come to perform almost automatically after the long years behind bars. But there were no bars now, no locks, no warders. It wasn't freedom, but in the narrow personal context it was the next best thing. Just stepping outside for a walk among the trees, he later recalled, 'was a moment of private glory'.

Meanwhile, rudimentary lines of communication were established between Mandela, the four senior ANC men still in Pollsmoor and the ANC in exile.

The talks, though, were deadlocked on three fundamental issues: violence, majority rule, and what Mandela saw as Botha's determination to perpetuate minority rule. Pressures were mounting beyond the tranquil precincts in which the discussions were being held. Sensing victory, or at least a crumbling of the monumental state facade, the by-now somewhat fragmented United Democratic Front allied itself with the new and even more energetic trade union federation COSATU to form the Mass Democratic Movement (MDM) and to launch a countrywide civil disobedience campaign.

Tens of thousands of Capetonians joined in the first of the great peace marches in 1989, enormous street congregations that moved slowly along the broad thoroughfares and demonstrated both the power of the people and their capacity for non-violent action. Abroad, Tambo was talking to key politicians in the Soviet Union, Britain and the US, the Harare Declaration providing the framework for these and other discussions. The declaration reiterated the call for prisoner release and the retreat of troops from the townships, and went on to demand the removal of those obstacles to negotiations which the regime itself had erected.

On 4 July 1989, Mandela met with PW Botha in secret – a long-awaited coming together that, in the event, brought the peace process no closer. Botha was not a well man. He had suffered a mild stroke, and although he was still the country's president, he had relinquished the National Party leadership to FW de Klerk, an unknown quantity who appeared to the ANC to be 'nothing more than a cipher'.

The meeting nevertheless proved worthwhile, if only because Mandela had heard of his host's aggressive personality and fearsome temper, and was to be delightfully surprised. Botha received his visitor with courtesy, even deference, and the two chatted amiably, their conversation ranging across the spectrum of South African history and culture. Mandela compared the liberation struggle with the Afrikaner's own, final rebellion: the 1914 uprising.

Voices of compromise

Real progress, however, was being made in the continuing talks with the government's negotiating team, which now included the brilliant constitutional expert and classical scholar Gerrit Viljoen.

On 10 October, in a goodwill move, the regime released the ageing Walter Sisulu, his Pollsmoor colleagues and Oscar Mpetha, Robben Island's oldest political inmate. More prisoners were released soon afterwards.

De Klerk, who had replaced Botha as president in the interim, also initiated the abolition of the remaining apartheid laws and of the National Security Management System, a sinister network that had usurped much of the civil authority and whose hidden arm was the blandly named but murderous Civil Cooperation Bureau (CCB). These shadowy organisations had drawn support from diehard conservative elements within the bureaucracy, the armed services and the police at a level senior enough to obstruct the Harms Commission of Inquiry, appointed in January 1990. The commission was obliged to exonerate the Defence Minister, General Magnus Malan, and other leading political and military figures, but nevertheless found that the CCB was involved in 'more crimes than the evidence shows'. The people whose interests the CCB served would continue to do what damage they could to the reconciliation process, most violently through the agency of what came to be known as a 'third force'.

When Mandela met De Klerk at Tuynhuis on 13 December 1989, he was pleased to discover that the new man in the presidential suite was anything but a 'cipher'. He listened carefully to what Mandela had to say about the ANC's preconditions and the hidden agenda that lay behind the regime's insistence on 'minority rights', and then, to Mandela's surprise, stated that the regime would simply have to change its stance. This was a hugely encouraging response. Shortly afterwards, Mandela wrote to Tambo in Harare. De Klerk, he said, 'is a man we can do business with'.

The pivotal moment

There have been few occasions in the political annals when a leader's words have caused such a startled reaction as those spoken by the state president at the opening of parliament on 2 February 1990.

Everyone had expected some sort of routine report-back on progress in the efforts to reach political accommodation. Instead, De Klerk announced that the bans on the ANC, the PAC, the SACP and other proscribed bodies would be lifted immediately, and

The floodgates open. Many of the massive multiracial peace marches around the country are led by a trio of clerics

that all political prisoners would be released. Mandela recalled that it was 'a breathtaking moment. In one sweeping action he [De Klerk] had virtually normalised the situation in South Africa.'

A week later, Mandela emerged through the gates of Victor Verster Prison to a rapturous reception from the waiting throng. He was then driven, along the back roads, into central Cape Town, where the crowd pressed in so closely (people were jumping on the car, hammering on its roof; the police presence, incredibly, was minimal) that the driver panicked and the party had to divert to a colleague's home for a breather. Eventually, though, Mandela got to the stately, baroque city hall, whose northern face looks onto the spacious Grand Parade.

Standing on an upstairs balcony, Mandela addressed the great multitude that had been waiting for many hours to greet him.

There were few fireworks in his first public address; these were very early times. He had yet to confer with the movement's leaders, some of whom suspected that he had already compromised its principles. In his rambling speech he professed his humility, stressed his loyalty to the ANC, called De Klerk a man of integrity, urged whites to join in the shaping of a new South Africa and insisted that the armed struggle would continue.

He then flew to Johannesburg, addressed a jubilant rally in Soweto, retired briefly with his wife Winnie to their beloved home in Orlando West ('the centre point of my world'), and then, on 27 February, set out on the first of a series of highly publicised foreign tours that took him across Africa and into Europe. In Lusaka, he met the leaders of the 'front-line states'; a million turned out to cheer him in Dar es Salaam; he found it impossible to make himself heard when he addressed a roaring Cairo audience; in Stockholm he met his friend and leader Oliver Tambo, who urged him to assume the ANC presidency.

Building bridges

Meanwhile, following Mandela's release, the two sides had made cautious formal contact, though the scheduled meeting was set back a month by the Sebokeng massacre, a senseless episode that took the lives of twelve innocents and injured many more.

Sebokeng heralded a grim, seemingly endless sequence of violent incidents that demonstrated, only too graphically, that there were groups – elements in the Zulu-dominated Inkatha Freedom Party, hard-line white conservatives, the as-yet undefined 'third force' – that had a vested interest in promoting chaos. Later in the year nearly thirty commuters on trains running between Johannesburg and Soweto were hacked to death, the first of many such attacks.

But by then the political process was under way in earnest, after being launched early in May 1990, when the two teams met as equals in Cape Town's splendid Groote Schuur mansion, once home to the arch-imperialist Cecil John Rhodes and to a succession of white premiers. Here, they discovered that their

De Klerk and Mandela herald the new order at Groote Schuur

'enemies' were serious, cultivated, good-humoured men and women who were determined to build bridges across the yawning cultural and racial gulf.

The ANC proposed the establishment of an interim government to oversee the transition and a multiparty negotiating conference to hammer out the thorny details – an arrangement soon to take shape in the Convention for a Democratic South Africa, a name shortened and celebrated as CODESA. The accord was sealed by the hope-filled Groote Schuur Minute, in which delegates pledged their commitment to a peaceful resolution.

The prodigal returns

To foreign onlookers, a miracle seemed to be unfolding. Few observers had predicted a racial entente, even the hesitant beginnings of one; many had long expected outright civil war as the logical end to decades of bitter confrontation between opposing ideologies.

When Nelson Mandela visited New York, a million Americans lined the ticker-tape route. In a packed Yankee Stadium and in Harlem he spoke of the great affinity that existed between people of colour everywhere. In Washington, he addressed a joint sitting of the US Congress. In Canada, to his wonderment, a group of Inuit (Eskimo) teenagers at the airport shouted 'Viva ANC!' How remarkable, thought this long-time exile from the modern world, that the course of events on the southern tip of Africa should have attracted attention in the cold remoteness of the far, far north! How things had changed since he had been quietly consigned to what most believed was political oblivion nearly thirty years before.

Mandela had embarked on the tour determined to persuade the major nations to sustain sanctions. These, and the armed struggle, were needed to keep the regime on course, he said. But here he was playing a losing game, especially in London, where Margaret Thatcher gave him a stern, schoolmarmish lecture on effective diplomacy. In December 1990 the European Community lifted its voluntary ban on new investments, and six months later the US Congress, 'recognising a profound change in South Africa', scrapped the Comprehensive Anti-Apartheid Act and all remaining embargoes.

South African athletes, entertainers and artists soon found themselves back in the international fold, a reconciliation formally confirmed when Colin Cowdrey, who had been at the crease when the very last England–South Africa test match ended, announced the demise of the International Cricket Council's boycott in July 1992.

The following year was a memorable one for South African sport. The cricketers contested their first World Cup, held in Australia, managing to beat their hosts and squeak into the semi-finals, and the athletes entered Barcelona's Olympic stadium to a roar of welcome from the vast crowd. The prodigal had returned, the image given memorable substance when Ethiopia's Derartu Tulu, winner of the 10 000 metres, completed her lap of honour hand in hand with the silver medallist, South Africa's Elana Meyer.

The first forum

Sporting integration was the easy part; the political programme was proving rather more difficult. Negotiations were being conducted, often painfully and always slowly, within the CODESA forum by nineteen leading groups. They came together in the draughty halls of the World Trade Centre at Kempton Park near Johannesburg in 1991, a super-talkshop that started well enough by immediately agreeing a keynote Declaration of Intent to create a post-apartheid South Africa 'by consensus' – in effect, by majority vote within the convention. This more or less guaranteed that the smaller, generally more extreme groupings couldn't obstruct the decision-making process. It also embraced the concepts of an independent judiciary, a Bill of Rights and a vote for every adult South African.

Negotiating at CODESA: Mandela and Jacob Zuma

'the domination of one group by another' – in other words, a system that entrenched white rights and was, Mandela suspected, simply a device intended to sustain aspects of white supremacy. The ANC, by contrast, wanted a unitary state with a strong central authority and a winner-takes-all electoral arrangement, or simple majority rule.

Each side had its bargaining chips. Pressured by an increasingly impatient black constituency, the ANC was desperate for progress, and De Klerk's white regime was in no hurry: it could threaten the entire transition exercise simply by stonewalling. Hard-liners could also (as some of them were already doing) give moral and material support to Inkatha in its bid for ethnic independence. For its part, the ANC commanded huge popular support and could, at any time it chose, trigger a crippling campaign of 'rolling mass action'. Moreover, it was able to use international sanctions as a coercive weapon, although this was a fast-diminishing resource. The world was increasingly willing to welcome South Africa back.

The first CODESA session came to a stumbling end when De Klerk, in his closing speech, infuriated Nelson Mandela with an astonishing attack on the ANC for retaining its arms caches and 'private armies', and generally for showing bad faith. Clearly, the white right was still exerting its malign influence.

Notable absentees from the deliberations were the radical Pan-Africanist Congress, which rejected suggestions that there was a role for whites in a future dispensation, and Mangosuthu Buthelezi, who wanted a fair degree of Zulu autonomy and was pressing for representation of Zulu interests not by a single lobby, but by three delegations (speaking for the Zulu royal house, the homeland of KwaZulu and the Inkatha Freedom Party).

The issues were immensely complicated, the path forward labyrinthine. Delegates, however, overcame the first hurdle – the question of governance in the interim – quite early on by agreeing that CODESA itself would have the power to make laws and that De Klerk's ruling National Party would use its parliamentary majority to push through progressive legislation. Where the two principals deadlocked was on the exact nature of a future and final South African body politic. De Klerk held out for a loose federal arrangement and built-in checks against

The Making of a Nation

The breakthrough

Much of the trust built up over months had suddenly been lost with De Klerk's ill-advised speech and, anxious perhaps to acquire fresh credentials and certainly to restore momentum to the talks, he decided on a make-or-break gamble. On 17 March 1992, white South Africans flocked to the referendum polls to answer the question: 'Do you support the continuation of the reform process which the state president began on 2 February 1990 and which is aimed at a new constitution through negotiation?'

The gamble paid off. The answer was a resounding 'yes' from nearly 70 per cent of the electorate.

The referendum result created new hope, even confidence, in both the corridors of state and among ordinary people. But therein lay a threat. De Klerk felt he was now in a much stronger bargaining position, and his negotiating stance hardened. Moreover, two man-made crises threatened political disaster. On 17 June 1992, a 200-strong gang of suspected Inkatha extremists attacked sleeping residents of the Boipatong informal settlement near Johannesburg with pangas (machetes) and guns, killing thirty-nine and injuring many more. A subsequent commission of inquiry revealed the massacre to be symptomatic of a wide-ranging dirty-tricks campaign sanctioned by white military officers.

Boipatong was not an isolated incident, but a tragically prominent part of a simmering, sometimes

A satisfied De Klerk. White South Africans vote overwhelmingly for change

People run towards the stadium in Bisho, Ciskei, minutes before the Bisho massacre

political, sometimes criminal wave of public blood-letting that threatened to consume the country. It was estimated that 3 500 people died in township violence during 1992 alone.

Then, on 7 September, a column of ANC demonstrators marching on Bisho, capital of the much scorned 'independent' homeland republic of Ciskei, was fired upon by the mini-state's ill-disciplined troops. Thirty were killed, more than 200 injured.

Once again the negotiations faced imminent collapse. But Mandela and De Klerk now had the ultimate prize within their grasp and were quite determined to let nothing, and certainly not a fracas that could have been avoided with a bit of common sense on both sides of the Ciskei border, take it away

from them. Two weeks after the shooting, they signed a statesmanlike Record of Understanding that committed the two parties to a single, elected constitutional assembly. This would serve as the transitional authority and in due course approve a new constitution. An agreed 'sunset clause' proposal (put forward by no less than Joe Slovo, the perceived ogre in the collective white consciousness) made provision for the creation of a transitional executive council, a government of national unity and an all-party cabinet. Members of the new 400-strong national assembly would be elected on the basis of proportional representation.

Much of the hard grind that lay behind these successful negotiations fell to two talented and

Cyril Ramaphosa and Chris Hani at a press conference in 1992

agreement, and they must be ranked among the heroes of racial reconciliation.

One more near-disaster would endanger the fragile peace process when, on 10 April 1993, the hugely popular communist leader Chris Hani, hero to a whole generation of black youth and one of the few personalities capable of keeping the extremists of the left in order, was assassinated. Widespread unrest was pre-empted when the conspirators, Polish-born Janusz Walus and far-right political fringe figure Clive Derby-Lewis, were adjudged to have been acting on their own. The talks continued to a successful conclusion.

immensely hard-working backroom boys. Representing the ANC's interests was Cyril Ramaphosa, a prominent trade unionist. It was he who had organised the first legal strike by black miners in 1984. In the years before then, he had suffered both detention under the terrorism and other apartheid-era statutes and constant police harassment, at one point surviving a four-month period of non-stop interrogation. Following full democracy in 1994, he was widely regarded as Mandela's heir apparent, but was ultimately beaten to the post by Thabo Mbeki. His opposite number during the CODESA talks, Roelf Meyer, was one of the moving spirits within the National Party's progressive wing and highly regarded for his profound insight into the workings of modern governance. Together, these two provided the skills that put flesh on the bones of broad

Youth hero Chris Hani's assassination jeopardises the whole peace process

Two months later, Nelson Mandela and FW de Klerk shared the Nobel Peace Prize. Against all the odds – despite the difficulties imposed by history, by contrasting cultures and the demands and fears of their separate constituencies – the two men had developed respect (if not affection) for each other and, in partnership, had constructed a solid framework for the future.

Shortly before Christmas 1992, a new transitional executive council effectively replaced the national parliament.

The last mile home

The second CODESA round had started with an almost full complement of delegates. The Inkatha Freedom Party, the Pan-Africanist Congress and the Conservative Party had suspended their reservations to take part in the final deliberations. None, though, was happy with the settlement terms. To the CP they were 'hostile to Afrikaner interests', and the generally admired ex-soldier General Constand Viljoen departed to form the Afrikaner Volksfront; the PAC held to its Africanist stance (though this had been considerably modified); and the IFP's Buthelezi, who wanted a final constitution in place before a general election, as well as greater regional powers, walked out.

In the event, little of this mattered. A special electoral commission set about the Herculean task of staging free elections in a country whose great majority had never seen the inside of a voting booth. Ten thousand polling stations needed to be manned and monitored; only a massive security presence could reduce – hopefully eliminate – the risk of violence (especially in KwaZulu-Natal) and deliberate sabotage (notably in the country's northern regions).

But the omens were favourable and became even more so when, at the eleventh hour, Buthelezi decided to rejoin the process. Enthusiasm ran high; the ANC, still much more of a liberation movement than a political party, launched a series of 'people's forums', which provided it with a good idea of what the ordinary citizen-to-be wanted from imminent freedom, and it then produced a 150-page document that laid out its planned Reconstruction and Development Programme (RDP). This promised jobs, a million new homes, ten years of free education, universal health care and affirmative action – a seductive package indeed. But in doing so, of course, the ANC risked a crisis of expectation. In the real world, manna rarely falls from heaven; wealth has to be earned. Mandela was well aware of this.

Into the fold: Buthelezi participates in the 1994 election

The end of a long, hard process: Nelson Mandela is sworn in as president of a free South Africa

'Don't expect a Mercedes the day after the election,' he warned the people.

There were indeed some incidents in the run-up to the elections: bombings carried out by right-wing white groups killed twenty-one individuals; ANC snipers fired into a massive Zulu procession armed with 'cultural weapons' while making its way through Johannesburg's streets. But for the rest, campaigning proceeded in lively, rather chaotic and, incredibly in view of past antagonisms, good-humoured style.

Came the great day itself, and long lines began forming well before the first light of dawn. No disturbances were reported. The elections would be adjudged 'free and fair'.

Predictably, the ANC won handsomely. It gained just less than the two-thirds majority that it would need if it wanted to make any unilateral changes to the Constitution, and captured six of the nine regional parliaments, sharing power with the National Party in the seventh (Northern Cape). However, it was by no means a clean sweep. The National Party, backed by the largely conservative coloured vote, triumphed in the Western Cape, and Inkatha won on its home ground, KwaZulu-Natal.

A month later, on 9 May 1994, Nelson Mandela mounted the podium in the amphitheatre of Pretoria's graceful Union Buildings and, in front of the greatest assembly of foreign luminaries ever to gather in Africa, took the oath of office as the first president of a free South Africa. 'Out of our experience of an extraordinary human disaster that has lasted too long,' he told his distinguished audience, 'must be born a country of which all humanity will be proud.'

THE NEW SOUTH AFRICA

*The long journey to freedom is
over and South Africa's first
democratic government takes office.
Its paramount objectives are
to heal the wounds of the past
and to steer the new ship of state
safely through the turbulent
waters of a changing world.*

President Mandela congratulates Springbok captain François Pienaar after his team's memorable victory in the 1995 Rugby World Cup. The country felt united as never before – and, perhaps, never since

The first few years of the new dispensation belonged to Nelson Mandela, executive president and leader of an all-party government of national unity. They were, on the whole, hugely successful years, even inspiring ones. By the time the old man handed over the reins to his successor Thabo Mbeki, the country was a going concern, drawing stability and strength from a range of solid democratic structures. These included, most especially, one of the world's most progressive constitutions and a Bill of Rights that, in theory, served as unassailable guardian of each individual's civil liberties.

Of all the ingredients for a trouble-free political transition, racial harmony was the most critical. Without it, there could be nothing but tragic decline and ultimate fall. No one had any illusions about the risks. Underlying the entire four-year peace process had been the largely unspoken but very real fear that the majority would exact revenge, or at least impossibly heavy compensation, for the centuries of oppression.

These concerns persisted after the handover, certainly among white South Africans, despite the ANC's constant assurances and the concessions it made to De Klerk.

Mandela was well aware of the destructive power of disharmony and of the need to purge the country of its past. His campaign for reconciliation, conducted in something approaching the spirit of a crusade, enabled the infant nation to hold together during its first and most vulnerable years.

Freedom through truth

Among the most positive features of the transition period was the national soul-searching conducted within the framework of the Truth and Reconciliation Commission, a mobile inquiry established, under the chairmanship of Nobel laureate Desmond Tutu, on the biblical principle that 'the truth shall make you free'. From April 1996 the commission set about exposing (and, when appropriate, forgiving) crimes within the

Setting the country free: the Truth and Reconciliation Commission begins hearings.
Deputy chairperson Alex Boraine (left) sits next to Archbishop Desmond Tutu

apartheid system, conducting hearings around the country and, finally, in October 1998, winding up the great confessional with a monumental report.

The apartheid state, said the TRC – the government, civil service and security forces – had been the 'primary perpetrator' of gross human rights violations. Racism 'constituted the motivating core of the South African political order, an attitude largely endorsed by South Africa's major trading partners'. Whites had adopted a 'dehumanising' position towards black citizens and had 'largely labelled them as the enemy. This created a climate in which the atrocities committed against them were seen as legitimate.'

Among the very worst of the individual criminals was a chillingly mild-mannered man named Eugene de Kock, a former police colonel and killer who, as testimony unfolded, became known to an incredulous public as 'Prime Evil'. De Kock, who had commanded the infamous Vlakplaas hit squad, was described as a psychopath who performed his grisly job with patience and painstaking care, murdering dozens of people before incinerating (and occasionally blowing up) their corpses.

If Prime Evil had any redeeming quality, it was his willingness to confess, to express remorse and to identify those who gave him his orders. Not so the political and military leaders of the apartheid regime, who kept their heads down and blamed the whole tragedy on a few rotten apples in the state barrel. Only one former cabinet minister applied for amnesty.

But the blame didn't stop there. The TRC red-carded plenty of other players, among them big business, the media – the Afrikaans press 'chose to provide direct support for apartheid', while their English-speaking colleagues 'adopted a policy of appeasement' towards the state – and the presidency in the person of PW Botha. All had contributed to a climate in which deliberate killings and widespread torture were allowed to occur. Nor did the ANC and PAC escape censure.

The face of 'Prime Evil': killer Eugene de Kock

Both had committed violations 'for which they are morally and politically accountable'. Umkhonto we Sizwe had actually killed more civilians than members of the security forces.

On the whole, the exercise was a success. The TRC went some way towards cleansing the collective spirit, bringing a degree of closure to a decades-long nightmare. It also set a hope-filled precedent for other troubled communities around the world to follow.

Socialism bows out

Crucially, there were also progressive developments on the economic front. The African National Congress had been one of the chief architects of the 1955 Freedom Charter, a socialistic document that had inspired the liberation movement and formed the basis of its programme for four decades. Many of the principles and objectives enshrined in the charter were still valid, among them the exercise of governance through the will of the people, a non-racial democracy, equal rights under and the protection of the law, and equal job and education opportunities.

But the charter now had a lot less relevance in its advocacy of a command economy, nationalisation and the wholesale redistribution of wealth. Radical socialism, the systemic bedrock of the old Soviet Union, its East European satellites and other unhappy states, had been discredited; only poverty-stricken Cuba and starving North Korea were clinging firmly to a strict Marxist ideology. The realities of globalisation, the dynamics of the new, bewildering age of information and the need to compete in new ways in order to survive prompted a sea change in ideology. South Africa was to remain a capitalist country. Wealth would of course have to be much more equitably shared, but society would be sustained and the poor uplifted through the free play of market forces and the economic growth they generated.

First steps towards equity

Nobody really expected a smooth ride towards social equity, and indeed the government's Reconstruction and Development Programme did prove too ambitious, largely because the delivery systems weren't in place. There simply wasn't the infrastructure or the administrative expertise to make it work. Nevertheless, some progress was made, notably in the provision of housing, electricity, clean water and sanitation to disadvantaged communities. Schooling, though, was proving a tough nut to crack. The system was deeply infected by the malignancy of the old Bantu Education Act, and the evils were now being compounded by an amateurish minister's first, disastrous attempts at restructuring. In the interests of transformation, thousands of experienced, often dedicated white teachers were leaving the classroom with expensive severance packages, to be replaced by raw recruits of the 'correct' colour.

There were and are, though, a few islands of progress in the ocean of mediocrity, centres of excellence that would be underpinned by the proposed African Institute of Science and Technology, a pan-continental facility designed to turn out 5 000 scientists and engineers each year. Among specific such centres in southern Africa are the leading universities and a raft of astronomical enterprises, including the SALT (South African Large Telescope) complex near Sutherland; HESS, the world's most powerful cosmic ray telescope (in Namibia); major involvement in NASA's Deep Space Network, in the Group on Earth Observation, and in the global Square Kilometre project. Other focal points of progress are an advanced telecommunications industry, an initiative to create Africa-friendly genetically modified crops, cutting-edge medical research projects (including cancer-curing nanotechnology), and a number of experimental renewable energy programmes, including wind turbine and solar thermal ('field of mirrors') initiatives, the revolutionary pebble bed nuclear reactor, and significant fuel-cell breakthroughs in nanotechnology-based catalysts and membranes that represent another step towards a hydrogen-powered economy.

All these and more have kept the technological flag flying in post-apartheid South Africa, but they are exceptional examples of endeavour in an otherwise deeply challenged society. From the beginning, public health was especially problematic. According to official estimates, more than two million South Africans were in 'urgent need of nutritional support'; seventy-two children were dying each day from malnutrition and related conditions, and the HIV/AIDS pandemic was beginning to take a serious toll, putting what threatened to become an almost intolerable strain on medical services already stretched by the decision to provide universal health care.

Above all, there was a desperate need to create jobs. This was a challenge that no administration, however well intentioned and decisive, could meet with confidence. The traditional labour-intensive smokestack economies of the post-industrial revolution belonged to the past; this was the age of technology and electronic information, and it needed the type and volume of expertise that the South African workforce simply did not possess. Around 80 per cent of the economically active population was either semi-skilled, unskilled or unemployed, and the jobless numbers were steadily rising as companies and state enterprises 'downsized' (a mild word for a brutal process) to meet the needs of a new, more competitive, smarter era.

Bearing the burdens

Government recognised the need for a bold strategy that would, eventually and after considerable sacrifice, create a dynamic economy. In due course it launched its Growth, Employment and Redistribution (GEAR) policy, a market-friendly macroeconomic programme to lower trade barriers, stabilise national finances and, most importantly, control inflation.

GEAR was intended, among other things, to attract massive foreign investment, and a healthy amount of new money did indeed flow into the country during the honeymoon period, but it never reached the volumes that were generally expected, or at least hoped for.

'Afro-pessimism' was a worrying factor despite the reassuring message the new regime was sending out to the capitalist world. The continent as a whole was, with some shining exceptions, widely perceived as something of an abyss of mismanagement and corruption, unstable and ravaged by regional violence that in many cases had been provoked by the Cold War superpowers. Africa had been serving for decades as a battlefield for the world's giants and their proxies; now that the war was over, the outsiders had all departed, bequeathing to the continent a legacy of disintegrating state structures, social dislocation and, in places, plain anarchy.

Moreover, South Africa's workforce was pushing for a new deal; COSATU, now closely linked with the ANC and the Communist Party in a tripartite alliance, had backed the liberation movement at every step along the road, and it expected a dividend. For its part, the government desperately needed to ensure social stability. It met its debt by a worker-friendly body of legislation that included the basic Conditions of Employment Act (minimum hours, overtime rates), the Skills Development Act (training schemes) and the Employment Equity Act (affirmative action, gender equality). Each was progressive and, arguably, helpful to social transformation. But collectively they were based on models that had evolved in much more advanced economies, notably those of Germany and Sweden, and even in those countries they had proved too onerous. Here, some believed, they simply added to the financial and administrative burden that enterprises had to bear, and injected an unwelcome degree of inflexibility into the labour market at a time of high unemployment and low productivity.

Sport: the new breed

Over the first few years, South Africans generally and Nelson Mandela in particular basked in the warmth of global admiration for having accomplished the 'miracle' of racial accommodation.

This had its benevolent effect on national self-esteem, and it helped forge a sense of unity, fragile as yet but remarkable in the light of the country's hugely divisive past. Sporting endeavour also played its part. South Africa's athletes did the country proud in a number of disciplines before the century's end.

Football success ranked among the highlights. One of the first of the sports to become racially integrated (the process began in the 1970s), the national squad, now known as Bafana Bafana, achieved some notable triumphs, most memorable of which was perhaps their winning run in the 1996 Africa Cup of Nations.

They then went on to compete, albeit with modest results, in the Football World Cup (held in France) for the first time, their very presence among the world's best a signal victory in itself.

In 1996, too, South Africa distinguished itself in the biggest arena of all. The Atlanta Olympic Games produced fine performances from, among others, swimmer Penny Heyns (two golds, one world record) and, most movingly, marathon specialist Josiah Thugwane. The latter's victory was perhaps an appropriate conclusion to a century during which local distance runners had done consistently well ever since Potchefstroom policeman Kenneth McArthur had breasted the tape in the 1912 Stockholm Olympics

Marathon man: gold-medallist Josiah Thugwane on his victory run

(he was followed home by another South African, Christopher Gitsham, in his first ever marathon attempt). The diminutive Thugwane was a surprising heir to this fine legacy. Abandoned at birth, he had grown up illiterate and in poverty, and in adult life worked as a janitor, living in a humble shack with his wife and four children. Not the ideal conditions, one would think, for an athlete, and the odds had lengthened further when, a few months before the Games, he was shot in the face by car hijackers.

The highlight of the decade, though, was played out in 1995 in the rugby arena and watched by billions around the world.

South Africans had entered international rugby just over a century before, in 1891, when they'd been trounced by WE Maclagen's British touring side, but they made their mark within a decade, winning their first 'test' in 1896. Ten years later, as the inaugural Springboks (led by the legendary Paul Roos), they won their first series. In the succeeding decades, the Springboks remained among the very best and, for long periods, dominated the world scene. Sporting isolation in the 1980s deeply affected a white community to whom rugby had become something close to a religion.

All that was forgotten in 1995 when François Pienaar, flanked by an ecstatic President Mandela (who wore Springbok colours for the occasion), raised the Rugby World Cup aloft to the roars of the Ellis Park crowd. This was the crest of the new wave, the instant when the people of the country – all the people – came together in their pride and purpose. It was also, recalled rugby great Morné du Plessis, a moment tinged with a hint of sadness for the fleeting nature of glory. 'I knew I would never experience anything like that again,' he said. 'It was a once-in-a-lifetime moment. That was it for me. I knew I had had my moment. It was gone.' A poignant recollection, and perhaps a prophetic one.

After Mandela

All through the first years, Nelson Mandela enjoyed iconic status both at home and abroad, attracting universal admiration for his courage, integrity, humility (a rare quality in politicians) and statesmanship. But at the end of the decade, when he was into his eighties, he called it a day. In any case, the period of grace, the honeymoon, was over. It was time to tackle the nuts and bolts of running a country that had its share of problems, many of them residual, some of them new.

Mandela was a hard act to follow. No successor could really match his stature, because he was one of a kind and he had conjured a miracle that could never be repeated. The celebrations were over; now the task, an unglamorous one, was to create a workable and equitable social system in a country with massive unemployment, widespread poverty and a critical shortage of skills, a schooling system seemingly incapable of reform, a deepening HIV/AIDS crisis, growing grassroots impatience with the lack of services; crime and corruption; and a labour movement locked into the ideologies of the past.

Few men were better equipped to take charge than Thabo Mbeki. A brilliant technocrat and skilled manager (albeit with a weakness for micro-managing), he had been through the political and diplomatic mills to become one of the shining lights of the liberation movement in exile, picking up university degrees and a host of invaluable international contacts on his way up. He was a prominent figure in the initial, crucial Groote Schuur discussions that led to the full-on CODESA dialogues and in the constitutional negotiations themselves. In 1993, with the backing of the ANC Youth League, among others, he was elected deputy

Thabo Mbeki, second democratic president

president of the ANC and heir apparent to the president, though the succession was by no means a foregone conclusion. The respected trade unionist and negotiator Cyril Ramaphosa was also a strong candidate for the post, and it took all of Mbeki's backroom political skills for him to meet the challenge and emerge the victor.

Diplomacy was Mbeki's strength, and it was needed in large measure in the first years of his presidency, certainly on the domestic front, where the seemingly conflicting interests of the major ideological elements – privileged whites and disadvantaged blacks, liberal democrats and Africanists, free-marketeers and socialists – needed to be reconciled. In general, his

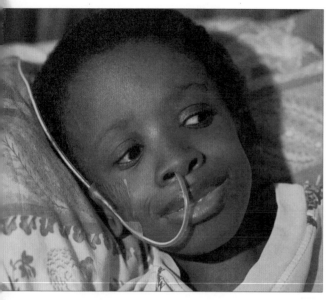

One of the countless victims of AIDS: Nkosi Johnson, months before he died at age twelve

efforts proved remarkably successful, though he drew criticism, mild enough, for his views on residual racism and his long absences from the country, and more forthright disapproval for his apparent denial of the nature of the AIDS crisis.

Mbeki's diplomatic skills were shown to especially dramatic effect in the international forum, where his well-articulated vision embraced no less than a total African 'renaissance' that would, with outside help, lift the lagging continent from its place at the bottom of the development heap. The key element in his imaginative and hugely ambitious scheme was the New Partnership for African Development, or NEPAD, a multinational agreement that he personally engineered and which would see vast amounts of investment funds shared among those African countries that committed themselves to good governance and a significant reduction in prevailing levels of corruption. Here, the South African president set a good example, not only of competent administration but of courage, too, when he fired the popular Jacob Zuma, his deputy (and contender for the next presidency), following the latter's alleged involvement in an arms deal scandal and later allegations of sexual misconduct.

A major part of the NEPAD deal, of course, was a concerted drive to eliminate regional African conflicts, and here Mbeki proved himself a consummate peace-broker, though a major setback was his inability, or unwillingness, to intervene in Zimbabwe, or even to condemn that country's dictatorial regime.

Mbeki confers with Jacob Zuma. Troubles were to follow

The Making of a Nation

By the middle of the millennium's first decade, the economy, girded by sound financial and fiscal management and riding on the coat-tails of rising global demand (notably from India and China) for commodities, was beginning to boom.

The body economic, though, has to grow at a minimum of 6 per cent a year (2004 rate: 4.5; 2005 rate close to 5.5) to sustain social stability, and in order to achieve *that*, it has to produce more engineers, technicians, mathematicians and science graduates, as well as competent administrators, a better educated and more productive workforce, a less regulated business environment and, most crucially, more efficient delivery systems.

The focal points of this last requirement are the new, expanded municipalities that are at the coalface of service provision. Unhappily, the need for transformation and the imperatives of party politics have prompted wholesale and often ill-advised changes at local and provincial government levels. Precious skills have been lost in the scramble for well-paid senior positions; cronyism and corruption threaten to become endemic in an area where good governance matters most to ordinary men and women.

As Thabo Mbeki approached the end of his second and final term of office, the battle for the succession became more intense. But whoever the president is, he or she, the cabinet and their party colleagues will be well aware of the risks posed by unfulfilled promises and the need to take remedial steps. Things should improve – but only if bold decisions are made. We shall have to see whether the governing elite can grasp the nettles, put party and self-interest aside and properly serve the people who elected them, or whether South Africans will have to put their faith, or at least their hopes, in some sort of new political alignment. The signs, so far, are hopeful.

Elder statesman: Nelson Mandela and his new wife Graça, widow of Mozambique's President Machel

MAJOR EVENTS

1990: President FW de Klerk releases Nelson Mandela and other political prisoners, unbans liberation organisations. **1991:** Multiparty talks held within the CODESA framework; sanctions lifted; South Africa re-enters sporting arena. **1992:** White South Africans vote in favour of reform. Massacres threaten process but leaders sign a Record of Understanding. **1993:** Youth hero Chris Hani assassinated. Transitional executive council replaces parliament as supreme authority. Mandela and De Klerk share Nobel Peace Prize. **1994:** South Africa holds first free elections; Nelson Mandela becomes first black South African president. **1995:** South Africa wins Rugby World Cup. **1996:** Truth and Reconciliation Commission (TRC) begins work. **1999:** Mandela retires, to be succeeded by Thabo Mbeki. **2001:** Mbeki launches NEPAD initiative, part of his overall 'African Renaissance' mission. **2002:** South African computer tycoon Mark Shuttleworth becomes second 'space tourist'. **2003:** South Africa hosts the Cricket World Cup. **2006:** Deputy President Jacob Zuma indicted on rape (acquitted) and corruption (pending at time of writing) charges, an important political issue as the long run-up to the presidential election begins.

PEOPLE

Oliver Tambo, father of the liberation movement, dies in 1993. He has been in the vanguard of the struggle ever since creating (with the help of Mandela and Walter Sisulu) the ANC Youth League in the early 1940s. He fled into exile after the Sharpeville massacre (1960), going on to serve as head of the ANC's external mission until suffering a stroke in 1989.

The decade sees the passing of Laurens van der Post (1997), friend and mentor to Britain's Prince Charles and a writer noted both for his lyrical prose and his mystical perceptions of the human and natural worlds. Among his best known books is *The Lost World of the Kalahari*, which tells of the San (Bushmen). Also going to his long home (in the same year) is //Am//Op, venerable leader of the Kalahari's //Komeni clan and known for his skill with the mouth-bow.

His name means 'survivor', an allusion to his childhood escape from German colonial Bushman hunters at the end of the nineteenth century. Says a musicologist: 'His song was the survivor's song. He is gone now and with him an era, a language, and a lot of knowledge.'

Welkom-born Mark Shuttleworth, a young Capetonian with a flair for innovation and adventure and extensive knowledge of the computer world, sells his Thawte company (which specialises in Internet security and digital certification) for R3.5 billion and becomes the first African, and the second 'tourist', to be rocketed into space (2002). He then founds Ubuntu, a computer-orientated public service enterprise.

First African in Space:
IT billionaire Mark Shuttleworth

The Making of a Nation

AWARDS

Mandela and De Klerk are not the only South Africans to win top accolades. The 1991 Nobel Prize for Literature is scooped by prolific local author Nadine Gordimer, whose books – unsentimental novels that dwell on alienation, social justice and the reconciliation of the personal with the ideological – were banned by the apartheid regime. Another fine South African writer, John Maxwell Coetzee, continues to turn out his critically acclaimed, rather bleak works, among them *The Master of Petersburg* (1994) and *Boyhood: Scenes from a Provincial Life* (1997). His novel *Disgrace* is his latest before he, too, earns Nobel honours.

JM Coetzee, the first author to win the Booker Prize twice, and winner of the Nobel Prize for Literature

Three South Africans – Percy Mtwa, Athol Fugard and Mbongeni Ngema – are inducted into the New York Playwrights' Sidewalk, the US theatre's equivalent of Hollywood's Walk of Fame.

DISCOVERIES

Two archaeological finds reveal further evidence that Africa was indeed the 'cradle of humankind'. Capetonian Dave Roberts discovers the 117 000-year-old 'Eve's Footprint' at Langebaan on the West Coast. It is the oldest mark of a modern human being yet found. Far to the north, in the Sterkfontein caves near Krugersdorp, Ron Clarke unearths the almost complete skeleton of four-million-year-old 'Little Foot', which has features of both ape and human (it climbed trees and walked upright).

ARTS & ENTERTAINMENT

South African film-maker Leon Schuster pulls in the audiences with his irreverent, basic, politically incorrect and hilarious *There's a Zulu on my Stoep* and *Mr Bones*. More notable are two South African successes on the international front. Charlize Theron, a Benoni-born beauty who survives childhood trauma (she witnesses her mother shoot her father,

From Benoni to Hollywood: Charlize Theron wins the 2004 Oscar for Best Actress

More Oscar success: the triumphant *Tsotsi* director, Gavin Hood, arrives
back in Johannesburg with his two lead actors, Presley Chweneyagae and Terry Pheto

became an international entertainer in the 1950s with such hit songs as 'Sugarbush' and 'Pickin' a Chicken', and Basil Coetzee, composer and jazz instrumentalist whose moving, eleven-minute 'Manenberg' became a kind of anthem for the freedom movement. He dies virtually penniless.

SPORT

Rugby: Victory in the World Cup takes South Africa to the pinnacle of sporting achievement; among the game's stars is Chester Williams, one of the first players of colour to gain Springbok colours (though not the first: that distinction

an abusive alcoholic) to model in Milan (at the age of 16), after which she turns to ballet, injures her knee, is discovered 'on the street' and begins to take Hollywood by storm with roles in films such as *The Devil's Advocate*, *The Cider House Rules* and *Mighty Joe Young* before receiving the 2004 Oscar for Best Actress for her lead role in *Monster*, the story of serial killer Aileen Wuornos (for which she makes herself thoroughly unattractive). Two years later, the South African film *Tsotsi*, featuring six days in the life of a Johannesburg gangster, is awarded the Oscar for Best Foreign Film. The story is taken from a novel by leading South African author and playwright Athol Fugard; its tagline is: 'In this world, redemption comes just once'; its star is twenty-two-year-old Sowetan Presley Chweneyagae.

The musical world loses two of its more impressive talents with the deaths in 1998 of veteran singer Eve Boswell, who

belongs to the brilliant Errol Tobias, chosen for the national squad in 1980). Williams, strong and elusive rather than speedy, is a prolific try-scorer, crossing the line three times in one test (against Wales in 1994).

Cricket: South Africa competes in its first World Cup, in Australia in 1992, memorably defeating the hosts before going down against England in an absurd, weather-spoilt semi-final (twenty-two runs required off one ball). There is even more drama in the 1999 tournament in the UK, when Herschelle Gibbs, in frivolous mood, drops a crucial catch, and an equally critical match is tied when Alan Donald and Lance Klusener fail to take the winning run when it's there for the asking. Klusener, though, wins the Man of the Series award (280 runs at an average of 140, plus 17 wickets). South Africa, despite its depth, strength and knack of winning consistently, compete without great distinction in both the 2003 Cup (which it hosts)

The Making of a Nation

and the 2007 event held in the West Indies. The Australians prove virtually unbeatable on both occasions.

Golf: The decade of the 1990s belongs to big Ernie Els, whose best year is 1997. He wins the Johnnie Walker Classic, the US Open and, a week later, the Buick Classic, then helps South Africa win the Alfred Dunhill world team event at St Andrews and goes on to triumph in the PGA Grand Slam in Hawaii. The next five years belong to Retief Goosen, a Limpopo golfer who survived a lightning strike in his youth but put the setback behind him to win the US Open in 2001 and 2004, to head the earnings-based European Tour Order of Merit in 2001 and 2002, and to win at least one PGA tour event in each year from 2001 to 2005.

Boxing: Best of a fine crop of local fighters are Vuyani Bungu (IBF junior featherweight, 1994) and, most notably, diminutive, gutsy 'Baby Jake' Matlala, who holds the WBA junior flyweight title for most of the decade.

Yachting: South Africa's *Shosholoza* team surprises the international sailing fraternity with its skill in the America's Cup, which starts its run-up in 2004. However, the sleek, high-tech craft, designed and built in South Africa, ultimately fails to advance in the years-long contest.

Swimming: The SA 4 x 100 metre relay team of Roland Schoeman, Lyndon Ferns, Darian Townsend and Ryk Neethling

Mandela cheers as captain Neil Tovey holds the cup aloft after winning the Africa Cup of Nations

snatch Olympic gold at the 2004 Athens Games, beating the Netherlands and the US into second and third places with a time of 3:13.17, a world record. The American foursome include the great Michael Phelps, whose team's failure denies him the medal he needs to top Mark Spitz's seven golds at a single Olympics.

Football: The national squad, known as Bafana Bafana, plays its way to continental glory with victory in the final of the 1996 Africa Cup of Nations, with a 2-0 win against Tunisia, and then, for the first time ever, competes in the finals of the 1998 Football World Cup – in itself a signal victory. Key figure in its success is team captain Lucas Radebe, who is a member and latterly captain of the English Premiership club Leeds United. Early in the new millennium South Africa is named as host to the 2010 FIFA World Cup, a huge vote of confidence in the fledgling nation.

On the ball: Bafana Bafana captain Lucas Radebe

FURTHER READING

A number of secondary sources were used in the preparation of this book. Repositories of anecdotal material include *South Africa's Yesterdays* (Cape Town: Reader's Digest Association, 1981); *Standard Encyclopaedia of South Africa* (Cape Town: Nasou Ltd, multiple volumes, 1970–1976); John Wentzel, *A View from the Ridge* (Cape Town: David Philip, 1975); and four of the author's own published works, namely *The Rise and Fall of Apartheid* (Cape Town: Struik, 1990); *South Africa in the 20th Century* (Cape Town: Struik, 2000); *A Concise Dictionary of South African Biography* (Cape Town: Francolin Publishers, 1999); and *The South African Family Encyclopaedia* (Cape Town: Struik, 1989). Among other titles, either consulted for this book or suggested for further reading, are the following:

Alhadeff, Vic. *A Newspaper History of South Africa*. Cape Town: Don Nelson, 1976

Arnold, Guy. *South Africa: Crossing the Rubicon*. London: Macmillan, 1992

Attwell, Michael. *South Africa: Background to the Crisis*. London: Sidgwick & Jackson, 1986

Bhana, S, and B Pachai. *A Documentary History of Indian South Africans*. Cape Town: David Philip, 1984

Bond, Patrick. *Elite Transition: From Apartheid to Neoliberalism in South Africa*. London: Pluto Press, 2000

Bunting, Brian. *The Rise of the South African Reich*. London: Penguin, 1964

Callinicos, Luli. *Oliver Tambo: Beyond the Engeli Mountains*. Cape Town: David Philip, 2004

Davenport, Rodney. *South Africa: A Modern History*. Johannesburg: Macmillan, 1987

First, Ruth. *Power in Africa*. New York: Pantheon, 1970

Gandhi, Mohandas K. *An Autobiography: The Story of My Experiments with Truth*. London: Phoenix Press, 1949

Gumede, William Mervin. *Thabo Mbeki and the Battle for the Soul of the ANC*. Cape Town: Zebra Press, 2005

Harrison, David. *The White Tribe of Africa*. Johannesburg: Macmillan, 1981

Holland, Heidi. *The Struggle: A History of the African National Congress*. London: Grafton, 1989

Huddleston, Trevor. *Naught for Your Comfort*. London: Fontana, 1956

Jacobs, Sean, and Richard Calland. *Thabo Mbeki's World: The Politics and Ideology of the South African President*. Pietermaritzburg: University of Natal Press, 2002

Johnson, Shaun. *Strange Days Indeed: South Africa from Insurrection to Post-election*. London: Bantam Press, 1993

Kruger, Rayne. *Goodbye Dolly Gray*. London: Cassell, 1983

Ingham, Kenneth. *Jan Christiaan Smuts: The Conscience of South Africa*. Johannesburg: Jonathan Ball, 1986

Leach, Graham. *The Afrikaners: Their Last Great Trek*. London: Macmillan, 1989

Lewis, Gavin. *Between the Wire and the Wall*. Cape Town: David Philip, 1987

Lodge, Tom. *Black Politics in South Africa since 1945*. Johannesburg: Ravan, 1983

———. *Mandela: A Critical Life*. New York: Oxford University Press, 2006

Luthuli, Albert. *Let My People Go*. London: Collins, 1962

Mandela, Nelson R. *Long Walk to Freedom*. London: Little, Brown, 1994

Mbeki, Govan. *The Peasants' Revolt*. London: Penguin, 1964

Meredith, Martin. *In the Name of Apartheid: South Africa in the Post War Period*. London: Hamish Hamilton, 1988

Modisane, Bloke. *Blame Me on History*. Johannesburg: AD Donker, 1986

Odendaal, André. *Vukani Bantu! The Beginnings of Black Protest Politics in South Africa to 1912*. Cape Town: David Philip, 1984

Pakenham, Thomas. *The Boer War*. London: Weidenfield & Nicolson, 1979

Pampallis, John. *Foundations of the New South Africa*. Cape Town: Maskew Miller Longman, 1991

Plaatje, Sol. *Native Life in South Africa*. Johannesburg: Ravan Press, 1982

Reader's Digest Association. *Illustrated History of South Africa: The Real Story*. Cape Town: 1988

Reitz, Deneys. *Commando: A Boer Journal of the Boer War of 1899–1902*. London: Faber & Faber, 1929

Slabbert, Frederik van Zyl. *The Last White Parliament*. London: Sidgwick & Jackson, 1985

Sparks, Allister. *The Mind of South Africa: The Story of the Rise and Fall of Apartheid*. London: Heinemann, 1990

———. *Beyond the Miracle: Inside the New South Africa*. Chicago: University of Chicago Press, 2003

Spies, SB. *Methods of Barbarism*. Cape Town: Human & Rousseau, 1977

Swan, Maureen. *Gandhi: The South African Experience*. Johannesburg: Ravan Press, 1985

Thompson, Leonard. *A History of South Africa*. New Haven: Yale University Press, 1990

Van der Ross, Richard. *The Rise and Decline of Apartheid*. Cape Town: Tafelberg, 1986

Warwick, P (ed.). *The South African War*. London: Longman, 1980

Welsh, Frank. *A History of South Africa*. London: HarperCollins, 1998

Wilkins, Ivor, and Hans Strydom. *The Super-Afrikaners*. Johannesburg: Jonathan Ball, 1978

Wilson, Monica, and Leonard Thompson (eds.). *The Oxford History of South Africa, Vol. 2 (1870–1966)*. Oxford: Oxford University Press, 1978

Wolpe, Harold. *Race, Class and the Apartheid State*. London: James Currey, 1988

PICTURE CREDITS

6–7: Anglo-Boer War Museum

9: National Archives

10 (top and bottom): Anglo-Boer War Museum

11: MuseuMAfricA

12: Anglo-Boer War Museum

13 (top and bottom): Anglo-Boer War Museum

14 (top): Anglo-Boer War Museum; (bottom): McGregor Museum

15: Killie Campbell Collection

16 (top): National Archives; (bottom): Cape Town Archives Repository

17: Cape Town Archives Repository

18 (top and bottom): Anglo-Boer War Museum

19 (top and bottom): Anglo-Boer War Museum

20: Anglo-Boer War Museum

21: Cape Times

22–3: National Archives

24: Anglo-Boer War Museum

27 (top): Cory Library; (bottom): Cape Town Archives Repository

28: Anglo-Boer War Museum

29 (top): Cape Town Archives Repository; (bottom and right): MuseuMAfricA

30: Topham Picturepoint/INPRA

31 (top and bottom): Anglo-Boer War Museum

32: Source unknown

34: UWC–Robben Island Museum Mayibuye Archives

35: UWC–Robben Island Museum Mayibuye Archives

36: UWC–Robben Island Museum Mayibuye Archives

37 (top right): Cape Town Archives Repository; (top left): Source unknown; (bottom): MuseuMAfricA

38–9: UWC–Robben Island Museum Mayibuye Archives

40 (top): Cape Town Archives Repository; (bottom): National Library of South Africa

41: National Library of South Africa

42: UWC–Robben Island Museum Mayibuye Archives

44: Local History Museums' Collection, Durban

45: Source unknown

46 (top): Museum of Military History; (bottom): MuseuMAfricA

47 (top): National Archives; (bottom): Museum of Military History

48: McGregor Museum

49 (top left): Pondo woman, by Irma Stern © DALRO 2007; (top right): MuseuMAfricA; (bottom): Source unknown

50–51: McGregor Museum

52 (top): National Archives; (bottom): Courtesy of Cape Town Photographic Society

53 (top): National Library of South Africa; (bottom): National Archives

54 (top): Cape Town Archives Repository; (bottom): MuseuMAfricA

55: PE Municipal Library

56: National Library of South Africa

58: National Archives

59: National Library of South Africa

61 (top): SA Railways; (bottom): Transnet Heritage Museum

62–3: Gallo Images/Getty Images

64: Cape Town Archives Repository

65: Cape Town Archives Repository

67: UWC–Robben Island Museum Mayibuye Archives

68 (top and bottom): UWC–Robben Island Museum Mayibuye Archives

69: Carnegie Commission Reports/ National Library of South Africa

70: National Archives

71 (top): Cape Town Archives Repository; (bottom): MuseuMAfricA

72: Cape Town Archives Repository

73 (top): UWC–Robben Island Museum Mayibuye Archives; (bottom): The Star

74: National Library of South Africa

75 (top left): MuseuMAfricA; (top right): Source unknown; (bottom): South African Institute for Aquatic Biodiversity

76–7: UWC–Robben Island Museum Mayibuye Archives

78 (top): Source unknown; (left): Museum of Military History; (bottom right): Source unknown

79 (left): Museum of Military History; (top, middle and bottom right): Source unknown

80 (top left): Source unknown; (top right): Museum of Military History; (bottom): Museum of Military History

81: National Cultural History Museum

82: UWC–Robben Island Museum Mayibuye Archives

83 (left and right): UWC–Robben Island Museum Mayibuye Archives

84: UWC–Robben Island Museum Mayibuye Archives

85: UWC–Robben Island Museum Mayibuye Archives

86 (left): National Archives; (right): National Library of South Africa

87: TopFoto/INPRA

88–9: UWC–Robben Island Museum Mayibuye Archives

90: Camera Press/INPRA

91: Source unknown

93 (top and bottom): UWC–Robben Island Museum Mayibuye Archives

94: Jürgen Schadeberg

95: UWC–Robben Island Museum Mayibuye Archives

96: Cape Times

97: Source unknown

98: Jürgen Schadeberg

99: UWC–Robben Island Museum Mayibuye Archives

100: UWC–Robben Island Museum Mayibuye Archives

101: UWC–Robben Island Museum Mayibuye Archives

102: UWC–Robben Island Museum Mayibuye Archives

103: Daily News

104 (**top, bottom left and right**): UWC–Robben Island Museum Mayibuye Archives

106: UWC–Robben Island Museum Mayibuye Archives

107: UWC–Robben Island Museum Mayibuye Archives

108 (**top and bottom**): UWC–Robben Island Museum Mayibuye Archives

109 (**top and bottom**): UWC–Robben Island Museum Mayibuye Archives

110 (**top**): Jewish Chronicle Archive/HIP/ TopFoto/INPRA; (**bottom**): BAHA/ africanpictures.net

111 (**top**): The ArenaPAL Picture Library/ INPRA; (**bottom**): Topfoto/INPRA

113: UWC–Robben Island Museum Mayibuye Archives

114 (**top and bottom**): Argus

115 (**top and bottom**): Argus

116–17: National Library of South Africa, Cape Times Collection

118: National Library of South Africa

119: UWC–Robben Island Museum Mayibuye Archives

120 (**left**): MuseuMAfricA; (**right**): The Star

121: UWC–Robben Island Museum Mayibuye Archives

122: UWC–Robben Island Museum Mayibuye Archives

123 (**top**): Herb Shore; (**bottom**): UWC– Robben Island Museum Mayibuye Archives

124 (**top and bottom**): UWC–Robben Island Museum Mayibuye Archives

126: UWC–Robben Island Museum Mayibuye Archives

127 (**left, right and bottom**): UWC– Robben Island Museum Mayibuye Archives

128: UWC–Robben Island Museum Mayibuye Archives

129: Argus

130: Cape Times

131 (**left**): Johncom/PictureNET; (**right**):

IMAGES24.co.za/Die Burger/ Pierre Schoeman

132 (**top and bottom**): Jürgen Schadeberg

133 (**top and bottom**): Johncom

134–5: UWC–Robben Island Museum Mayibuye Archives

136: UWC–Robben Island Museum Mayibuye Archives

137: UWC–Robben Island Museum Mayibuye Archives

139 (**top**): National Library of South Africa; (**bottom**): Gallo Images/Getty Images

140: UWC–Robben Island Museum Mayibuye Archives

141: UWC–Robben Island Museum Mayibuye Archives

142: UWC–Robben Island Museum Mayibuye Archives

143: UWC–Robben Island Museum Mayibuye Archives

144: Argus

145: UWC–Robben Island Museum Mayibuye Archives

146: Christo Crous

147: Source unknown

148: UWC–Robben Island Museum Mayibuye Archives

149: Die Burger

150 (**top**): Charles Knight/Rex Features/ INPRA; (**bottom**): Source unknown

151: IMAGES24.co.za/Die Burger

152–3: Graeme Williams/South Photographs/Bigger Picture

154: Independent Newspapers/Trace Images

155: Source unknown

156: IMAGES24.co.za/Die Burger

157 (**top**): UWC–Robben Island Museum Mayibuye Archives; (**bottom**): The Star

158: Paul Weinberg/South/Bigger Picture

159: Cedric Nunn/PictureNET

160 (**top**): Source unknown; (**bottom**): UWC–Robben Island Museum Mayibuye Archives

161: Johncom/PictureNET

162 (**top and bottom**): UWC–Robben Island Museum Mayibuye Archives

164: IMAGES24.co.za/Die Burger

165: UWC–Robben Island Museum Mayibuye Archives

166: IMAGES24.co.za/Die Burger

167 (**top and bottom**): UWC–Robben Island Museum Mayibuye Archives

169: Sunday Times/PictureNET

170: Ruphin Coudyzer

171 (**top**): Johncom; (**bottom**): AP Photo/ PictureNET

172–3: TopFoto/ImageWorks/INPRA

174: UWC–Robben Island Museum Mayibuye Archives

176 (**left**): National Archives; (**right**): UWC–Robben Island Museum Mayibuye Archives

178: UWC–Robben Island Museum Mayibuye Archives

181: Gallo Images/Getty Images

182: IMAGES24.co.za/Die Burger

184: IMAGES24.co.za/Die Burger

185: Gallo Images/AFP

186: IMAGES24.co.za/Die Burger

187 (**top**): Graeme Williams/South Photographs/africanpictures.net; (**bottom**): Gallo Images/AFP

188: Gallo Images/AFP

189: David Sandison/Sunday Times/ Johncom

190–91: TopFoto/EMPICS/INPRA

192: Eye Ubiquitous/Rex Features/INPRA

193: IMAGES24.co.za/Beeld/Leon Botha

196: AP Photo/Doug Mills/PictureNET

197: Obed Zilwa/Trace Images/ africanpictures.net

198 (**top**): Gallo Images/Getty Images; (**bottom**): Thembinkosi Dwayisa/ Sunday Times/PictureNET

199: IMAGES24.co.za/Beeld/Johann Hattingh

200: Gallo Images/Getty Images

201 (**left**): Sunday Times/Johncom; (**right**): Rex Features/INPRA

202: IMAGES24.co.za/Beeld/Alan Murdoch

203 (**top**): Gallo Images/Getty Images; (**bottom**): Gallo Images/Getty Images

INDEX

Page numbers in **bold type** *indicate illustrations*

The Making of a Nation

The Making of a Nation

The Making of a Nation

The Making of a Nation

Do you have any comments, suggestions or
feedback about this book or any other Zebra Press titles?
Contact us at **talkback@zebrapress.co.za**